Expectations

Expectations
A Reader for Developing Writers

Anna Ingalls
Southwestern College

Dan Moody
Southwestern College

New York San Francisco Boston
London Toronto Sydney Tokyo Singapore Madrid
Mexico City Munich Paris Cape Town Hong Kong Montreal

Vice President and Editor in Chief: Joseph Terry
Senior Acquisitions Editor: Steven Rigolosi
Development Manager: Janet Lanphier
Marketing Manager: Melanie Craig
Supplements Editor: Donna Campion
Production Manager: Joseph Vella
*Project Coordination, Text Design,
    and Electronic Page Makeup:* Shepherd, Inc.
Cover Design Manager: John Callahan
Cover Designer: Kay Petronio
Senior Manufacturing Buyer: Dennis J. Para
Printer and Binder: Courier–Stoughton
Cover Printer: The Lehigh Press

For permission to use copyrighted material, grateful acknowledgment is made to the copyright holders on pp. 241–244, which are hereby made part of this copyright page.

Library of Congress Cataloging-in-Publication Data

Expectations : a reader for developing writers / [compiled by] Anna Ingalls [and] Dan Moody.
    p. cm.
  Includes bibliographical references and index.
  ISBN 0-205-32937-3 (alk. paper)
    1. College readers. 2. English language—Rhetoric—Problems, exercises, etc. 3. Report writing—Problems, exercises, etc. I. Ingalls, Anna. II. Moody, Dan.

PE1417 .E95 2001
808'.0427—dc21

2001038405

Copyright © 2002 by Pearson Education, Inc.

All rights reserved. No part of this publication may be reproduced, stored in a retrieval system, or transmitted, in any form or by any means, electronic, mechanical, photocopying, recording, or otherwise, without the prior written permission of the publisher. Printed in the United States.

Please visit our website at http://www.ablongman.com

ISBN: 0-205-32937-3

1 2 3 4 5 6 7 8 9 10—CRS—04 03 02 01

Dedication

It is with great respect and affection that we dedicate this book to the phenomenal staff, the talented faculty, and above all, the wonderful students of Southwestern College.

Contents

Rhetorical Contents   x
Preface   xiii

1 / Strategies for Active Reading   1

Humans and the Environment by Robert E. Gabler, Robert J. Sager, Daniel L. Wise, and James F. Petersen   3

2 / Cultural and Social Issues   9

American Fish by R. A. Sasaki   10
Listen to Me Good by Margaret Charles Smith and Linda Janet Holmes   18
Boomer Parents by Sandy Banks   23
Spanglish Spoken Here by Janice Castro   29
The Ambitious Generation by Barbara Schneider and David Stevenson   35
Saffron Sky by Gelareh Asayesh   40
Suspect Policy by Randall Kennedy   46

3 / Education and Career   51

Stop! by Sam Quinones   52
How to Write with Style by Kurt Vonnegut, Jr.   57
The Reading Debate by Laura E. Berk   63
Possible Lives by Mike Rose   68
Breaking Through the Barriers by James M. Henslin   75
The Rich Heritage of Public Speaking by Steven A. Beebe and Susan J. Beebe   80

viii ◆ Contents

Emergency Medical Technicians by Joseph J. Mistovich, Brent Q. Hafen, and Keith J. Karren   85
Internet Job Search by A. C. "Buddy" Krizan, Fatricia Merrier, Carol Larson Jones, and Jules Harcourt   91

4 / Media and Popular Culture   97

Taking Potluck by Tom Bodett   98
Color TV by Richard Breyer   103
Breaking the Habit by Mike Duffy   109
Shoeless Joe by W. P. Kinsella   116
Elvis Culture by Erika Doss   122
Dressing Down by John Brooks   127

5 / Fitness and Health   133

Strive to Be Fit, Not Fanatical by Timothy Gower   134
Procrastination and Stress by Lester A. Lefton   139
Managing Time by Rebecca J. Donatelle and Lorraine G. Davis   144
Computer Addiction Is Coming Online by William J. Cromie   148
Playing for Keeps by Andy Steiner   154
Can You Afford to Get Sick? by Helen Martineau   159

6 / Nature and the Outdoors   165

Journey of the Pink Dolphins by Sy Montgomery   166
In the Shadow of Man by Jane Goodall   171
Life in the Treetops by Margaret D. Lowman   175
Nature's R_x by Joel L. Swerdlow   182
Monarchs' Migration: A Fragile Journey by William K. Stevens   187

Heavy Traffic on the Everest Highway by Geoffrey Tabin   193
Death Valley by Doug and Bobbe Tatreau   199

7 / Technology and the Future   205

What'll They Think of Next? by Melissa Melton and Barbra Murray   206
The 10-Minute Tech Inspection by Peter Bohr   211
Tourist Trap by James Hebert   217
Indistinguishable from Magic by Robert L. Forward   222
The Mars Direct Plan by Robert Zubrin   227
The World After Cloning by Wray Herbert, Jeffrey L. Sheler, and Traci Watson   233

Text Acknowledgments   241
Index   245

Rhetorical Contents

Readings are categorized here according to their predominant rhetorical modes. In cases where readings clearly exemplify two different modes of thinking and writing, they are listed in both categories. However, because of the nature of professional writing, readers will find that many authors have employed a variety of other modes in addition to those listed here.

Narration

American Fish by R. A. Sasaki   10
Listen to Me Good by Margaret Charles Smith and Linda Janet Holmes   18
Boomer Parents by Sandy Banks   23
Saffron Sky by Gelareh Asayesh   40
Shoeless Joe by W. P. Kinsella   116
Playing for Keeps by Andy Steiner   154
In the Shadow of Man by Jane Goodall   171
Life in the Treetops by Margaret D. Lowman   175

Description

Possible Lives by Mike Rose   68
Taking Potluck by Tom Bodett   98
Journey of the Pink Dolphins by Sy Montgomery   166
Life in the Treetops by Margaret D. Lowman   175
Heavy Traffic on the Everest Highway by Geoffrey Tabin   193
Death Valley by Doug and Bobbe Tatreau   199

Cause and Effect

Boomer Parents by Sandy Banks   23
Spanglish Spoken Here by Janice Castro   29
Breaking Through the Barriers by James M. Henslin   75
Elvis Culture by Erika Doss   122
Procrastination and Stress by Lester A. Lefton   139
Computer Addiction Is Coming Online by William J. Cromie   148
Nature's R_x by Joel L. Swerdlow   182
Tourist Trap by James Hebert   217
The World After Cloning by Wray Herbert, Jeffrey L. Sheler, and Traci Watson   233

Instructions

How to Write with Style by Kurt Vonnegut, Jr.   57
Internet Job Search by A. C. "Buddy" Krizan, Patricia Merrier, Carol Larson Jones, and Jules Harcourt   91
Strive to Be Fit, Not Fanatical by Timothy Gower   134
Managing Time by Rebecca J. Donatelle and Lorraine G. Davis   144
The 10-Minute Tech Inspection by Peter Bohr   211

Comparison/Contrast

The Ambitious Generation by Barbara Schneider and David Stevenson   35
Stop! by Sam Quinones   52
The Reading Debate by Laura E. Berk   63
Tourist Trap by James Hebert   217

Persuasion

Boomer Parents by Sandy Banks   23
Suspect Policy by Randall Kennedy   46
Color TV by Richard Breyer   103
Breaking the Habit by Mike Duffy   109
Indistinguishable from Magic by Robert L. Forward   222

Classification

Emergency Medical Technicians by Joseph J. Mistovich, Brent Q. Hafen, and Keith J. Karren   85

Exposition (Informative)

The Rich Heritage of Public Speaking by Steven A. Beebe and Susan J. Beebe   80
Dressing Down by John Brooks   127
Can You Afford to Get Sick? by Helen Martineau   159
Monarchs' Migration: A Fragile Journey by William K. Stevens   187
What'll They Think of Next? by Melissa Melton and Barbra Murray   206
The Mars Direct Plan by Robert Zubrin   227

Preface

Expectations: A Reader for Developing Writers features a carefully chosen collection of popular readings for developmental writing students, with questions, discussion topics, and assignments to develop active reading techniques, critical thinking skills, and effective writing strategies. *Expectations* is specifically designed to meet the needs of pre-freshman composition students who can benefit from instruction in reading, critical thinking, and writing skills.

Reading Selections

Expectations features a wide variety of readings on topics of interest and value to today's students. Many of the 40 readings reflect the multicultural and pluralistic nature of our society, including articles that feature the Japanese-American experience, gender issues in the workplace, disabled athletes, and the experience of an African-American midwife in the deep South.

In addition to cultural issues, topics range from useful readings on managing time, keeping fit, and conducting an Internet job search, to nature topics, such as pink dolphins and climbing Mt. Everest, to technology-oriented subjects like cloning and computer addiction. The topics, the lengths, and the difficulty levels of the readings are appropriate for developing writers.

Most of the readings originally appeared in nationally known magazines or contemporary nonfiction books. Several excerpts from textbooks in communication, health, physical geography, and other fields of study are also included to help students build the kinds of reading skills they will need in order to be successful in college courses across the curriculum. Other readings originated as newspaper articles, and, to enhance students' reading experience, a few examples of fiction are also included.

The readings exemplify a broad range of rhetorical modes, organizational styles, and effective stylistic techniques that students are encouraged to apply to their own writing. An underlying emphasis on the reading-writing connection is apparent throughout the text.

Organization

Expectations is organized by themes that relate to students' lives and personal interests, as well as to our society and directions for the future: social and cultural issues, education and career, media and popular culture, fitness and health, nature and the outdoors, and technology and the future. Within each theme, easier readings are placed first, while readings with a higher vocabulary level, more complicated sentence structure, or a denser text style appear later in the section. To give instructors the flexibility of following either a thematically based instructional outline or a rhetorically based outline, readings are also cross-referenced by their predominant rhetorical modes: narration, description, cause and effect, instructions, comparison/contrast, persuasion, classification, and exposition (informative).

Strategies for Active Reading

An initial section called Strategies for Active Reading introduces such skills as previewing, recognizing audience and purpose, identifying the main idea, discovering meaning through context clues, making inferences, evaluating for logic and bias, reviewing, and reflecting on the reading. These skills are reinforced throughout the book in comprehension questions, critical thinking questions, and language and vocabulary questions.

Features

Within each lesson, pre- and post-reading features make the content and vocabulary accessible, as well as promoting analysis, discussion, and written expression.

- A short **introduction** sets the stage for each reading by presenting information about the topic or the source.
- **Prereading questions** provide a conceptual framework by asking students to start thinking about the topics and issues reflected in the reading.
- A **Vocabulary** list for preview or quick reference provides simple and concise definitions of difficult or unusual vocabulary.
- **Comprehension** questions allow students to check their understanding of the reading.
- **Critical Thinking** questions focus on the author's purpose and audience, the main point of the reading, awareness of bias, and application to society. Skills such as inference, extrapolation, and deductive reasoning are emphasized.

- **Language and Vocabulary** questions range from general, technical, and specific vocabulary of particular fields to broader topics, such as synonyms, discovering meaning from context, and figurative language.
- **Style, Structure, and Organization** questions lead students to examine the writers' techniques and to build an awareness of rhetorical methods.
- **Topics for Discussion or Journal Writing** include a selection of creative, imaginative, and personal response topics to stimulate class discussion and informal writing.
- **Writing Topics for Paragraphs or Essays** are based on the topics and the rhetorical modes of the readings, as well as incorporating a variety of other modes. Each lesson includes one or more writing projects that encourage students to use outside sources, such as library materials, oral interviews, and information obtained via the Internet.

To the Teacher

Expectations: A Reader for Developing Writers is designed to be both teacher- and student-friendly. It is our hope that students will find the topics to be interesting and relevant to contemporary society, as well as useful for the improvement of their writing techniques and styles.

Teachers may choose to rely heavily on this reader for classroom use or to use it as an adjunct to a comprehensive writing text—and possibly a basic handbook, such as *Check It Out: A Quick and Easy Guide for Writers,* by the same authors.

With 40 reading selections, teachers are able to choose readings that best fit their courses, students, and teaching methods. Some may choose to work extensively with one or more of the themes or to select readings across several themes, based on the difficulty level. Other teachers will prefer to choose those readings that illustrate lecture points or that match the type of writing that students are engaged in learning. Finally, there will be teachers who allow students to choose their own readings as homework assignments to enrich the core curriculum of the classroom. This book is intended to be an effective tool in the hands of many capable and creative teachers.

The Teaching and Learning Package

A complete instructor's manual to accompany *Expectations* is available (ISBN 0-321-09484-0). In addition, a series of other skills-based supplements is available for both instructors and students. All of these supplements are available either free or at greatly reduced prices.

For Additional Reading and Reference

The Dictionary Deal. Two dictionaries can be shrinkwrapped with any Longman Basic Skills title at a nominal fee. *The New American Webster Handy College Dictionary* is a paperback reference text with more than 100,000 entries. *Merriam Webster's Collegiate Dictionary*, tenth edition, is a hardback reference with a citation file of more than 14.5 million examples of English words drawn from actual use. For more information on how to shrinkwrap a dictionary with your text, please contact your Longman sales representative.

Penguin Quality Paperback Titles. A series of Penguin paperbacks is available at a significant discount when shrinkwrapped with any Longman Basic Skills title. Some titles available are Toni Morrison's *Beloved*, Julia Alvarez's *How the Garcia Girls Lost Their Accents*, Mark Twain's *Huckleberry Finn*, *Narrative of the Life of Frederick Douglass*, Harriet Beecher Stowe's *Uncle Tom's Cabin*, Dr. Martin Luther King, Jr.'s *Why We Can't Wait*, and plays by Shakespeare, Miller, and Albee. For a complete list of titles or more information, please contact your Longman sales consultant or visit our website: http://www.ablongman.com/penguin.

100 Things to Write About. This 100-page book contains 100 individual assignments for writing on a variety of topics and in a wide range of formats, from expressive to analytical. Ask your Longman sales representative for a sample copy (ISBN 0-673-98239-4).

The Longman Textbook Reader. This supplement, for use in developmental reading courses, offers five complete chapters from Addison-Wesley/Longman textbooks: computer science, biology, psychology, communications, and business. Each chapter includes additional comprehension quizzes, critical thinking questions, and group activities. Available FREE with the adoption of this Longman text. For information on how to bundle *The Longman Textbook Reader* with your text, please contact your Longman sales representative. Available in two forms: with answers and without answers.

Newsweek **Alliance.** Instructors may choose to shrinkwrap a 12-week subscription to *Newsweek* with any Longman text. The price of the subscription is 57 cents per issue (a total of $6.84 for the subscription). Available with the subscription is a free "Interactive Guide to *Newsweek*"—a workbook for students who are using the text. In addition, *Newsweek* provides a wide variety of instructor supplements free to teachers, including maps, Skills Builders, and weekly quizzes. For more information on the *Newsweek* program, please contact your Longman sales representative.

Electronic and Online Offerings

The Writer's Warehouse. This innovative and exciting online supplement is the perfect accompaniment to any developmental writing course. Written by developmental English instructors especially for developing writers, The Writer's Warehouse covers every part of the writing process. Also included are journaling capabilities, multimedia activities, diagnostic tests, an interactive handbook, and a complete instructor's manual. The Writer's Warehouse requires no space on your school's server; rather, students complete and store their work on the Longman server, and are able to access it, revise it, and continue working at any time. For more details about how to shrinkwrap a free subscription to The Writer's Warehouse with this text, please consult your Longman sales representative. For a free guided tour of the site, visit **http://longmanwriterswarehouse.com**.

The Writer's ToolKit Plus. This CD-ROM offers a wealth of tutorial, exercise, and reference material for writers. It is compatible with either a PC or Macintosh platform, and is flexible enough to be used either occasionally for practice or regularly in class lab sessions. For information on how to bundle this CD-ROM FREE with your text, please contact your Longman sales representative.

The Longman English Pages Web Site. Both students and instructors can visit our free content-rich Web site for additional reading selections and writing exercises. From the Longman English pages, visitors can conduct a simulated Web search, learn how to write a resume and cover letter, or try their hand at poetry writing. Stop by and visit us at **http://www.ablongman.com/englishpages**.

The Longman Electronic Newsletter. Twice a month during the spring and fall, instructors who have subscribed receive a free copy of the Longman Developmental English Newsletter in their e-mailbox. Written by experienced classroom instructors, the newsletter offers teaching tips, classroom activities, book reviews, and more. To subscribe, visit the Longman Basic Skills Web site at **http://www.ablongman.com/basicskills**, or send an e-mail to **Basic Skills@ablongman.com**.

For Instructors

Electronic Test Bank for Writing. This electronic test bank features more than 5,000 questions in all areas of writing, from grammar to paragraphing, through essay writing, research, and documentation. With this easy-to-use CD-ROM, instructors simply choose questions from the electronic test bank, then print out the completed test for distribution (ISBN CD-ROM: 0-321-08117-X. Print version: 0-321-08486-1).

Competency Profile Test Bank, Second Edition. This series of 60 objective tests covers ten general areas of English competency, including fragments; comma splices and run-ons; pronouns; commas; and capitalization. Each test is available in remedial, standard, and advanced versions. Available as reproducible sheets or in computerized versions. Free to instructors (Paper version: 0-321-02224-6. Computerized IBM: 0-321-02633-0. Computerized Mac: 0-321-02632-2).

Diagnostic and Editing Tests and Exercises, Fourth Edition. This collection of diagnostic tests helps instructors assess students' competence in Standard Written English for purpose of placement or to gauge progress. Available as reproducible sheets or in computerized versions, and free to instructors (Paper: 0-321-10022-0. CD-ROM: 0-321-10459-5).

ESL Worksheets, Third Edition. These reproducible worksheets provide ESL students with extra practice in areas they find the most troublesome. A diagnostic test and post-test are provided, along with answer keys and suggested topics for writing. Free to adopters (ISBN 0-321-07765-2).

Longman Editing Exercises. 54 pages of paragraph editing exercises give students extra practice using grammar skills in the context of longer passages. Free when packaged with any Longman title (ISBN 0-205-31792-8).

80 Practices. A collection of reproducible, ten-item exercises that provide additional practices for specific grammatical usage problems, such as comma splices, capitalization, and pronouns. Includes an answer key, and free to adopters (ISBN 0-673-53422-7).

CLAST Test Package, Fourth Edition. These two 40-item objective tests evaluate students' readiness for the CLAST exams. Strategies for teaching CLAST preparedness are included. Free with any Longman English title. (Reproducible sheets: 0-321-01950-4. Computerized IBM version: 0-321-01982-2. Computerized Mac version: 0-321-01983-0).

TASP Test Package, Third Edition. These 12 practice pre-tests and post-tests assess the same reading and writing skills covered in the TASP examination. Free with any Longman English title. (Reproducible sheets: 0-321-01959-8. Computerized IBM version: 0-321-01985-7. Computerized Mac version: 0-321-01984-9).

Teaching Online: Internet Research, Conversation, and Composition, **Second Edition.** Ideal for instructors who have never surfed the Net, this easy-to-follow guide offers basic definitions, numerous examples, and step-by-step information about finding and using Internet sources. Free to adopters (ISBN 0-321-01957-1).

Teaching Writing to the Non-Native Speaker. This booklet examines the issues that arise when non-native speakers enter the developmental classroom. Free to instructors, it includes profiles of international and permanent ESL students, factors influencing second-language acquisition, and tips on managing a multicultural classroom (ISBN 0-673-97452-9).

For Students

The Longman Writer's Journal. This journal for writers, free with any Longman English text, offers students a place to think, write, and react. For an examination copy, contact your Longman sales consultant (ISBN 0-321-08639-2).

***Researching Online,* Fifth Edition.** A perfect companion for a new age, this indispensable new supplement helps students navigate the Internet. Adapted from *Teaching Online,* the instructor's Internet guide, *Researching Online* speaks directly to students, giving them detailed, step-by-step instructions for performing electronic searches. Available free when shrinkwrapped with this text (ISBN 0-321-09277-5).

Learning Together: An Introduction to Collaborative Theory. This brief guide to the fundamentals of collaborative learning teaches students how to work effectively in groups, how to revise with peer response, and how to co-author a paper or report. Shrinkwrapped free with any Longman Basic Skills text (ISBN 0-673-46848-8).

***A Guide for Peer Response,* Second Edition.** This guide offers students forms for peer critiques, including general guidelines and specific forms for different stages in the writing process. Also appropriate for freshman-level course. Free to adopters (ISBN 0-321-01948-2).

***Thinking Through the Test,* by D.J. Henry.** This special workbook, prepared specially for students in Florida, offers ample skill and practice exercises to help students prep for the Florida State Exit Exam. To shrinkwrap this workbook free with your textbook, please contact your Longman sales representative. Available in two versions: with and without answers. Also available: Two laminated grids (one for reading, one for writing) that can serve as handy references for students preparing for the Florida State Exit Exam.

Acknowledgments

First of all, we would like to express our appreciation to our editor, Joe Opiela, Vice President of Allyn and Bacon/Longman, without whom this book would not have come into existence. Joe has been instrumental in shaping both the form and the content, as well as providing encouragement and assistance at every stage of the writing process. He has our sincere thanks.

Dan would like to thank his wife, Kathleen, and his four daughters, Rachel, Sarah, Hannah, and Elizabeth, for the love and support they give him, and his parents for always believing in him. He also owes a debt of gratitude to the many friends and colleagues who have supported him by encouraging him and keeping him in their prayers.

Anna would like to express her appreciation to friends and colleagues who have helped her survive the pressures of writing and editing, especially her traveling companions—Bobbe Tatreau, Meredith Morton, Tori Rowden, Nancy Evans, Donald Pratt, Frank Giardina, and Denis Callahan—whose wit and generosity of spirit are unsurpassed.

Professor Eliana Santana has our thanks for explaining a Brazilian legend and helping us with Portuguese phrases. We also wish to thank the many capable librarians who assisted us in our search for excellent readings. Additionally, we wish to acknowledge our dean, Dr. Renée Kilmer, for her knowledge of and enthusiasm for English literature and language, and for her support of our project.

Finally, we would like to thank the astute reviewers who generously took the time to offer their thoughtful, professional advice on the development of this text: Judy Covington, Trident Technical College; Eileen Eliot, Broward Community College; Ruth H. Greer, Ivy Tech State College; Priscilla Underwood, Quinsigamond Community College; R. J. Willey, Oakland Community College.

Anna Ingalls
Dan Moody

1

Strategies for Active Reading

Active Reading

There is a strong connection between reading and writing; in fact, reading is one of the best ways to become an effective writer. Through reading, we can learn, both consciously and subconsciously, how to use language more effectively.

When we read an effective article or story, for example, we often soak up some of the writer's techniques *intuitively*, at a subconscious level, without even being aware of it, and occasionally one of these techniques will surprise us by showing up in our own writing. This can happen even (or especially!) when we are reading for pleasure. We might get caught up in the story and not pay any attention to the writer's techniques or style, but still, at some level, we learn. This is one of the great benefits of reading for pleasure.

In addition to reading for pleasure, those who want to become better writers should learn to read *actively*. Active reading means consciously analyzing the author's techniques to see what works well. By focusing on and evaluating such things as the author's *purpose, point of view, organization, style, vocabulary,* and *grammatical structures*, we can add to our own collection of writing tools and be ready to try them out ourselves in the next papers we write.

Writing is like any other craft: writers have their own specialized tools of the trade. By increasing the number of tools we have to choose from, we can learn to be more effective writers. This book of readings provides a close look at a number of writing tools as they are used by some very effective authors.

The following pages present an illustrated example of active reading. On the left side of each page, you will find a specific strategy for active reading, as well as notes that show how a reader could apply these strategies to the reading on the right, "Humans and the Environment."

Active Reading Strategies

By reading actively, you will get the most out of each selection that you read. An active reader interacts with the words on the page (or on the screen), analyzes the reading, and takes note of effective techniques for use in his or her own writing.

There are several methods of active reading. Nearly all of them include the following steps in one form or another:

I. **Preview the reading.**
   Before you read the selection word for word, look ahead to get a general idea of the topic and other important information.
   A. Read the title, any writing at the top or in the margins, and any words that are boldface or in italics.
   B. Read the first paragraph, the first sentence of each paragraph, and the last paragraph.

(From Robert E. Gabler, Robert J. Sager, Daniel L. Wise, and James F. Petersen. *Essentials of Physical Geography,* Sixth Edition, Saunders College Publishing, 1999.)

Humans and the Environment

Environment—Ecology—Ecosystem

One of the great advantages of considering subsystems when studying physical geography is that they serve to illustrate the relationships among the various elements within a system. As scientists, geographers are keenly interested in relationships, and they pay special attention to the relationships between humans and the physical environment. In no way can the human-environment relationship be better illustrated than through the examination of human impact on ecosystems. In the last half of the twentieth century, people have become increasingly conscious of their environment. We talk about the environment and ecology and worry about ecological damage caused by human activity. Newspapers and news magazines often devote entire sections to discussions of environmental issues. But what are we really talking about when we use words like *environment, ecology,* or *ecosystem?*

In the broadest sense, our **environment** can be defined as our surroundings; it is made up of all the physical, social, and cultural aspects of our world that affect our growth, our health, and our way of living. Humans also share environments with plants and animals. We can speak of a plant's environment and include in our discussion the soil in which a plant grows, the amount of sunlight and rainfall it receives, the gases that surround it, the range of air temperatures, and the nature of the plants that grow nearby, which also serve to block winds, sunlight, and rain.

SOURCE: "Humans and the Environment." Excerpts from *Essentials of Physical Geography,* Sixth Edition, by Robert Gabler, Robert Sager, Daniel Wise, and James Petersen, copyright © 1999 by Harcourt Inc., reprinted by permission of the publisher.

II. **Understand the reading.**
   As you read, use several strategies to get more out of your reading.
   A. Analyze the selection to understand who the author is writing for—the general public or a specific target audience. *General public, college students?*
   B. Figure out the author's purpose—to inform, to entertain, to persuade, a combination of these, or a different purpose. *To inform, to persuade?*
   C. Look for the main idea of the reading, the key points, and important details and examples. *Changing one member of an ecological system affects all of the other members.*
   D. Try to guess the meaning of new words and unfamiliar expressions from the words around them (the context). Use a dictionary only when it's absolutely necessary in order to understand the key points of the reading. *Ecosystem = ecological system, a community of organisms; depleted = affected, reduced, destroyed?*
   E. Read between the lines (make inferences). Look to see if the author makes any points indirectly, even if they are not stated directly. *Humans are messing up the environment?*
   F. Use your judgment to decide if the author is presenting unbiased information and using clear logic. *It sounds logical, but I'm going to look for some examples later in the reading before I decide.*

Just as humans interact with their environment, so do other animals and plants. The study of relationships between organisms, whether animal or plant, and their environments is a science known as **ecology**. Ecological relationships are complex but naturally balanced "webs of life." Disrupting the natural ecology of a community of organisms may have negative results (although this is not always so). For example, filling in or polluting coastal marshlands may disrupt the natural ecology of such areas. As a result, fish spawning grounds may be destroyed and the food supply of some marine animals and migratory birds could be greatly depleted. The end product is the destruction of valuable plant and animal life.

The word **ecosystem** is a contraction of **ecological system**. An ecosystem is a community of organisms and the relationships of those organisms to their environment. An ecosystem is dynamic in that its various parts are always in flux. For instance, plants grow, rain falls, animals eat, and soil matures—all changing the environment of a particular ecosystem. Since each member of the ecosystem belongs to the environment of every other part of that system, a change in one alters the environment for all the others. As those components react to the alteration, they in turn continue to transform the environment for the others. A change in the weather, from sunshine to rain, affects plants, soils, and animals. Heavy rain may carry away soils and plant nutrients so that plants may not be able to grow as well and animals then may not be able to eat as much. On the other hand, the addition of moisture to the soil may help some plants grow, increasing the amount of shade beneath them and thus keeping other plants from growing.

The ecosystem concept (like other systems models) can be applied on almost any scale, in a wide variety of geographic locations, and under all environmental conditions in which life is possible. Hence, your backyard, a farm pond, a grass-covered field, a marsh, a forest, or a portion of a desert can be viewed as an ecosystem.

Strategies for Active Reading ◆ 5

III. **Interact with the reading.**
As you read, mark important information with a highlighter, marker, or pen. Then look back over the reading again and mark anything you missed the first time.

A. Make a note in the margin next to the main idea of the reading, or write the main idea in your own words.
People should not alter the environment without seriously considering the consequences.

B. Highlight the key points that the author makes.

C. Circle or underline important details and examples.

D. Make marginal notes of anything you think is important.

Ecosystems are found wherever there is an exchange of materials among living organisms and where there are functional relationships between the organisms and their natural surroundings. Ecosystems are open systems, as both energy and material move across their boundaries. Although some ecosystems, such as a small lake or a desert oasis, have clear-cut boundaries, the limits of many others are not as precisely defined. Often the change from one ecosystem to another is obscure and transitional, occurring slowly over distance.

Ever since human beings first walked Earth, they have affected each ecosystem they have inhabited, and in modern times, humans' ability to alter the landscape has been increasing. For example, a century ago the interconnected Kissimmee River—Lake Okeechobee—Everglades ecosystem constituted one of the most productive and stable wetland regions on Earth. But sawgrass marsh and slow-moving water stood in the way of urban development. Intricate systems of ditches and canals were built, and since 1900, half of the original 4 million acres of the Everglades has disappeared. The Kissimmee River has been channelized into an arrow-straight ditch, and wetlands along the river have been drained. Levees have prevented water in Lake Okeechobee from contributing sheet flow to the Everglades, and highway construction has divided the region, further disrupting natural drainage patterns. Fires have been more frequent and destructive, and entire biotic communities have been eliminated by lowered water levels. During excessively wet periods, portions of the Everglades are deliberately flooded to prevent drainage canals from overflowing. As a result, animals drown and birds cannot rest and reproduce. South Florida's wading bird population has decreased by 95 percent in the last hundred years. Without the natural purifying effects of wetland systems, water quality in South Florida has deteriorated, and with lower water levels, saltwater encroachment is a serious problem in coastal areas.

So if we change one ecosystem, we might mess up others too?

6 ♦ Part 1 / Strategies for Active Reading

IV. **Review the reading.**
   After you read, fix the important information from the selection firmly in your mind.
   A. Ask yourself or your classmates about the reading, including *who, what, when, where, how,* and *why* questions, and jot down short answers in your notebook.

   Who—people all over the world
   What—natural habitats are being destroyed, along with the birds and animals that live there; now we need to pay more attention
   When—now more than ever before
   Where—all over the world; the Everglades in Florida is the example used in the reading
   How—people have blocked up rivers and changed the land in other ways too; scientists are working to heal some of the most damaged ecosystems
   Why—if people continue to change the natural landscape drastically, there will continue to be drastic reductions in plant, bird, and animal species

   B. Write a short summary of the selection or make a list of important points. One way to do this is to start with the main idea of the reading, and then summarize the main point or topic of each paragraph.

Today, backed by regional, state, and federal agencies, scientists are struggling to restore South Florida's ailing ecosystems. There are extensive plans to allow the Kissimmee River to meander again across its former flood plain, to return agricultural land to sawgrass marsh, and to restore historic water-flow patterns through the Everglades. The problems of South Florida should serve as a useful lesson. Alterations of the natural environment should not be undertaken without serious consideration of all the consequences.

Summary:

People should not change the environment without considering the effect the changes will have on the ecological systems of the area. Geographers study the relationships between humans and the physical environment. Humans share the environment with plants and animals. Humans have had a big impact on the environment. Ecology is the study of the complex relationships that exist between plants, animals, and the physical environment. An ecosystem (ecological system) is the whole community of organisms that share an environment. Ecosystems can be very small or very large: a backyard or part of a desert, for example. Ecosystems are open systems (matter and energy go in and out of an ecosystem); some ecosystems have clear boundaries, but others transition gradually into different ecosystems. Humans have altered the landscape more in recent times; for example, the Everglades ecosystem has lost 95 percent of its wading bird population in the past 100 years due to artificial river channels, ditches, and highways. Today, South Florida is being restored and should serve as a lesson.

V. Reflect on the reading.
Evaluate if and how the reading can be useful to you for your own writing.

    A. Respond to the reading by writing down new ideas that interest you, related thoughts you have on the topic, your opinion of the value of this reading, things to reflect on, or even how you felt when you read it.[1]

    B. Observe what types of writing are used and how the selection is organized.

    C. Take note of any special techniques or styles that the author uses effectively.

    D. Memorize key vocabulary or keep a personal vocabulary list in your notebook.

    E. Note any effective grammar structures that might work well in your own writing.

A. *This might explain why the animal population near here has been changing, with more wild animals being forced into populated areas as their own habitat is destroyed for more houses. I wonder if humans caused the melting of the glaciers around the world, and the ice caps, and the change in rainfall that many areas have experienced recently. This is interesting but depressing, because I don't know what I can do to help.*

B. *The writing seems to be a clear statement of human actions and our effects on the ecosystems we live in. I guess this reading is a combination of explanatory and cause-and-effect writing.*

C. *This selection has good definitions of several key words, such as <u>ecology, environment</u>, and <u>ecosystems</u>, early on.*

D. • *environment = everything around us, our surroundings*
    • *ecology = the study of relationships between plants, animals, and their environment*
    • *ecosystem = an ecological system; the whole community of plants and animals that live in one area*
    • *biotic = related to life (I had to look this one up)*

E. *(Present perfect tense)*
    • *Humans . . . <u>have affected</u> each ecosystem*
    • *half of the . . . Everglades <u>has disappeared</u>*
    • *the Kissimmee River <u>has been</u> channelized*
    • *Fires <u>have been</u> more frequent*

---

[1]Adapted from Anna Ingalls and Dan Moody, *Check It Out: A Quick and Easy Guide for Writers* (Boston: Allyn & Bacon, 1999), pp. 15–16.

2

Cultural and Social Issues

American Fish   R. A. Sasaki   10

Listen to Me Good   Margaret Charles Smith and Linda Janet Holmes   18

Boomer Parents   Sandy Banks   23

Spanglish Spoken Here   Janice Castro   29

The Ambitious Generation   Barbara Schneider and David Stevenson   35

Saffron Sky   Gelareh Asayesh   40

Suspect Policy   Randall Kennedy   46

American Fish

R. A. Sasaki

Each group of immigrants to the United States has made unique contributions to our multi-ethnic, multi-cultural society. The following short story by Japanese-American writer R. A. Sasaki consists almost entirely of a conversation between two Japanese-American women. The story is interesting because of what lies beneath the surface—their attitudes toward each other and how they have both been affected by their experiences in America.

Prereading Questions

1. What kinds of things do people talk about when they haven't seen each other for a long time?
2. Do you think that different cultures have different unwritten rules about how one is expected to be polite and courteous to others?

Vocabulary

daikon radish a long white radish from Japan
burdock a weedy plant
boasting bragging, glorifying oneself
consoling reassuring, offering comfort
refrained held back, used self-control to resist doing something
aggravating annoying
peeved irritated
shriveled dried out and shrunken
groped tried uncertainly to find
redeem to compensate or make up for something, such as a previous mistake
bumped into met accidentally

SOURCE: "American Fish" Copyright 1991 by R. A. Sasaki. Reprinted from *The Loom and Other Stories* with the permission of Graywolf Press, St. Paul, Minnesota.

American Fish

Mrs. Hayashi was inspecting a daikon radish in the American Fish Market in Japantown when she recognized a woman who was heading toward the burdock roots.

2   I know her, she thought. What was her name? Suzuki? Kato? She decided to pretend not to see the woman, and see if the woman recognized her. She put down the radish and picked up another.

3   "Oh . . . hello," said the woman, who was now standing next to her.

4   Mrs. Hayashi looked up and smiled enthusiastically. "Oh, hi!" she said. "Long time no see." Immediately she regretted the remark. What if it was someone she had just seen yesterday?

5   "How've you been?" the woman asked.

6   "Fine, just fine," Mrs. Hayashi said. I should ask her about her husband, she thought. Did she have a husband?

7   "How's your husband?" the woman asked.

8   Mrs. Hayashi's husband had died ten years before. Obviously, the woman was someone she had not seen in quite some time. Thank goodness, she thought. Then it had been appropriate to say "long time no see."

9   "He passed away several years ago," Mrs. Hayashi said.

10 "Oh, so sorry to hear that," the woman said.

11 I should ask her about her children, Mrs. Hayashi thought. But since she still did not know if the woman had a husband or not, she couldn't very well assume that she had children. Wouldn't it be awful if I asked her about her children and it turned out she wasn't even married! And even if she was married, and did have children, what if they had died, or committed crimes? After all, everyone couldn't have a son in law school, and Mrs. Hayashi did not like to appear to be boasting. No, she'd better avoid the subject of children.

12 "How are your kids?" the woman asked.

13 "Oh, Bill is just fine," Mrs. Hayashi replied. She couldn't stand it. "He'll be graduating from law school next spring," she added, consoling herself with the thought that at least she had refrained from mentioning that her son was at the top of his class.

14 "That's nice," said the woman. "And what about your daughter?"

15 "I don't have a daughter," Mrs. Hayashi said stiffly. "Just a son." She was beginning to think that the woman wasn't anyone she knew very well.

16   "Stupid me," said the woman. "I was thinking of someone else."

17   "How are *your* children?" Mrs. Hayashi asked, throwing caution to the wind.

18   "Fine," the woman said. "Emily and her husband live in San Jose and have two little girls."

19   "How nice," Mrs. Hayashi said.

20   There was a pause. Mrs. Hayashi did not know anyone named Emily. Who was this woman?

21   It occurred to her that the woman might be someone she didn't like. How aggravating, she thought, not to be able to remember whether to be pleasant to someone or not.

22   "I'm so sorry," the woman said, "But I have a real bad memory for names. It was Suzuki-san, wasn't it?"

23   "Hayashi," Mrs. Hayashi said, peeved. "Grace Hayashi."

24   "Of course," said the woman, somewhat vaguely. "Hayashi . . ."

25   "And . . . forgive me," said Mrs. Hayashi, seizing the opportunity, "but you're . . . ?"

26   "Nakamura," the woman said. "Toshi Nakamura."

27   The name did not even ring a bell.

28   "Is that the family that runs the bakery on Fillmore?" Mrs. Hayashi asked.

29   "No," the woman said, "not that Nakamura."

30   "Then you must be related to Frank Nakamura."

31   "No."

32   "How odd," Mrs. Hayashi said without thinking, and was embarrassed when she realized she had spoken aloud.

33   "My maiden name was Fujii," Mrs. Nakamura said.

34   "Fujii . . . " Mrs. Hayashi said, thinking hard.

35   "Maybe you know my sister Eiko."

36   "Eiko Fujii . . . " Mrs. Hayashi said, frowning.

37   Then a horrible thought occurred to Mrs. Hayashi. Perhaps she did not know this woman at all; perhaps Mrs. Nakamura just looked like someone she knew, or someone she should know—a Japanese-American lady in her late fifties, the same age as Mrs. Hayashi, wearing a somewhat faded but sensible raincoat even though it was not raining outside. But then, Mrs. Nakamura had recognized her, too.

38   "Did I know you in Topaz?" Mrs. Hayashi asked.

39   "Oh, no," Mrs. Nakamura said. Mrs. Hayashi waited, but the other woman said nothing further.

40   "You weren't in Topaz?" Mrs. Hayashi continued.

41   "No."

42   "Where were you—Manzanar?" Mrs. Hayashi asked pleasantly.

43   "No."

44 "Oh, well," Mrs. Hayashi said, becoming flustered. "Perhaps you weren't in camp during the war. I don't mean to pry."

45 "I was in Tule Lake," Mrs. Nakamura said, turning to pick through the burdock roots. She rejected a shriveled bunch of roots and put a fresh bunch in her cart.

46 "Oh," Mrs. Hayashi said. She felt her face go hot. Tule Lake was where all those branded "disloyal" had been imprisoned during the war. "I see," Mrs. Hayashi said, searching for a way to change the topic.

47 "Do you?"

48 Mrs. Hayashi was startled. "I'm sorry," she said. "I don't know what you mean."

49 "And I don't know what you see," Mrs. Nakamura said.

50 "Nothing," Mrs. Hayashi said. "I just meant—oh."

51 "Oh," Mrs. Nakamura said.

52 Mrs. Hayashi by this time was extremely uncomfortable and groped for a way to redeem the situation.

53 "I knew some people who were in Tule Lake," she said. "The Satos. From Watsonville. Did you know them?"

54 "No," Mrs. Nakamura said.

55 "It was the silliest thing, really," Mrs. Hayashi went on. "Mr. Sato was a Buddhist priest, and after Pearl Harbor, his name got on some list, and the FBI picked him up. Imagine that."

56 Mrs. Nakamura was silent.

57 "As if being Buddhist was a crime," Mrs. Hayashi added, trying to make clear where her sympathies lay. She was not a Buddhist herself, but she thought Mrs. Nakamura might be one.

58 "My father said he wanted to go back to Japan," Mrs. Nakamura said suddenly. "That's why we were in Tule Lake."

59 "Oh," Mrs. Hayashi said.

60 "They took his boat away after Pearl Harbor," Mrs. Nakamura continued. "He was a fisherman down in Terminal Island. Without a boat, he couldn't make a living. he thought the only thing to do was to go back to Japan."

61 "I know," Mrs. Hayashi said. "My father was forced to sell his store to the first person who offered to buy. A lifetime of hard work, just thrown away!"

62 "It made my father mad," Mrs. Nakamura went on. "He said why stay in a country that doesn't want us?"

63 "That's perfectly logical," Mrs. Hayashi reassured. "Why indeed?"

64 "Why did *your* parents want to stay?" Mrs. Nakamura asked.

65 "Well," Mrs. Hayashi said, startled. "I don't know." She thought for a moment, then said, "I guess they knew that we, I mean my brothers and sisters and I, would never want to go to Japan. I mean, we were born here. We belonged here. And they wanted the family to stay together."

66 "That's how my mother and I felt," Mrs. Nakamura said. "That's why we said we wanted to go back to Japan, too—so we'd be all together. Except in those days, that made you disloyal."

67 "Well, it was ridiculous," Mrs. Hayashi said firmly. "And it caused so much grief."

68 There was a silence.

69 "Where did you go back to, in Japan?" Mrs. Hayashi asked gently.

70 "Oh, we didn't go back," Mrs. Nakamura replied cheerfully. "My father changed his mind when he remembered that they didn't have central heating in Japan."

71 Both women burst out laughing.

72 Mrs. Hayashi, still laughing, threw a bunch of burdock roots into her cart.

73 "Well, I should be getting along," Mrs. Nakamura said. "I'm so glad I bumped into you . . ." She stopped, embarrassed.

74 "Hayashi."

75 ". . . Hayashi-san," she finished. "Now if I could just remember who you are."

76 They laughed again.

77 "I'm sure it'll come back to us," Mrs. Hayashi said. "Everything does."

78 "Do you go to the Buddhist church?" Mrs. Nakamura asked. "Maybe I've seen you there."

79 "I doubt it," Mrs. Hayashi replied. "I'm Methodist. But I've been to funerals at the Buddhist church, so maybe."

80 "That must be it—we must have met at someone's funeral," Mrs. Nakamura agreed. "I'm sure it'll come to me as soon as I walk out of here with my groceries. Isn't it always like that?"

81 "It can't be that mysterious," Mrs. Hayashi said. "I mean, our lives aren't so terribly complicated. If we didn't know each other in camp, then we knew each other before the war, or after the war. I'm sure I won't be able to sleep until I remember which it was," she added cheerfully. "I hate to forget things. That is, unless they're the sort of things you'd rather not remember."

82 Mrs. Nakamura looked at her watch.

83 "My goodness," she said. "I have to run. I have to be at work in an hour."

84 "Work?" Mrs. Hayashi said.

85 "Yes; I work at Macy's," Mrs. Nakamura said. "I'm in . . ."

86 "Gift wrap!" Mrs. Hayashi said, remembering.

87 The two women stared incredulously at each other for an instant, then broke into raucous laughter. Then they bowed slightly, and continued on their separate ways.

◆◆◆

Comprehension

1. At the beginning of the story, why does Mrs. Hayashi have trouble deciding whether or not to speak to Mrs. Nakamura and what to say to her?
2. In what ways do the two women seem to be alike?
3. At what point in the story do the two women seem to be a little bit annoyed with each other, possibly even angry? How does the topic of their conversation affect their feelings?
4. Why do the women laugh together three times near the end of the story? What does their laughter tell us about the change in their relationship?

Critical Thinking

1. If the two women had been Mexican-American, African-American, Anglo-American, or another ethnic combination, do you think their conversation would have been different? How so? Give reasons for your answer.
2. Why does Mrs. Hayashi feel that she ought to be careful about the kinds of questions she asks and the things she says? Give at least two examples from the story.
3. Do the two characters in this short story seem believable and realistic (that is, like real people)? Why or why not?
4. Why is it especially difficult for the two women to talk about the time when their families were in camps? How do you think they feel about that period of their lives?
5. Do you think the women will become friends? Why or why not?

Language and Vocabulary

1. Had you ever heard the expression "throwing caution to the wind" before you read it in the story? What does it sound like it means? Take your best guess at the meaning, and look it up if you need to. Then write a sentence about a time when you or someone else threw caution to the wind.
2. At first, much of the conversation consists of ordinary, everyday comments and questions. Find at least three examples of these routine phrases or sentences near the beginning of the story. Are these typical greetings that Americans exchange with acquaintances or with friends they have not seen in a while?

Style, Structure, and Organization

1. Whose point of view is "American Fish" told from? To answer this question, look at the story to see which character's thoughts and feelings are frequently included. How do these thoughts and feelings help us understand the story?
2. Does the ending make the story seem complete? Why or why not?

Topics for Discussion or Journal Writing

1. Have you ever had a similar experience of seeing someone you weren't sure you knew? How did you feel?
2. If you were in Mrs. Hayashi's or Mrs. Nakamura's place, how would you have handled the situation? Would you have said or done anything differently?
3. Do you come from a mixed cultural background, or do you know someone else who does? Are you aware of any conflicts or differences between the two cultures?
4. Based on what you learned in this story, do you think Japanese Americans were treated unfairly during World War II? Explain your answer.

Writing Topics for Paragraphs or Essays

1. Write about some of the problems that you or someone you know has had in adjusting to a move from one culture to another.
2. Write a short story similar to "American Fish," based on a conversation between two people. Choose two characters who are in an uncomfortable situation or who disagree with each other. Make their conversation, or *dialogue*, sound as real as possible. You may also want to include some of the thoughts of one or both characters.
3. Read another short story by R. A. Sasaki or by another Asian-American author, such as Amy Tan. Write a summary of the story, plus your evaluation and personal response. You may also want to comment on any similarities you see between that story and "American Fish."

4. Look up information about the United States' internment of Japanese citizens and Japanese Americans during World War II. Write a paper about what you learn. Include your opinion about the internment camps.
5. Write an imaginary scene with *dialogue* (conversation) between you and Mrs. Hayashi. How would you get acquainted? What would you talk about? If you wish, you may imagine that you know her son or grandson.

Listen to Me Good

Margaret Charles Smith and Linda Janet Holmes

Margaret Charles Smith learned to be a midwife at a time when very few doctors were available in rural areas of the United States, and the overwhelming majority of African-American babies were born at home. As you read this collection of short selections from *Listen to Me Good: The Life Story of an Alabama Midwife,* look for evidence of the conflict between traditional African-American midwives and the medical establishment of doctors and nurses.

Prereading Questions

1. In this country, where do most women choose to have their babies, at home or in the hospital? Why do you think that is?
2. Is modern medicine always better than traditional methods of healing people?

Vocabulary

walk a pain off in this case, walk around until the birth contraction stops again

to get a kick out of something to enjoy something very much

lantern light light from a kerosene lantern (because many houses had no electricity)

incubator in this case, a small tent or box that keeps premature, underweight, or sick babies warm

the pen short form of *penitentiary,* a prison where inmates often serve extended sentences

getting out in this case, becoming known (dialect)

tea in this case, a hot drink made from local plants and herbs that is supposed to help ease a mother's labor pains

clinic a local medical center, not as big as a hospital

Listen to Me Good

Listen to me good. Back when I started, it was kind of poor. At that time, the people didn't have nothing. You couldn't get nothing. They had to do the very best they could. Some of them didn't have places to sit. They didn't even have a piece of white sheet, clean or nothing. I'd have to get up sometime and go to the next-door house and ask her to give me some clean rags, if she had 'em. Just barely living.

. . .

2   I took training courses, but the midwife had already trained me, Ella Anderson. I learned everything, learned how to ask the mother if she was ready—does she have all her equipment ready? You know—the newspaper, something to boil the water in, something for the baby. But you just didn't need nothing new for the baby. Somebody else may have some things you could borrow or use. See what I mean? But everything, everything I learned, I learned from Miss Anderson. See, Miss Ella Anderson had done learned me, and I didn't forget it.

. . .

3   Then sometimes, I'd tell the mother to go take a hot bath, and that hot water helps a lot. I sit their feet in hot water or let them sit in that tub, if they got it, a number three tub. I was willing to let them have their way until push comes to shove. Some of them would say, "I don't want to take a bath."

4   I'd say, "Just get in the tub, and I'll bathe you." I was right there to get them out, but some of them just wouldn't do it.

. . .

5   Sometime they want to get up, and I'd help them up. Walk around in the room. Walk a pain off then get back in the bed. A lot of people get a kick out of walking. Go into different rooms and sit in different chairs, or get down on their knees—anywhere they think they can get ease. But there's no ease for birth till it's over with. It's good to walk, but you'll have to stop sometime.

. . .

6   The houses would be so cold, you would almost freeze sitting beside her bed. The fireplace up here in the front of the house, and you back yonder on the bed. You had to peep to see what's happening down there, and you have to do it by lantern light until the people got to the place where they had better lights.

. . .

7   The nurse would come after the baby was born, if I gave her word to come. If you weighed the baby, and the baby is underweight, then you call your nurse to bring out the incubator. They used to have the one that runs with hot water bottles.

. . .

8   Now, the nurses didn't know what was good and what was bad. You can't take too much of anything. You just need enough to warm you up inside and get those pains a-moving, if you done done everything you can do on the outside.

9   I had to stop fooling with those teas and things in labor because my name was getting out.

. . .

10   They said, "They better not catch nobody giving nobody no tea of no kind. If they do, she was going to jail and from there to the pen."

11   So, I didn't figure I wanted to go to the pen, but they had a couple midwives that still gave a woman teas. They had the nurses to come and the doctor that was the head of the clinic, and a couple more white ladies. I don't know who they were or where they were from. But they sure got that midwife ripped about them teas. They told her the best thing you do when you go home, get your bag and come back to town. Bring your bag in because you're going to kill somebody.

12   You know, they're quick to think teas and things are going to kill somebody. One midwife told the nurse when we had the meeting, she just told her, "I think I'll bring my bag in and give it to you all because you all are not there when this labor is going on. You don't know how it goes. Rubbing helps and teas help. If I can't give them some hot teas which I know will help, I just as well ought to give it up."

. . .

13   All they wanted was the midwives off. Training was the last thing they wanted. They wrote me at the health department that I couldn't be no more midwife. I had to bring my bag and my equipment in, not only me, but all of them that was delivering.

. . .

14   Everybody goes to the hospital now. Some of them feel pretty good about it, and some don't. But if you go to the hospital, you're going to pay some money.

15   The doctors have made them so much money. They take two thousand, three thousand for delivering one baby. That's a lot of money, and you're doing all the work.

16   I think it's just better to stay home than to go to the hospital. Go to the hospital, have your baby, get up and go home the next day? I'd have the baby at home and let that do.

17   You can have your way more at home. You can have your own freedom at home. You won't have to lay down until your time come. You can get up and do things. The baby won't have to be drugged before birth from giving you those shots to knock you out.

. . .

18   I'm worth millions of dollars for what I've done done. I thought I was doing a big thing. I was proud of it. The lives that I've saved, going to deliver all these babies, till I got something to be thankful for. The children have grown so. Some of them have to bend their heads down to hardly get in that door. They have grown just that way. I am thankful, yeah.

◆◆◆

Comprehension

1. How did Margaret Smith learn to be a midwife?
2. What things did a midwife need in order to deliver a baby?
3. Why did a nurse sometimes come to the house after a baby was born?
4. According to the selection, what are some benefits of having a baby at home?

Critical Thinking

1. Based on the reading, what social and economic changes led to fewer midwives delivering babies?
2. How does the author, Margaret Smith, feel about doctors, nurses, and hospitals? Find at least two examples in the reading to support your answer.
3. Do you think the author's viewpoint might be biased against modern medicine?
4. Do you think that the doctors and nurses in this selection were biased against traditional midwives and delivering babies at home?

Language and Vocabulary

1. What does the author mean when she writes, "But they sure got that midwife ripped about them teas"?
2. Using her rural dialect, the author writes, "At that time, the people didn't have nothing. You couldn't get nothing." In the past, even well-known authors such as William Shakespeare used double negatives. Is it acceptable to use double negatives in academic writing today, such as in papers for college classes?

Style, Structure, and Organization

1. The author of these selections writes in her own voice, the dialect of one area of the rural South. Does using dialect make the selections feel richer and more authentic?

2. This reading consists of selections taken from various places in the book. Do you think these selections give a good picture of a midwife's job in the mid 1900s in a poor area of the country?
3. How does the conclusion wrap up the topic and make the selection feel finished?

Topics for Discussion or Journal Writing

1. Do you believe in natural methods of healing and childbirth, or do you think that births should take place in hospitals?
2. What is alternative medicine? Is it as effective as modern medical practices, such as surgery and drugs?
3. In your opinion, what are some benefits of having a baby in a hospital? What are some benefits of having a baby at home?
4. Why do you think the doctors and nurses in the story didn't want the midwives giving herbal teas (made from local plants) to expectant mothers? Do you agree?
5. Some religions do not approve of certain medical techniques, such as blood transfusions. Should people have the right to refuse medical treatment that they don't want?

Writing Topics for Paragraphs or Essays

1. Describe a hospital experience you have had, or interview someone else who has been a patient in a hospital.
2. If you have had a baby, give some advice to an expectant mother or father.
3. Look up information in a library or on the Internet about one or more of the following health professionals: osteopaths, chiropractors, homeopaths, and acupuncturists. Then write a report about what you learn. How well are they accepted by the medical establishment? What is your opinion about them?
4. Interview a midwife, a nurse, an obstetrician, an anesthesiologist, or any other person who helps deliver babies. Prepare a list of questions in advance. After the interview, write about what it's like to help babies come into this world.
5. Choose one of the following health-related topics. Find out more about the topic by searching online or in a library; then write about it.
    a. What is alternative medicine? Are some types of alternative medicine as effective as modern medical methods?
    b. Compare two different methods of labor and delivery, such as Lamaze, Bradley, Leboyer, or Waterbirth (underwater delivery).

◆◆◆

Boomer Parents

Sandy Banks

The baby boomer generation grew up with events such as the Vietnam War protests, the Civil Rights Movement, and the assassination of President John F. Kennedy. A popular saying, "Don't trust anyone over 30," showed that many boomers questioned all forms of authority.

Now that boomers are raising their own teenagers, they must deal with being authority figures themselves. As you read this newspaper article, think about how strict—or how lenient—parents should be with their teenage sons and daughters.

Prereading Questions

1. Who are the "baby boomers"?
2. Do most parents share the same standards for raising their children?

Vocabulary

catered food party food delivered and served by a restaurant or catering service

bellied up came forward and stood close (slang)

swig swallow quickly, gulp

grimaced made a face, frowned

adhered stuck

disabuse (oneself) of stop believing something false

thicket in this case, a large number (of difficult choices), tangle

blissfully very happily

off-guard with one's defenses down

SATs Scholastic Aptitude Tests, a widely used college entrance exam

unwittingly without meaning to, without realizing

albeit although

risqué daring and possibly offensive

spill out my contrition tell them how sorry I am

obscenity-laced full of offensive language
schlep carry, transport
ambivalence lack of enthusiasm
lyrics words

Boomer Parents

They were new neighbors, decent enough people with nice cars, a well-maintained home, one handsome, well-behaved young son. Their housewarming party was an all-night affair, with good music, catered food, a poolside bar.

2 It was long past midnight when the kids began crowding the patio bar. A bunch of 12-year-olds, arms outstretched, paper cups in hand. "Can you put a little vodka in this, please," the young son of the hostess politely inquired.

3 The bartender eyed him suspiciously. "For you?" she asked. "You must be kidding."

4 "For me," he said, thrusting his cup toward her. "C'mon . . . my mom said it's OK." The bartender shook her head and put the vodka bottle away. "I don't serve children." Then mom breezed up, uncapped the bottle and poured a short stream of vodka into her son's cup. "Just a capful," she announced resolutely, as if she were handing out candy on Halloween. Her son's buddies bellied up to the bar . . . capfuls of vodka all around.

5 A few party-goers raised voices in protest: Aren't they a little young? Isn't that illegal? But we grew quiet when Mom waved us off, as if she were guilty of nothing more serious than serving cake before dinner. "Oh, it's not going to hurt them. It's just a capful . . . what's the big deal?"

6 I rose to leave, feeling heartsick as I watched these little boys swig vodka. They grimaced as they choked it down, then slapped high-fives to celebrate. And I couldn't help but think about their mothers. Blissfully ignorant at home, never dreaming that a sleepover would make social drinkers of their preteen sons.

7 Or maybe not. Maybe they serve their kids liquor too.

. . .

8 It was easy when my three children were small to imagine that every family was just like ours, followed the same conventions, adhered to the same set of parenting rules. But the older they get, the more I realize how little I know about what goes on in homes that once seemed very much like my own.

9 I have had to disabuse myself of the notion that every "good" parent is raising his or her kids just like I am, that there is one universal

set of behavioral standards that guides us all through this thicket of parenting choices.

10 Still, I am caught off-guard by what I see and hear:

11 An 11-year-old lets loose with a string of swear words. Her mother shushes her gently with this admonition: "Now you know you're not to talk that way in public." How can that be? These are good parents, responsible, well-educated. Mom stays at home with her kids, sends them to Catholic school . . . and lets them curse around the dinner table.

12 My baby-sitter opens her mouth to show my daughters her birthday present—a giant gold stud pierced through her tongue. She is 16, still wears braces on her teeth, is deemed by her mom too young to date. Yet piercing her tongue seems somehow not extreme. "My mom got hers pierced too," she tells us. "And if I do well on my SATs, she might let me get a tattoo for Christmas."

13 I question their choices, then suddenly, unwittingly, I land on the outlaw mother side.

14 I've invited my daughters' friends to join us for a movie. They are 9- and 11-years-old—suburban girls like mine, sheltered, but not naive. The movie—"Nutty Professor II"—is PG-13.

15 It is raucously funny, albeit a little risqué. I laugh but cringe at the off-color gags and four-letter words. But the theater is full of children, so how bad can this be? Very bad, I realize later, when I'm confronted by a disapproving 11-year-old. "Did you guys like the movie," I ask, as we gather our things to leave.

16 My daughter glances at her friend, who shakes her head and looks away. "It was inappropriate, Mommy," my daughter says firmly. "I didn't think you'd let us watch something with so many bad words."

17 Our guests are quiet as I drive them home. Could it be this is unlike anything their own mothers would have let them see? I rehearse in my mind the apologies I'll have to deliver. And when I drop them off and spill out my contrition, I see in the eyes of their mothers disappointment, and this unspoken question:

18 "What kind of mother is she?"

. . .

19 They are not the "family values" politicians crow about, these micro issues we confront in the day-to-day raising of our kids. But they are the choices that go to the heart of who we are as parents and families today.

20 How much freedom is too much for our children? At what age do you let them go off alone to Magic Mountain? Is a 9-year-old too young for a second hole in her ear? Should I let my 15-year-old see an R-rated movie, my 11-year-old listen to her friend's obscenity-laced rap CD?

21 I imagine I am no different than many parents, caught in a middle of confusion over shifting standards and sensibilities.

22 "It's not hard to know how we feel about the big issues," says USC sociology professor Constance Ahrons. "What's harder is the small stuff that comes up day to day, the decisions that raising children forces you to make. That's where we're bombarded with pressures, and every parent is not going to respond the same way."

23 Surveys show that more than half of parents today think they are doing a worse job raising kids than their parents did. They admit that they're often confused by the choices they face, and disappointed in the course they take.

24 "The problem is not neglectful parents," says David Blankenhorn, director of the research group the Institute for American Values.

25 "It's us—the baby boomers . . . folks with nice homes, two cars in the garage, who love our kids, schlep them to soccer practice and piano lessons, make enormous sacrifices to give them the best we can," yet shortchange them in a very important way.

26 "Because we were raised to be skeptical of authority, we have this fundamental ambivalence about being authoritative," he says. "Remember, 'Don't trust anybody over 30'? . . . Well, now here we are, middle-aged people with teenage kids and young children, and we don't want to tell them what to do. So we don't."

27 So before we blame the lyrics in the music, the trash on TV, the violence of video games, perhaps we ought to look in the mirror and ask ourselves: Who is really in charge? Are we leading or following, guiding or giving up? Are we making our children choose on their own which road to stumble down?

◆◆◆

Comprehension

1. What did the bartender tell the children when they wanted some vodka?
2. In some of today's families, certain standards of behavior are different from the standards that most families had in the past. What are two examples from the reading?
3. How did the author's daughter and her friends feel about the PG-13 movie that the author took them to see?
4. Besides parenting styles, what other influences on children are listed in the article?

Critical Thinking

1. Who is the author's intended audience—in other words, who is the writer primarily directing this article to?
2. What is the main idea of the reading?
3. According to the article, who is responsible for the way children turn out?
4. How do you think the author feels about her own parenting skills?
5. How do you think the generation called "baby boomers" got that name? How old are the baby boomers now?

Language and Vocabulary

1. What does "mom breezed up" mean (in the fourth paragraph)? Besides the basic meaning, what impressions does the expression "breezed up" give the reader?
2. One of the sentences in this article says that the girls are "sheltered, but not naive." What is the difference between *sheltered* and *naive* in this sentence?

Style, Structure, and Organization

1. In this article, the author uses many personal examples to *show* the reader what she means rather than just *tell* her points. Do these personal examples make the article more effective? Why?
2. The author includes a lot of *questions* in this article. Find and underline at least five of the author's questions. How does using so many questions help set the *tone* (or *feel*) of the reading?
3. There are many short paragraphs in this reading, each with a small chunk of meaning. How is this style, which is commonly used in newspaper articles, different from the style used in papers written for college classes?

Topics for Discussion or Journal Writing

1. What would you do if you learned that your child had been exposed to something you don't approve of at a friend's house?
2. Is raising children more difficult today than it was in the past? Why?

3. People need a license to drive a car, open a business, or teach school, but anyone can have children. In a perfect world, what qualifications would parents have before they started raising children?
4. Do you think the author of this article is a strict parent? Is that good or bad?
5. In your opinion, will raising children in the future be easier or harder? Why?

Writing Topics for Paragraphs or Essays

1. What is the best way to raise children? Provide some advice for new parents.
2. Write about some things your parents did well in raising you or that you have done well in raising your own children.
3. Describe some of the bad or dangerous influences on children in today's society, and recommend a way for parents and young people to deal with these influences.
4. Compare a typical day in the life of two children, one in the 1960s or 1970s and one today.
5. Choose one of the following topics. Find out more about the topic by searching online or in a library; then write a short paper on the effects of that activity.

   a. How can learning to drink alcohol at a young age affect a person later in life?

   b. What effect does watching violence on TV, in movies, and in video games have on children?

Spanglish Spoken Here

Janice Castro

The United States contains an exciting mix of people from all over the world, each group contributing to our unique culture. The fastest-growing immigrant group in recent decades has been the Hispanic population; as a result, many Spanish words have entered mainstream English and added to its richness. Likewise, many English words are used by Spanish speakers on a daily basis. As you read this article that was first published in 1988, think about which facts may have changed since then (such as statistics) and which situations have not changed.

Prereading Questions

1. Do most people in the United States know at least a few words of Spanish? What other languages are spoken in your area of the country?
2. Immigrant groups have always faced prejudice from some people. Do you think that Hispanics face more, less, or about the same levels of prejudice as previous waves of immigrants, such as Africans, Italians, Irish, and Germans?

Vocabulary

bemused puzzled

miss a beat hesitate

personnel officer a person who accepts job applications and sometimes interviews applicants

free-form without specific rules or boundaries

mode in this case, a way of speaking

syntax grammar, especially word order

handier easier to use

melting pot the idea that the United States "melts" all cultures together into one common culture

Anglo English-speaking

Hispanic of Spanish-speaking origin or family background

Latinos in this case, people of Latin-American origin or background, often used to mean Hispanics

gaffes, blunders, goofs mistakes

inadvertently without intending to, accidentally

mangled badly mistreated

Spanglish Spoken Here

1. In Manhattan a first-grader greets her visiting grandparents, happily exclaiming, "Come here, *siéntate!*" Her bemused grandfather, who does not speak Spanish, nevertheless knows she is asking him to sit down. A Miami personnel officer understands what a job applicant means when he says "*Quiero un* part time." Nor do drivers miss a beat reading a billboard alongside a Los Angeles street advertising CERVEZA—SIX-PACK.

2. This free-form blend of Spanish and English, known as Spanglish, is common linguistic currency wherever concentrations of Hispanic Americans are found in the U.S. In Los Angeles, where 55% of the city's 3 million inhabitants speak Spanish, Spanglish is as much a part of daily life as sunglasses. Unlike the broken-English efforts of earlier immigrants from Europe, Asia, and other regions, Spanglish has become a widely accepted conversational mode used casually—even playfully—by Spanish-speaking immigrants and native-born Californians alike.

3. Consisting of one part Hispanicized English, one part Americanized Spanish and more than a little fractured syntax, Spanglish is a bit like a Robin Williams comedy routine: a crackling line of cross-cultural patter straight from the melting pot. Often it enters Anglo homes and families through the children, who pick it up at school or at play with their young Hispanic contemporaries. In other cases, it comes from watching TV; many an Anglo child watching *Sesame Street* has learned *uno dos tres* almost as quickly as one two three.

4. Spanglish takes a variety of forms, from the Southern California Anglos who bid farewell with the utterly silly "*hasta la* bye-bye" to the Cuban-American drivers in Miami who *parquean* their carros. Some Spanglish sentences are mostly Spanish, with a quick detour for an English word or two. A Latino friend may cut short a conversation by glancing at his watch and excusing himself with the explanation that he must "*ir al* supermarket."

5. Many of the English words transplanted in this way are simply handier than their Spanish counterparts. No matter how distasteful the subject, for example, it is still easier to say "income tax" than *impuesto sobre*

la renta. At the same time, many Spanish-speaking immigrants have adopted such terms as VCR, microwave and dishwasher for what they view as largely American phenomena. Still other English words convey a cultural context that is not implicit in the Spanish. A friend who invites you to *lonche* most likely has in mind the brisk American custom of "doing lunch" rather than the languorous afternoon break traditionally implied by *almuerzo*.

6 Mainstream Americans exposed to similar hybrids of German, Chinese or Hindi might be mystified. But even Anglos who speak little or no Spanish are somewhat familiar with Spanglish. Living among them, for one thing, are 19 million Hispanics. In addition, more American high school and university students sign up for Spanish than for any other foreign language.

7 Only in the past ten years, though, has Spanglish begun to turn into a national slang. Its popularity has grown with the explosive increases in U.S. immigration from Latin American countries. English has increasingly collided with Spanish in retail stores, offices and classrooms, in pop music and on street corners. Anglos whose ancestors picked up such Spanish words as *rancho, bronco, tornado* and *incommunicado*, for instance, now freely use such Spanish words as *gracias, bueno, amigo* and *por favor*.

8 Among Latinos, Spanglish conversations often flow easily from Spanish into several sentences of English and back again. "It is done unconsciously," explains Carmen Silva-Corvalan, a Chilean-born associate professor of linguistics at the University of California who speaks Spanglish with relatives and neighbors. "I couldn't even tell you minutes later if I said something in Spanish or English."

9 Spanglish is a sort of code for Latinos: the speakers know Spanish, but their hybrid language reflects the American culture in which they live. Many lean to shorter, clipped phrases in place of the longer, more graceful expressions their parents used. Says Leonel de la Cuesta, an assistant professor of modern languages at Florida International University in Miami: "In the U.S., time is money, and that is showing up in Spanglish as an economy of language." Conversational examples: *taipiar* (type) and *winshi-wiper* (windshield wiper) replace *escribir a máquina* and *limpiaparabrisas*.

10 Major advertisers, eager to tap the estimated $134 billion in spending power wielded by Spanish-speaking Americans, have ventured into Spanglish to promote their products. In some cases, attempts to sprinkle Spanish through commercials have produced embarrassing gaffes. A Braniff airlines ad that sought to tell Spanish-speaking audiences that they could settle back *en* (in) luxuriant *cuero* (leather) seats, for example, inadvertently said they could fly without clothes (*encuero*). A fractured

translation of the Miller Lite slogan told readers the beer was "filling, and less delicious." Similar blunders are often made by Anglos trying to impress Spanish-speaking pals. But if Latinos are amused by mangled Spanglish, they also recognize these goofs as a sort of friendly acceptance. As they might put it, *no problema.*

❖❖❖

Comprehension

1. What is Spanglish? How does it reflect the culture of those who speak it?
2. What Spanish words listed in the article are commonly used among English speakers in the United States? List at least five.
3. How much spending power did Spanish-speaking Americans control in 1988, when this article was written?
4. What is the most popular foreign language among U.S. high school and university students?

Critical Thinking

1. How do you think the author feels about Latino immigration and Spanglish? Is her attitude negative or positive?
2. Is the author's purpose only to inform or also to entertain? How informative is the article and how entertaining?
3. The author's name is Janice Castro. What might that tell you about her family background? Do you think having a Hispanic background could give someone a special insight into the topic of this article?
4. Is this article objective (based on facts and numbers), subjective (based on personal experience and opinion), or both?

Language and Vocabulary

1. In this article, the author uses many *adjectives*—words that describe a noun (person, place, thing, animal, or idea). In the final paragraph, the first five adjectives are *major, eager, spending, Spanish-speaking,* and *embarrassing.* Highlight or underline five more adjectives in the final paragraph. Do these adjectives make the reading more interesting?
2. The author uses many Spanish words as examples in this article. If you are unsure of the meaning of any of these Spanish words, look them up in a Spanish-English dictionary.

Style, Structure, and Organization

1. Who do you think the author is writing for (who is her intended audience)? Why do you think so?
2. The author uses several quoted phrases and sentences throughout the article, such as "Come here, *siéntate!*" How do these quotations help make the article interesting?
3. The conclusion of this article ends with an example of Spanglish: "*no problema.*" How does this technique support the author's point by *showing* rather than *telling*?

Topics for Discussion or Journal Writing

1. What are some benefits of learning and speaking a second language?
2. Do you speak any other languages? Which ones? Do any of your relatives or friends speak another language? What languages did your ancestors speak?
3. Have you ever used any Spanish words while speaking English? What are some examples?
4. Have you ever spent time in a foreign country where a different language is spoken or in an area of the United States where Spanish is commonly spoken, such as California, Texas, Florida, or New York City? Describe your experience.
5. What languages have you heard spoken in the United States? What foods from other countries have you eaten? Describe your experiences.

Writing Topics for Paragraphs or Essays

1. Is the United States more like a melting pot of different cultures or more like a salad bowl? Why?
2. Write about a trip you took to another place, or write about a trip you would like to take. Include information about language and customs.
3. Write about your own experience studying and practicing a foreign language. How did you feel when you were learning it? How do you feel about your ability to speak it now?
4. Write an instructions paper that gives useful tips on learning to speak another language. How can a second language learner become really proficient?

5. Choose one of the following topics. Find out more about the topic by searching online or in a library; then write a paragraph or short essay.

   a. Compare how many languages (and which languages) are spoken by schoolchildren in your area with the number of languages that are spoken by schoolchildren in a large city, such as New York or Los Angeles. Give examples and information on where the students in each area have come from.

   b. Find updated information to replace the 1988 statistics in the reading. Compare how the statistics have changed and how these numbers have affected the society in the United States.

The Ambitious Generation

Barbara Schneider and David Stevenson

Barbara Schneider, a professor of sociology at the University of Chicago, and David Stevenson, assistant director for social and behavioral sciences in the U.S. government Office of Science and Technology Policy, have collected and analyzed a great deal of information about the teenage experience and how it has changed over the years. As you read the following selection from their book, *The Ambitious Generation,* consider how the social world of adolescents during the 1950s differed from the social world of today.

Prereading Questions

1. In what ways do you think today's teenagers are different from the teenagers of 50 years ago?
2. What qualities make some people more popular in school than others? Does being an athlete, a cheerleader, or a member of certain organizations contribute to a person's popularity in high school or college?

Vocabulary

bounded having specific boundaries

booster clubs clubs that promote and support certain school activities

social status in this context, a high social position

peer group people of approximately the same age and social position

markers indications or signs

confer to award an honor or a position

elite considered to have a high social position; above others

Sloan sample a reference to participants in a survey called the Sloan Study of Youth and Social Development, which the authors used as a source of information

misperception an inaccurate perception or viewpoint

SOURCE: "The Ambitious Generation" by Barbara Schneider and David Stevenson. From *The Ambitious Generation: America's Teenagers, Motivated but Directionless,* copyright © 1999, published by Yale University Press. Reprinted by permission.

fostered encouraged
prevalent common or widespread
fluid in this context, frequently changing
criteria guidelines or requirements

The Ambitious Generation

The social world of adolescents in the 1950s was very different from that of adolescents today. Public high schools then drew their students primarily from bounded residential communities where families were likely to know their neighbors' children, as well as the children's grandparents, other relatives, and close friends. Some families lived in the same communities for several generations, and it was not uncommon for children to attend the same schools their parents had and even to have the same teachers. In these communities, parents and their children shared common understandings of what it meant to be popular and successful in adolescent society.

2   Adolescents in the 1950s lived in a world where participation in certain activities, such as athletics and booster clubs, could give one social status in the school as well as among adults within the community. Other school organizations, such as the honor society and debate club, were for "good students," but participation in these activities did not result in popularity among teenagers at school. Academic excellence was rarely helpful in achieving peer-group popularity; only about a quarter of high school seniors would enroll in college. School dances and other social activities were important, and "dating" and "going steady" were highly valued by most teenagers. The social life of the high school was an important part of courtship, because most boys and girls married soon after high school.

3   The social world of today's teenagers is very different, and the markers of adolescents' social status are not as clear or as widely held by them or their parents. Being an athlete, a cheer-leader, or homecoming queen does not necessarily confer high social status. For the increasing number of young people who plan to attend college, getting good grades and participating in such organizations as academic clubs are important for college admission. And being admitted to a competitive college is an important marker of social status.

4   Peer groups have changed substantially since the 1950s. There are few dominant elite crowds that most students desire to become members of. There are, however, numerous smaller social groups whose composition changes from year to year. These changes in peer groups are reflected in adolescents' views of themselves. Adolescents in the 1990s are more likely to see themselves as popular. Ten percent of students in the Sloan sample considered themselves very popular, 65 per-

cent reported that they were somewhat popular, and 25 percent said they were not popular. Considering oneself popular is probably not a misperception if one is referring to a smaller friendship group.

5   The creation of numerous small groups is fostered, in part, by large high schools that draw students from many different neighborhoods. Because school friends often live far apart, it can be difficult to get together outside school. Some young people have school friends whom they eat lunch with and talk with but do not see otherwise. During the past decade, many facilities like recreational parks and programs that cater to adolescents after school have closed. With fewer places to go after school other than work, adolescents can spend long periods of time alone at home.

6   The tight, closed peer groups so prevalent in the 1950s have been replaced by fluid friendship groups. Students often move from one group to another, and friendships change over a period of a few weeks or months. Best friends are few, and students frequently refer to peers as "acquaintances" or "associates." Building close, intimate ties with a special boyfriend or girlfriend that could lead to long-term commitment or marriage is viewed as undesirable. Few teenagers "date"; instead, they "go out" with someone, which can mean anything from spending time together to a casual relationship that is recognized by the peer group as some form of special emotional attachment. Not only has the premise of dating changed, so have the criteria for whom one can go out with. Mixed-race couples and even same-sex couples are part of the teenage social world today.

◆◆◆

Comprehension

1. Describe high school social life in the 1950s. Which school activities helped certain teenagers become popular in the 1950s?
2. According to the authors, have attitudes toward getting good grades and attending college changed since the 1950s? In what ways have they changed?
3. How are peer groups and friendship groups different now than they were in the 1950s?
4. In what ways has dating or going out with someone changed since the 1950s?

Critical Thinking

1. Why have young people's attitudes changed in so many ways since the 1950s?

2. Do you think that being popular is important to most teenagers? Why? Do people's attitudes about popularity tend to change as they grow older? If so, in what ways do they change?
3. Why do more people consider it important to attend college now than in the 1950s?
4. How did the authors acquire the information they used in writing *The Ambitious Generation*? In your opinion, how reliable is information obtained through surveys?
5. Which generation does the title *The Ambitious Generation* refer to? Do you agree with the authors' choice of title? Why or why not?

Language and Vocabulary

1. In the next to the last paragraph of the reading, the authors make a distinction between the terms *date* and *go out*. What do these terms mean to you? Do you agree with the difference in meaning that the authors suggest?
2. Find two paragraphs that are written entirely in the past tense, and highlight or underline all of the verbs. Look for regular verbs that have an *-ed* ending (such as *lived*), verbs that have an irregular past form (such as *was*, *were*, and *drew*), and verbs that use "did not" to make them negative. Are the auxiliary verbs *could* and *would* also used to express something about the past?

Style, Structure, and Organization

1. Which sentence states the authors' main point? Is this an effective place to state the main idea of the reading selection? Why or why not?
2. One method of organizing a comparison/contrast is to go back and forth between the two items being compared. Another method of organization, called the block method, first presents a fairly long block of information about one of the items, followed by a block of similar information about the other item. Which of these methods serves as the primary organization for this reading?

Topics for Discussion or Journal Writing

1. Would you like to have been a teenager during the 1950s? Why or why not?
2. Do you agree with the authors' observations about friendships and popularity among teenagers of the 1990s and today? Why or why not?

3. What similarities or differences do you see between your own high school experiences and the types of experiences described in the reading?
4. Do you prefer getting acquainted with new people fairly often and making new friends or keeping the same friends for many years? Why?
5. Do you think that mixed-race couples are more likely to be accepted nowadays than in the past? What are the attitudes toward mixed-race couples in your community?

Writing Topics for Paragraphs or Essays

1. Write about the social world at the high school you attended.
2. Compare and contrast the social world of high school with the social world of college.
3. Write a comparison/contrast paper about the similarities and differences between two friends, two teachers, two family members, or two other people you know well.
4. Using library resources or the Internet, look up information about some aspects of life during the 1950s, such as clothing styles, popular movies, kinds of music, or television programs of that decade. Write a paper telling what you learn about the 1950s.
5. Interview someone who attended high school during the 1960s, 1970s, or 1980s. Ask about the kinds of things mentioned in the reading, such as friends, peer groups, popularity, college expectations, and relationships. Then choose one of the following writing assignments:
    a. Write about some of the high school experiences of the person you interviewed.
    b. Based on your interview, contrast the social world of adolescents in the 1960s, 1970s, or 1980s with the social world of adolescents today. Use the reading selection as a model for your writing.

Saffron Sky

Gelareh Asayesh

Gelareh Asayesh is a talented and respected journalist who has written for a number of major newspapers in the United States. She grew up in Iran and immigrated to this country with her parents when she was a young teenager. In her book *Saffron Sky*, which this reading is taken from, she vividly portrays her experiences as an immigrant and her connections with other Iranian Americans.

Prereading Questions

1. What problems do you think an Iranian woman might experience living in the United States with her American husband?
2. To what extent do you think people who immigrate to another country should try to maintain the customs and traditions of their home country?

Vocabulary

emerged came out

feat accomplishment

Norooz the Persian/Iranian new year festival, celebrated at the time of the spring equinox

mike microphone

tar in this case, a stringed musical instrument

launching into beginning

reconcile to accept, to make compatible

infighting disagreement among members of a group

exiles people who for one reason or another cannot move back to their native land

Sizdah-bedar the thirteenth day of the new year

dawned on occurred to

reclusiveness a preference for isolation rather than socializing

schisms divisions

pits puts people or groups in opposition to each other
colloquialisms informal conversational phrases used by native speakers
consign to assign, to place permanently in that situation
spurious false
disenfranchisement loss of privileges or rights
ambivalence uncertainty, mixed feelings
invokes summons, calls for
angst strong anxiety, apprehension
cemented bonded, held together

Saffron Sky

April 1, 1998 (Farvardin 12, 1377)

My friend Forough is going to Tehran on Saturday.

2   I rush down to the outlet mall near Sarasota. After an hour in the dressing room of Westport Woman, I emerge with a cobalt blue outfit for my cousin Maryam and a red one for my cousin Soodi. This is no easy feat, finding long-sleeved clothes (short sleeves are not permitted in Iran in public) in Florida in Spring.

3   I call Forough to find out when I can bring by the clothes, which she will take to Iran for me. We make a date, then compare notes on Norooz parties. Forough and her husband, Ali, went to the one at the University of South Florida in Tampa—a less formal affair than the dinner my family and I chose to attend. "How was your party?" Forough wants to know. "I heard it was dreadful."

4   "I thought it was great," I tell her, surprised. "There were some problems with the mike and the dancing started too late for us, but I was impressed. So were my parents. They're used to pretty fancy parties in Toronto."

5   "I heard the *tar* player had a real attitude," Forough says, launching into the list of criticisms she heard from friends who attended our party. We keep talking, trying to reconcile these differing reports of the same event. We conclude that the problem is the tendency toward infighting that so often exists among exiles. I'm not sure what causes it, but suspect it has something to do with feeling threatened. I've noticed that groups under stress tend to pull apart—the losing side in a game of Pictionary, the passengers of the *Titanic,* the underclass in any society. Perhaps this is why the two Iranian cultural groups in Tampa Bay have devoted a fair bit of time, and a couple of mailings, to putting each other down.

6   Ali is trying to get the two groups to meet and work together, maybe even merge, Forough tells me. "I can't see it." I say. "Their styles are totally opposite. Besides, there's nothing wrong with having two groups, two events, two choices. If only they could get along."

7   Before we say good-bye, she asks me if I'm going to the Sizdah-bedar picnic. "The Sizdah-bedar picnic!" I say enthusiastically. "I'd like to go but I'm not sure. I'll have to talk to Neil."

8   I hang up the phone, vaguely ashamed. I know in my heart that we will not go to the picnic. Although our reasons vary from event to event, Neil and I rarely attend the picnics, concerts, and poetry nights sponsored by Iranians here.

9   Years ago, it dawned on me that just because someone was Iranian did not mean I had much in common with them. We have little enough leisure time as a family that we guard our weekends closely. But there is more to my reclusiveness.

10   Iranians in America, like many immigrants, are a troubled group. Take away the financial problems, language barriers, and emotional challenges of immigration, take away the political schisms that cause mutual distrust, and you are still left with the central dilemma of assimilation. The need to belong is a powerful thing. It pits those of us who are children of other worlds against ourselves and one another.

11   It made the Iranian clerk I encountered a few years ago at Bloomingdale's, in Rockville, Maryland, stare coldly when I spoke to her in Farsi. She rang up my sale without a word. A few months later, when an Iranian handed me the numbered tag I took into the dressing room of another department store, I was careful to thank her in English. I pretended that I did not recognize the almond skin, arched eyebrows, and glossy hair of a countrywoman.

12   A memory surfaces, one I haven't summoned in years. I am twenty-something, working at the *Miami Herald*. I fly up to Washington, D.C., to get a new passport. I stay at the Kalorama Guesthouse, near the zoo, and wake early in the morning to go to the Iranian Interests Section on Wisconsin Avenue. The Interests Section requires that applicants wear Islamic dress. Waiting on the steps of the guesthouse for a cab, I am painfully conscious of the scarf on my head. I try to catch the eyes of people passing by, hungry for an opportunity to show them that, despite my appearance, I am not one of *them*. Let me speak a sentence loaded with colloquialisms. See, I am fluent in English! I have no accent! I'm like *you*. Don't consign me to the trash heap, where the unforgivably different belong. Don't look at me as if I were an animal at the zoo, an object of curiosity and spurious compassion.

13   This inner dialogue fills me with shame, yet I am helpless against it. I have become a party to my own disenfranchisement. The worst part of

being told in a thousand ways, subtle and not, that one is inferior is the way that message worms itself into the heart. It is not enough to battle the prejudice of others, one must also battle the infection within.

14   I have struggled for years with my own ambivalence. Socializing with other Iranians invokes my angst in painful ways. Yet despite my discomfort, in every city I have lived I have sought out my countrymen and tried to establish meaningful connections with them.

15   Only in St. Petersburg, with our children as a common bond, have I succeeded. Only in Iran—or in Toronto, where relationships are cemented by family ties—is it easy to be with other Iranians. My closest friends, including my husband, are American.

16   Sometimes I get tired of the struggle.

17   So it is that each year I go to great lengths to travel to Iran. Each week I spend hours preparing our Farsi lesson.

18   Yet I won't make the effort to go to a picnic half an hour away in Clearwater.

Comprehension

1. Why is it difficult for Gelareh Asayesh to find appropriate gifts of clothing for her cousins in Tehran?
2. How does the author explain the existence of two different Iranian cultural groups in Tampa Bay?
3. What happened when the author spoke Farsi to an Iranian clerk in Bloomingdale's?
4. How did the author feel when she wore Islamic dress on the streets of Washington, DC, on her way to get a new passport?

Critical Thinking

1. Why isn't the author planning to attend the Sizdah-bedar picnic?
2. Why does the author say that "Iranians in America, like many immigrants, are a troubled group"?
3. Does the author still feel strong ties to Iran, or does she feel stronger ties to the United States? Give reasons for your answer.
4. Do you think that Gelareh Asayesh and Forough are close friends? Why or why not?
5. Do you think the author has experienced prejudice and discrimination in the United States? In what kinds of situations?

Language and Vocabulary

1. What do you think *dilemma* and *assimilation* mean? (Consult a dictionary if necessary.) After you know the meaning of these two key words, consider the meaning of the author's phrase "the dilemma of assimilation." Express in your own words the dilemma she is referring to.
2. What are *colloquialisms*? Why did the author say, "Let me speak a sentence loaded with colloquialisms"? Do you think it's important for immigrants from other cultures to learn American colloquialisms? Why or why not?

Style, Structure, and Organization

1. Find the one paragraph that is written completely in the *past tense*. Why do you think the author chose to put this particular paragraph in the past tense?
2. A good conclusion often leaves readers with something to think about. Is that true of the conclusion for this reading? What issue does it leave readers thinking about?

Topics for Discussion or Journal Writing

1. Which ethnic minority groups live in your area? What kinds of problems or conflicts do you think they experience because of cultural differences?
2. What can we do to reduce prejudice and discrimination against different ethnic groups?
3. Based on what you read in this selection from *Saffron Sky*, how do you think the position of women in Iran differs from the position of women in the United States?
4. Have you ever been in a situation where you had ambivalent feelings about something or felt pulled in two directions at the same time? How did you feel? How did you resolve the conflict?
5. Do you agree with the author that groups of people who are experiencing stress have a tendency to pull apart (in paragraph 5)? Why or why not? What examples can you think of?

Writing Topics for Paragraphs or Essays

1. Write a personal narrative about a time when you experienced discrimination or felt that you didn't fit in with a group.
2. Interview someone from another country. Ask about cultural differences between that person's native country and the United States, as well as

about any difficulties he or she has had in adjusting to life in this country. Write a paper about the experiences of the person you interviewed.
3. Write about your own national origins. What country (or countries) did your parents or your ancestors come from? In what ways do you still feel a connection with that culture (or those cultures)?
4. Access a web site that features information about Iranian culture, such as the Iranian Cultural Information Center at **http://tehran.stanford.edu/** or **http://netiran.com** or **http://www.persia.org/.** You may also want to follow links to other related sites. Then write a paper about something you have learned through your research.
5. Using library resources or the Internet, find out more about the Iranian celebrations of Norooz and Sizdah-bedar. Write a paper about what you learned, or compare and contrast Norooz with Western celebrations of the new year.

Suspect Policy

Randall Kennedy

Racial profiling is the practice by law enforcement officers of stopping and questioning people because of their race or ethnicity. It is a controversial issue, and many people have very strong feelings about it. In this excerpt from an article that originally appeared in *The New Republic* magazine, Randall Kennedy, a professor at Harvard Law School, examines various perspectives on the issue.

Prereading Questions

1. What are some of the challenges faced by law enforcement officers in ethnically diverse neighborhoods?
2. How do law enforcement officers decide which people to stop and question?

Vocabulary

flooding in this context, providing very large quantities

made a beeline went quickly and directly (an idiomatic expression)

deplaning getting off a plane

trafficking sales, dealing (of drugs, in this case)

v. abbreviation for *versus,* used in naming the two sides of a court case

constitutionality legality according to the Constitution of the United States

presumptively based on a presumption, not on actual evidence

detain in this context, hold for questioning

bona fide genuine, real

harassment systematic persecution, repeated threats or demands

hooligans troublemakers or lawbreakers

profile in this context, a general description of a likely suspect for certain crimes

rackets illegal businesses

empirically based based on statistics

denunciations strong criticisms, condemnations
corrosive destructive
undercuts undermines or takes away support for an idea

Suspect Policy

An officer from the Drug Enforcement Administration stops and questions a young man who has just stepped off a flight to Kansas City from Los Angeles. The officer has focused on this man for several reasons. Intelligence reports indicate that black gangs in Los Angeles are flooding the Kansas City area with illegal drugs, and the man in question was on a flight originating in Los Angeles. Young, toughly dressed, and appearing very nervous, he paid for his ticket in cash, checked no luggage, brought two carry-on bags, and made a beeline for a taxi upon deplaning. Oh, and one other thing: the officer also took into account the fact that the young man was black.

. . .

2   How should we evaluate the officer's conduct? Should we applaud it? Permit it? Prohibit it? Encounters like this take place every day, all over the country, as police attempt to battle street crime, drug trafficking, and illegal immigration. And this particular case study happens to be the fact pattern presented in a federal lawsuit of the early '90s, *United States* v. *Weaver,* in which the U.S. Court of Appeals for the Eighth Circuit upheld the constitutionality of the officer's action.

3   "Large groups of our citizens," the court declared, "should not be regarded by law enforcement officers as presumptively criminal based upon their race." The court went on to say, however, that "facts are not to be ignored simply because they may be unpleasant." According to the court, it made sense for the officer to regard blackness, when considered in conjunction with the other factors, as a signal that could be legitimately relied upon in the decision to approach and detain the suspect.

4   Other courts have agreed with the Eighth Circuit that the Constitution does not prohibit police from routinely taking race into account when they decide whom to stop and question, as long as they do so for purposes of bona fide law enforcement (not racial harassment) and as long as race is one of several factors that they consider.

. . .

5   Some police officers note that racial profiling is race-neutral in that various forms of it can be applied to persons of all races, depending on the circumstances. In predominantly black neighborhoods and other places in which white people stick out in a suspicious fashion (as potential drug customers or racist hooligans, for example), whiteness can

become part of a profile. In the southwestern United States, where Latinos often traffic in illegal immigrants, apparent Latin American ancestry can become part of a profile. In a Chinatown where Chinese gangs appear to dominate certain criminal rackets, apparent Chinese ancestry can become part of a profile. Racial profiling, then, according to many cops, is good police work: a race-neutral, empirically based and, above all, effective tool in fighting crime.

6 But the defenders of racial profiling are wrong.

7 Indeed, ever since the Black and Latino Caucus of the New Jersey State Legislature held sensational hearings a few months ago, complete with testimony from victims of the New Jersey State Police force's racial profiling, the air has been thick with public denunciations of the practice. In June, at a forum organized by the Justice Department on racial problems in law enforcement, President Clinton condemned racial profiling as a "morally indefensible, deeply corrosive practice." Vice President Al Gore has promised that, if elected president, he would see to it that the first civil rights act of the new century would end racial profiling.

. . .

8 Racial profiling undercuts a good idea that needs more support from both society and the law: that individuals should be judged by public authority on the basis of their own conduct and not on the basis—not even *partly* on the basis—of racial generalization

◆◆◆

Comprehension

1. Why do many law enforcement officers consider racial profiling an effective crime-fighting tool?
2. In the court case *United States v. Weaver*, which the author refers to, what decision did the judge make about racial profiling? What reasons did the judge give for his decision?
3. In what kinds of neighborhoods is whiteness likely to be part of a racial profile for criminal suspects?
4. According to Randall Kennedy, why should racial profiling be abolished?

Critical Thinking

1. Reread the first paragraph, which tells the story of a DEA officer stopping and questioning a young African-American man in Kansas City. Why did the officer decide to stop him? Do you think the officer's decision was reasonable? Give reasons for your answer.

2. Why do many police officers consider racial profiling "good police work"?
3. Do you think Randall Kennedy is well qualified to write on the topic of racial profiling? Why or why not?
4. If witnesses report seeing a white woman in her early thirties, about 5'6" tall, with blonde hair, running from the scene of a murder, should the police question every woman in the area who fits that description? Why or why not?

Language and Vocabulary

1. What do you think the author means by the term *racial harassment* in paragraph 4?
2. Because of the nature of the topic, the author uses a number of fairly technical words that relate to the legal system or law enforcement, such as *constitutionality* and *intelligence reports*. Find at least two other technical words or phrases related to law enforcement or the legal field. What do you think they mean? If you are not sure of the meaning, consult a dictionary.

Style, Structure, and Organization

1. At what point in the reading does Kennedy reveal that he is against racial profiling? Did you suspect his real stand on the issue earlier in the reading?
2. In which paragraphs does the author present evidence in favor of racial profiling? Label these paragraphs *Pro*. In which paragraphs does he argue against it? Label these paragraphs *Con*. Do you think this pattern of organization is effective?

Topics for Discussion or Journal Writing

1. Have you ever experienced discrimination because of your race or ethnicity? If so, how did you react?
2. Do you think that the law enforcement officers in your community usually treat people of different races and ethnicities fairly or unfairly?
3. What do you think would be the hardest part of being a police officer? Why?
4. How do you think someone who was falsely accused of a crime would feel?
5. What advice do you think Neighborhood Watch groups should give residents about keeping an eye out for strangers in their neighborhood? Should race or ethnicity be considered as a factor?

Writing Topics for Paragraphs or Essays

1. Look up information about the job of being a police officer in the *Occupational Outlook Handbook* online or in a library, or interview a police officer. Then write a paper about a police officer's duties and responsibilities. Also include several advantages and disadvantages of the job.

2. Write a short dramatic scene between a police officer making an arrest and an innocent suspect who is African American, Hispanic, Native American, or Asian. Try to create a believable story about what happens. Be sure to include realistic *dialogue*—that is, words that the two people might actually say to each other.

3. Watch a police drama on television. Notice how the police officers identify and question suspects and whether or not they use racial profiling. Then write a paper about the program, including your observations and your opinion of the program.

4. Have you ever been falsely accused of something by your parents, a teacher, a friend, or someone else? Write the story of what happened. Be sure to include your feelings and descriptive details, so that readers can picture what happened.

3

Education and Career

Stop!   Sam Quinones   52

How to Write with Style   Kurt Vonnegut, Jr.   57

The Reading Debate   Laura E. Berk   63

Possible Lives   Mike Rose   68

Breaking Through the Barriers   James M. Henslin   75

The Rich Heritage of Public Speaking   Steven A. Beebe and Susan J. Beebe   80

Emergency Medical Technicians   Joseph J. Mistovich, Brent Q. Hafen, and Keith J. Karren   85

Internet Job Search   A. C. "Buddy" Krizan, Patricia Merrier, Carol Larson Jones, and Jules Harcourt   91

52 ◆ Part 3 / Education and Career

Stop!

Sam Quinones

Sam Quinones is a freelance writer based in Mexico City. His article about women in the Mexico City police force originally appeared in *Ms.*, a magazine published in New York and intended primarily for women. However, the article deals with an issue that involves both men and women—gender roles in law enforcement.

Prereading Questions

1. What special qualities do you think a good police officer should have?
2. Are male and female police officers capable of doing the same kinds of jobs equally well?

Vocabulary

screws up makes a mess of something, makes a mistake (slang)
image in this case, the public perception
task an assigned duty or job
corruption immoral or dishonest activity
pyramid a structure with a broad base that narrows at the top
purportedly supposedly
commute traffic going to or from work
chaos confusion
apathy lack of interest, indifference
peso the monetary unit of Mexico
infraction minor violation of the law
root in this case, primary; the basic core of something
notoriously well-known in a negative way
empowered given power

SOURCE: *"Stop!"* by Sam Quinones, from *Ms. Magazine*, Vol. X, Num. 1. Reprinted by permission of *Ms. Magazine*, copyright © 1999–2000.

extortion illegal use of one's official position to obtain money by means of intimidation

tailgating following too closely behind (usually referring to one vehicle closely following another)

Stop!

What a man screws up, a woman will do right. This appeared to be the philosophy at work when Mexico City Police Chief and Secretary of Public Safety Alejandro Gertz Manero announced last August that only female officers would have the authority to write traffic tickets—in the belief, and hope, that women are more honest than men.

2   There are 950 women officers in the so-called Grupo Cisne, or Swan Group. (Each unit in the Mexico City Police Department is named after a bird. The swan was chosen for the women's traffic unit because it's "feminine.")

3   These birds are charged not only with issuing tickets, but with changing the image of traffic cops, which is no easy task. The Mexico City traffic cop is a worldwide symbol of police corruption, routinely stopping drivers to take a bribe, known as a *mordida,* or bite.

4   Traffic cops have always been at the lowest level in Mexico City's pyramid of police corruption. Each cop is rumored to have a daily quota of bribe money to meet. He purportedly keeps part for himself, then pays off his sergeant, who pays off the lieutenant, and so on.

5   And while cops are taking bribes, drivers are taking risks—running red lights, changing lanes without signaling, making illegal U-turns, making right turns from the left lane—all in a single commute.

6   Into this chaos step the women of Grupo Cisne. The officers are part of teams—including both men and women—that direct traffic, tow cars, and remove license plates from offending vehicles. Only the women, however, are allowed to write tickets.

7   "Why only women?" asks Raul Tovar, Mexico City police spokesman. "Because women are more dedicated and less able to be corrupted."

8   Officer María del Carmen García agrees. "I think it's because at some point women are more energetic," she told *Ms.* "We do work the way it should be done. There's a little more apathy in men."

9   Whatever the reason may be, Grupo Cisne is doing too well for the taste of many drivers who now find that, faced with the possibility of a 300-peso fine, a quick 50-peso bribe looks pretty good.

10   "When they commit some infraction, they'll immediately argue," says García. "They get out and say, 'Here, take this [money],' when we've never asked for anything.

11 "You'll pull someone over for an illegal U-turn, and he'll stand there watching to see who else does it. He'll say, 'Why are you stopping me? Look at him. Stop him.' I just say, 'Sir, we're all adults. We each have to correct our own behavior.' They never want to accept their error."

12 The women won't be able to do much about the root cause of corruption: officers' notoriously poor pay. García is typical of male and female officers. After eight years on the force, she takes home only about $83 a week. If the city officials can't improve that, then these newly empowered women might surrender to temptation just as easily as the men have.

13 "First, the people asked for this because there was extortion," says Officer Erika Alcaraz. "Now, they've seen they can't get away with anything with us, so they complain to our superiors!"

14 No female officer has yet been accused of demanding bribes. But then again, maybe it's just another case of women having to catch up with the men. So far, they're not even tailgating.

◆◆◆

Comprehension

1. According to the Mexico City police chief and Officer Maria del Carmen García, why has the job of writing traffic tickets been assigned only to women?
2. Why is the women's traffic unit called the Grupo Cisne?
3. What problems have Officers Maria del Carmen García and Erika Alcaraz encountered while issuing traffic tickets?
4. According to the author, what reputation do the Mexico City police have? Why have they acquired this reputation?

Critical Thinking

1. Do you think that the female police officers will be more honest and less likely to accept bribes than the male police officers in Mexico City? Why or why not?
2. Does author Sam Quinones present a fair and accurate picture of the differences between male and female police officers in Mexico City? Give reasons for your answer.
3. Why is it important to ensure that police officers are paid a good salary?
4. Do you agree or disagree with the differences between men and women that are mentioned in the article? Give reasons for your answer.

Language and Vocabulary

1. Who is the writer referring to in paragraph 3 when he says "these birds"? Why does he call them birds?
2. Explain the term *daily quota* in paragraph 4. If necessary, use a dictionary to find the meaning of *quota*. Can you think of any kinds of jobs that have legitimate daily quotas?

Style, Structure, and Organization

1. How does the author capture readers' attention with his first sentence? Do you think he believes that this statement is completely true? If not, why did he use it?
2. Newspaper articles and many magazine articles tend to use shorter paragraphs than academic writing requires. Why do you think this is so? Count the number of sentences in each of the first eight paragraphs. Which one has the most sentences?
3. In what ways do you think that the author's intended audience affected his style and his choices of what information to include? (Remember that he originally wrote the article for a women's magazine.)

Topics for Discussion or Journal Writing

1. Do you think that male and female police officers should be given different types of job assignments or exactly the same assignments? Why?
2. What are some of the major types of problems that law enforcement officers in any large city might experience?
3. What do you think are the hardest or most challenging parts of being a police officer? What are the most rewarding parts?
4. Do you think that people react differently to being issued a traffic ticket by a female officer than by a male officer? Why or why not? Would it make any difference to you personally?

Writing Topics for Paragraphs or Essays

1. Do you think there are any basic differences between men and women in the areas of personality, values, communication, and/or ability to deal with people? Think through the topic before you begin writing so that

you can compose a clear main idea statement, and then illustrate your main idea with examples from your own experience.

2. What are the requirements to become a police officer, a border patrol agent, a marshal, an FBI agent, or some other type of law enforcement officer? If your college has a career center, you can find information there about one of these careers. You can also inquire at a local law enforcement agency or use library resources.

3. Have you ever gotten a traffic ticket or been in the car with someone who did? How did the police officer treat you? How did you feel? Write a personal narrative about your experience.

4. Are there periods of heavy rush-hour traffic in your area when people are commuting to and from work? Are drivers generally polite, or do you see instances of road rage? Do most drivers obey speed limits and other laws? Choose one of the following writing topics about traffic in your area:

   a. Describe a typical drive in one of the worst traffic areas.
   b. Suggest ways to improve the traffic situation.
   c. Classify the kinds of drivers on the road into at least three categories and describe each category, giving specific examples of how drivers in each group act.

How to Write with Style

Kurt Vonnegut, Jr.

The author of this article, Kurt Vonnegut, Jr., is probably best known for his award-winning, best-selling science fiction books. In this short article, he offers the benefit of his years of experience as he shares his secrets for writing effectively. As you read this article, look for tips and examples that you can apply to your own writing.

Prereading Questions

1. Who are some popular modern authors? Why do people like to read their writing?
2. Do most people know how to write effectively? Where can they learn how to write better?

Vocabulary

wretches miserable beings
chowderhead blockhead, dummy
compelling engaging, extremely interesting
ramble to go on and on without a clear purpose
profound deep
frisky light-hearted and energetic
reputable well thought of
illuminate to shed light on
piquant colorful or spicy
locutions language expressions, especially those from a particular time period
vehemently angrily and forcefully
dialect a particular variety of a language
unambiguously very clearly

SOURCE: "How to Write with Style" by Kurt Vonnegut, Jr., from the *Power of the Printed Word* series, copyright © 1982 by International Paper Company. Reprinted by permission of International Paper.

How to Write with Style

Newspaper reporters and technical writers are trained to reveal almost nothing about themselves in their writings. This makes them freaks in the world of writers, since almost all of the other ink-stained wretches in that world reveal a lot about themselves to readers. We call these revelations, accidental and unintentional, elements of style.

2   These revelations tell us as readers what sort of person it is with whom we are spending time. Does the writer sound ignorant or informed, stupid or bright, crooked or honest, humorless or playful—? And on and on.

3   Why should you examine your writing style with the idea of improving it? Do so as a mark of your respect for your readers, whatever you're writing. If you scribble your thoughts any which way, your readers will surely feel that you care nothing about them. They will mark you down as an egomaniac or a chowderhead—or worse, they will stop reading you.

4   The most damning revelation you can make about yourself is that you do not know what is interesting and what is not. Don't you yourself like or dislike writers mainly for what they choose to show you or make you think about? Did you ever admire an empty-headed writer for his or her mastery of the language? No.

5   So your own winning style must begin with ideas in your head.

1. Find a Subject You Care About

6   Find a subject you care about and which you in your heart feel others should care about. It is this genuine caring, and not your games with language, which will be the most compelling and seductive element in your style.

7   I am not urging you to write a novel, by the way—although I would not be sorry if you wrote one, provided you genuinely cared about something. A petition to the mayor about a pothole in front of your house or a love letter to the girl next door will do.

2. Do Not Ramble, Though

8   I won't ramble on about that.

3. Keep It Simple

9   As for the use of language: Remember that two great masters of language, William Shakespeare and James Joyce, wrote sentences which were almost childlike when their subjects were most profound. "To be or

not to be?" asks Shakespeare's Hamlet. The longest word is three letters long. Joyce, when he was frisky, could put together a sentence as intricate and glittering as a necklace for Cleopatra, but my favorite sentence in his short story "Eveline" is this one: "She was tired." At that point in the story, no other words could break the heart of a reader as those three words do.

10   Simplicity of language is not only reputable, but perhaps even sacred. The *Bible* opens with a sentence well within the writing skills of a lively fourteen-year-old: "In the beginning God created the heaven and the earth."

4. Have the Guts to Cut

11   It may be that you, too, are capable of making necklaces for Cleopatra, so to speak. But your eloquence should be the servant of the ideas in your head. Your rule might be this: If a sentence, no matter how excellent, does not illuminate your subject in some new and useful way, scratch it out.

5. Sound Like Yourself

12   The writing style which is most natural for you is bound to echo the speech you heard when you were a child. English was the novelist Joseph Conrad's third language, and much that seems piquant in his use of English was no doubt colored by his first language, which was Polish. And lucky indeed is the writer who has grown up in Ireland, for the English spoken there is so amusing and musical. I myself grew up in Indianapolis, where common speech sounds like a band saw cutting galvanized tin, and employs a vocabulary as unornamental as a monkey wrench.

13   In some of the more remote hollows of Appalachia, children still grow up hearing songs and locutions of Elizabethan times. Yes, and many Americans grow up hearing a language other than English, or an English dialect a majority of Americans cannot understand.

14   All these varieties of speech are beautiful, just as the varieties of butterflies are beautiful. No matter what your first language, you should treasure it all your life. If it happens not to be standard English, and it shows itself when you write standard English, the result is usually delightful, like a very pretty girl with one eye that is green and one that is blue.

15.   I myself find that I trust my own writing most, and others seem to trust it most, too, when I sound most like a person from Indianapolis, which is what I am. What alternatives do I have? The one most vehemently recommended by teachers has no doubt been pressed on you, as well: to write like cultivated Englishmen of a century or more ago.

6. Say What You Mean to Say

16   I used to be exasperated by such teachers, but am no more. I understand now that all those antique essays and stories with which I was to compare my own work were not magnificent for their datedness or foreignness, but for saying precisely what their authors meant them to say. My teachers wished me to write accurately, always selecting the most effective words, and relating the words to one another unambiguously, rigidly, like parts of a machine. The teachers did not want to turn me into an Englishman after all. They hoped that I would become understandable—and therefore understood. And there went my dream of doing with words what Pablo Picasso did with paint or what any number of jazz idols did with music. If I broke all the rules of punctuation, had words mean whatever I wanted them to mean, and strung them together higgledy-piggledy, I would simply not be understood. So you, too, had better avoid Picasso-style or jazz-style writing, if you have something worth saying and wish to be understood.

17   Readers want our pages to look very much like pages they have seen before. Why? This is because they themselves have a tough job to do, and they need all the help they can get from us.

7. Pity the Readers

18   They have to identify thousands of little marks on paper, and make sense of them immediately. They have to *read*, an art so difficult that most people don't really master it even after having studied it all through grade school and high school—twelve long years.

19   So this discussion must finally acknowledge that our stylistic options as writers are neither numerous nor glamorous, since our readers are bound to be such imperfect artists. Our audience requires us to be sympathetic and patient teachers, ever willing to simplify and clarify—whereas we would rather soar high above the crowd, singing like nightingales.

20   That is the bad news. The good news is that we Americans are governed under a unique Constitution, which allows us to write whatever we please without fear of punishment. So the most meaningful aspect of our styles, which is what we choose to write about, is utterly unlimited.

8. For Really Detailed Advice

21   For a discussion of literary style in a narrower sense, in a more technical sense, I commend to your attention *The Elements of Style* by William Strunk, Jr., and E. B. White [the most recent edition is published by Longman, 2000]. E. B. White is, of course, one of the most admirable literary stylists this country has so far produced.

22   You should realize, too, that no one would care how well or badly Mr. White expressed himself, if he did not have perfectly enchanting things to say.

◆◆◆

Comprehension

1. How many tips for writing effectively does the author provide? What are they?
2. What did Vonnegut's English teachers want him to be able to do?
3. What reason does the author give for saying that we need to "simplify and clarify" our writing? Why can't we just express ourselves any way we want in everything we write?
4. According to the author, what is the single most important requirement for writing well?

Critical Thinking

1. Is Vonnegut's advice useful for everyone, or will some readers find it more helpful than others? Why?
2. Do you think Vonnegut is really interested in helping other writers? What is there in this article that makes you think so?
3. How do you think Kurt Vonnegut became such an expert on writing?
4. How much information about himself did Vonnegut reveal in this article? Do you think it was intentional or accidental?

Language and Vocabulary

1. Under point 7, "Pity the Readers," the author uses the expression "singing like nightingales." What does he mean when he says this?
2. The author uses a number of specialized words, such as *piquant* and *locutions*. Would Vonnegut's writing still be helpful if he used only everyday words, such as *colorful* for *piquant* and *expressions* instead of *locutions*? Would it be as interesting as it is now?

Style, Structure, and Organization

1. What does the author say about the necessity for writing standard English? Does his own writing style follow this advice?

2. This article contains several *similes*—expressions that compare one thing to something that is similar in a very specific way. One of these is "singing like nightingales." Choose two or three more similes that use *like* or *as*. What idea does each simile communicate?
3. Reread the concluding sentence of the article. Does it emphasize the author's main point effectively?

Topics for Discussion or Journal Writing

1. It is more important to write with your own voice or to write so that the reader will easily understand your message? Is it possible to do both?
2. How do you feel about your own writing ability? What writing skills would you like to improve?
3. Would you enjoy being a professional writer—making a living by selling your writing to publishers?
4. Which of Vonnegut's tips do you like the best? Why?

Writing Topics for Paragraphs or Essays

1. What steps do you follow when you write a paper? List each step and briefly describe it.
2. Rewrite a paper you wrote earlier, using some of Vonnegut's tips this time. Then write a paragraph telling which tips you used and how they seemed to work for you.
3. Write about how you felt when you had to write a paper for one of your college classes. If your feelings about writing have changed, compare your feelings now and in the past.
4. Give some practical advice about college to a new student. Include a short introduction, several points in the body, and a conclusion. Try to follow some of Vonnegut's tips for writing with style.
5. Check out a book by Kurt Vonnegut, Jr., from your local library and choose one of the following topics to write about:
    a. In your opinion, does Vonnegut follow his own rules for writing? Include several examples from one chapter of his book.
    b. Write a critique of at least one chapter of the book. Include the author, title, page numbers, publisher, and year and date of publication; a short summary of the story; a few comments on the author's style; and your own reaction to the story.

The Reading Debate

Laura E. Berk

In recent years, there has been a great deal of discussion about methods of teaching reading. In this selection from a textbook called *Child Development,* author Laura E. Berk compares two methods of teaching reading. Throughout the selection, she refers to a number of studies by experts in the field of education. As you read, look for advantages of each method of teaching reading.

Prereading Questions

1. Why is it important to learn how to read well?
2. How can reading ability affect a person's education and career?

Vocabulary

debate discussion or argument

whole-language approach a method of teaching reading that focuses on meaning and complete readings

basic-skills approach a method of teaching reading that focuses on the relationships between letters and sounds

clear-cut definite

gains improvements

text, text materials reading materials

process in this case, all of the skills involved in reading

intervention in this case, an additional lesson or learning experience

research in this case, studies done by experts

fluently easily, capably

meaning-based instruction same as whole-language approach

shift change

engaged with the text able to make critical judgments about what is being read

SOURCE: "The Reading Debate," from Laura E. Berk, *Child Development,* Fifth Edition, copyright © 2000 by Allyn & Bacon. Reprinted and adapted by permission.

The Reading Debate

Currently, psychologists and educators are engaged in a "great debate" about how to teach beginning reading. On one side are those who take a whole-language approach to reading instruction. They argue that reading should be taught in a way that parallels natural language learning. From the very beginning, children should be exposed to text in its complete form—stories, poems, letters, posters, and lists—so they can appreciate the communicative function of written language. According to these experts, as long as reading is kept whole and meaningful, children will be motivated to discover the specific skills they need as they gain experience with the printed word (Watson, 1989). On the other side of the debate are those who advocate a basic-skills approach. According to this view, children should be given simplified text materials. At first, they should be coached on *phonics*—the basic rules for translating written symbols into sounds. Only later, after they have mastered these skills, should they get complex reading material (Rayner and Pollatsek, 1989).

2   As yet, research does not show clear-cut superiority for either of these approaches (Stahl, McKenna, & Pagnucco, 1994). In fact, a third group of experts believes that children learn best when they receive a balanced mixture of both (Pressley, 1994; Stahl, 1992). Kindergartners benefit from an emphasis on whole language, with gradual introduction of phonics as reading skills improve (Sacks and Mergendoller, 1997). In the early grades, balancing the two methods seems most effective. In one study, 7-year-old poor readers showed greater gains when assigned to a "phonics/meaningful reading" intervention than to either a "phonics alone" or a "reading alone" teaching condition (Hatcher, Hulme, & Ellis, 1994).

3   Why might combining phonics with whole language work best? Learning the basics—relations between letters and sounds—enables children to decode words they have never seen before. As this process becomes more automatic, it releases children's attention to the higher-level activities involved in comprehending the text's meaning (Adams, Treiman, & Pressley, 1998). Yet if practice in basic skills is overemphasized, children may lose sight of the goal of reading: understanding. Many teachers report cases of pupils who can read aloud fluently but who comprehend very little. These children might have been spared serious reading problems if they had received meaning-based instruction with attention to basic skills.

4   Around age 7 to 8, a major shift occurs from "learning to read" to "reading to learn" (Elly, 1997). As decoding and comprehension skills reach a high level of efficiency, adolescent readers can become actively engaged with the text. They adjust the way they read to fit their current

purpose—at times seeking new facts and ideas, at other times questioning, agreeing, or disagreeing with the writer's viewpoint.

❖❖❖

Comprehension

1. What is the "great debate" mentioned in the first paragraph?
2. What is the difference between the two approaches used to teach reading?
3. What can happen if basic skills are overemphasized?
4. What shift in reading objectives occurs when children are about seven or eight years old?

Critical Thinking

1. Who is the selection written for (the intended audience)?
2. Does the author seem to prefer the whole-language approach, the basic-skills approach, or a combination?
3. Do you agree or disagree with the author's opinion?
4. Why does the author refer to so many studies and other publications in this reading? Do these citations make the reading more convincing?

Language and Vocabulary

1. In the third paragraph of the reading, the author writes, "Learning the basics—relations between letters and sounds—enables children to decode words they have never seen before." What do you think it means to *decode* words?
2. In this selection, the author uses several *compound adjectives* to describe other words. Three of these compound adjectives are *whole-language* approach, *clear-cut* superiority, and *phonics/meaningful reading* intervention. Highlight or underline two more compound adjectives. Do these adjectives seem to work well with this topic and style of writing?

Style, Structure, and Organization

1. In "The Reading Debate," the author refers to many studies on reading. In each case, she has included a *citation* in parentheses—the last name of

the author or researcher and the year that the information was published. Example: "Only later, after they have mastered these skills, should they get complex reading material (Rayner and Pollatsek, 1989)." Find and mark three of these citations in the reading.
2. In textbooks and other types of informative writing, the first sentence of a paragraph is often a topic sentence—that is, it expresses the main idea of the paragraph. How many of the paragraphs in "The Reading Debate" begin with a topic sentence?

Topics for Discussion or Journal Writing

1. Do you remember learning to read? What are some of the first materials you remember reading?
2. Do you sometimes read during your free time, or do you usually prefer doing something more active (or watching television)?
3. How do you feel about reading? Is reading easier for you when it's for personal enjoyment, as opposed to when it's a class assignment?
4. What kind of topics do you enjoy reading most—mystery, romance, police/detective stories, adventure, science fiction, horror, medical/disaster stories, classics, sports, true biographies, life problems, fashion, music, technology, history, or something else?
5. Do you know an adult who doesn't know how to read? How does he or she deal with situations that require the ability to read?

Writing Topics for Paragraphs or Essays

1. Write about your own experiences with reading and how your reading ability has affected you, for better or worse.
2. Obtain permission to observe two different reading lessons in two elementary classrooms. Compare the two lessons and report on your observations.
3. Interview an elementary school teacher or reading specialist. Ask why this person chose to become a teacher and what techniques he or she uses to teach reading. Then write a short report about the person you interviewed.
4. Check out some Internet web sites about reading. One good place to start is "Reading Is Fundamental" at **http://www.rif.org/resources/li_links.html**. Then report on what kind of reading help is available online.

5. Use the Internet, a library, or the Yellow Pages™ to find resources that help adults learn to read. Try adult schools, community colleges, community centers, or social services. Then choose one of the following writing assignments:

   a. Write a report describing the resources that you found. Include details about how to contact these places, such as phone numbers, URLs (web addresses), or street addresses.

   b. Volunteer to help in a literacy training program (or to read stories to children in a local library or hospital). Write about the experience.

Possible Lives
Mike Rose

Mike Rose is well known for examining the realities of American education today—the failures as well as the successes. In these selections from his book *Possible Lives*, he credits the successful elementary and high school programs in the low-income desert community of Calexico, California, to three factors. As you read, try to identify these factors.

Prereading Questions

1. Do you think that most people learned a lot in their K–12 schooling? How well does K–12 education prepare most students for college?
2. Do you know of some things that the school system in your local area does well? Can you think of some things that could be improved?

Vocabulary Preview

kiosk booth

bicultural sharing elements of two cultures

surveying mapping of landscape features and property boundaries

dropout rate the percentage of students who do not finish high school

Latino Latin-American, Hispanic; often used to mean Spanish-speaking people

unanimity complete agreement

district administration the management, those whose job it is to manage a school district on a daily basis

school board the elected officials who oversee the management of a school district and establish policies and guidelines for the administration to follow

bilingual education education in two languages (in this case, English and Spanish)

satellite campus a small campus that is not independent from a main campus

four-year degree the standard bachelor's degree, which usually takes at least four years to earn

rocanrol rock and roll (an attempt to represent the Mexican pronunciation)

precariously dangerously (in this case, in danger of falling)

listlessly without any excitement, interest, or energy

fecund foul-smelling

empathetic understanding

La Maestra the teacher (Spanish)

poverty line the income level that the U.S. government sets to officially decide who is "poor"

parcel out divide up

gender male or female

factored into played a part in

unilateral one-sided

cohesiveness sticking together

role part to play

Possible Lives

I drove out of Los Angeles on the 405, two hours or so, curving through San Diego, close to the Mexican border, heading east onto Highway 8, where the road narrowed from four lanes to two. I passed an abandoned government kiosk, various twists of scrap metal, and a thousand configurations of rock and brush, and began the slow descent onto the desert floor of the Imperial Valley. There were signs for—but no sight of—Lake Moreno, Kitchen Creek Road, the Tecate Divide, Manzanita, Jacumba, and Ocotillo. The sky was clear, deep blue, and the sun played off the rockface in the distance. I was the only car on the road. The air was warm and dry. In the distance: ROAD 98. The road that takes you along the border to Calexico.

2   Calexico is an American city that speaks two languages, a truly bicultural city. Border culture. Of the 21,000 residents, most are of Mexican ancestry, and the majority of Anglos speak so-so-to-fluent Spanish. This whole area of the Imperial Valley was converted from desert to arable land through water diverted from the Colorado River. The project began just after the turn of the century. Calexico was the surveying camp on the Mexican border—the name blends *Cali*fornia and M*exico*—and in 1908 was incorporated as a city. A few of the early buildings still stand on First Street, just this side of Mexicali.

3   Though many families in Calexico are poor—income is low and seasonal—and the school district is always scrambling for funds, the elementary schools exceeded the Imperial County average on recent statewide tests of language arts, mathematics, and science, and the high schools have the lowest dropout rate of any predominantly Latino school district in California. In fact, they are 9 percentage points below the statewide average for *all* schools. A significant number of graduates go on to two- and four-year colleges. One explanation has to do with the unanimity of goals between district administration and school board. Another with an effective bilingual education program. And a third has to do with the way teacher education develops out of respect for local history.

. . .

4   The Imperial Valley Campus of San Diego State University took up one square block of land six short blocks from the Mexican border. It was located on the site of the old Calexico High School, which had been boarded up and broken into for a long time. The campus retained three original, though refurbished, buildings—archways, white stucco, tile roofs—and had built a few classrooms and brought in some portable structures for administration, student services, and faculty offices. There were plans in the works for a complete reconstruction, but for over twenty-five years this small satellite campus, with its patchwork of buildings and bungalows, has served as the only means for Valley residents to get a four-year degree. Walking down Seventh Street, you came upon it like a park or a historical preserve, nestled between houses and parked cars and an occasional delivery van. Maybe you'd hear the buzz of a lawn mower. Little more.

5   Students at the campus would usually begin their work at IVC, Imperial Valley College, a two-year school about twelve miles north of Calexico, right up Highway 111, and transfer over to complete degrees in humanities or social science. They majored in liberal studies or Latin-American studies, English or Spanish or criminal justice administration, psychology or history, to prepare themselves for careers in business or law enforcement or education. Many hoped to teach. They were a serious student body—numbering four or five hundred in any given year—and they came to school in order to lead a better life here in the Valley. Most worked, and night courses were popular. Hardly anyone hung out. So unless you walked across campus right at those times when classes were starting up or winding down—noon, say, or four or seven or ten—you might, in fact, think the place *was* a historical monument. There would be the shade and rustle of Mexican fan palms and date palms and eucalyptus, and you might stop to hear the birds chirping in the trees and cooing in the red tile. As you made your way toward the north side

of campus—it's a short walk—you'd begin to hear faint music from behind the closed doors of the service bungalows: the hectic advertisements of the Mexican *rocanrol* stations or trumpets and guitars or the lyrics of North American oldies—"Angel Baby" or "Blue Velvet." A little farther, over toward the plywood and corrugated metal, and you'd come upon the faculty offices, faded and baking in the sun.

. . .

6   Evangelina Bustamante Jones sat in front of gray metal bookcases wedged tight against her brief office wall. The shelves were crammed with books on the teaching of writing, bilingual education, reading, and teacher education—her responsibilities here. Student papers and projects from semesters past were boxed or bundled or rolled up and stacked precariously on shelves or placed safely in a corner on the floor. Newspaper clippings about former students—weddings and awards—were taped to the wall. "It's such a small community," she said, leaning forward and loosely folding her hands on the desk, "that you kinda keep track of everyone."

7   We had just come from visiting a student teacher she was supervising—teaching over in Heber, a little agricultural town about three miles northwest of Calexico. Anthony Heber was one of the early developers of the Imperial Valley—many of the cities in the Valley and the streets within them were named after developers and civil engineers—and the town that bore his name had twenty-five hundred people, two schools, and a lot of cattle that listlessly regarded you as you drove in. The air was heavy and fecund. "You don't notice it," a local told me, "until you leave. Then when you return, it's well, it's the smell of home." Lori, the young teacher, was born in Heber and wrote in the journal Evangelina asked her to keep, "I am so happy and so lucky to be working in this school where I grew up."

8   "She's really good," Evangelina continued. "She's very creative, very responsible, and she's empathetic. She may not stay in Heber, but it's important for her to be there now." Evangelina absentmindedly touched a streak of silver in her hair. "You know, some of the teachers Lori had as a little girl are still there—and her principal, too. They gave her a lot of support." A pause here. "And in the eyes of her old neighbors. Imagine! 'Look at Lori. She's come back.' *La Maestra.*"

9   Education was highly valued in places like Heber and Calexico, as it was generally in Mexican culture. Teachers were respected, and school was seen as a place where children could learn the skills that would enable them to do better than their parents had done. This support of education played out, however, amid a complex of forces. Many of the families in the Valley were poor—35 percent of the residents lived below the poverty line—and sometimes had to make decisions between work and

school. As Evangelina put it, "Poverty forces you to parcel out your human resources." So some children would be selected to pursue their education, and others sent out to make money. "I was the oldest and had to work," one man explained, "but my brother was able to go to college." Traditional beliefs about gender factored into these decisions, but not in the unilateral way commonly portrayed. Some families still believed that girls don't need schooling as much as boys do, but I also heard from a number of professional women that it was their working-class fathers who urged them toward achievement. Such achievement could, though, conflict with other beliefs about family cohesiveness and a woman's role in maintaining it—and this could become a source of awful tension if a college-bound woman decided to leave the area to pursue her education. The local San Diego State campus made higher education possible for women who could not easily leave the Valley.

Comprehension

1. According to the author, what three factors explain the success of the high school program in Calexico?
2. Why did some residents of the Imperial Valley have to choose between school and work?
3. Who is Evangelina Bustamante Jones? What is her job?
4. How do the people in this region feel about education and teachers?

Critical Thinking

1. The author gives several details about the performance of students in Calexico schools. Do these facts support his point that the schools are successful?
2. Do you think there are still some parents in Calexico who don't want their daughters to go to college as much as they want their sons to go to college? What statement in the reading gives you that idea?
3. In another book, *Lives on the Boundary,* author Mike Rose talks about struggling college students whose K–12 educations left them underprepared for college. In *Possible Lives,* he focuses on successful educational programs. Do these book titles match the author's message?
4. What do you think is the author's purpose in writing about educational programs?

Language and Vocabulary

1. Had you ever read or heard the expression "arable land" before you read it in the second paragraph of this selection? Can you figure out the meaning by reading the other words around it?
2. In this reading, the author uses many adverbs that end in -*ly*. An *adverb* is a word that describes or changes the meaning of verbs, adjectives, and other adverbs, such as "Education was *highly* valued . . . ." Find and underline at least 8 -*ly* adverbs in the reading. (Do not underline four other words that end in -*ly* but are not used as adverbs—*early, only, hardly,* and *family.*)

Style, Structure, and Organization

1. Mike Rose includes a lot of background information about Calexico and the Imperial Valley in this selection. Find and list six or seven details about the community. Does this background information make the reading seem more interesting and realistic?
2. Of the three reasons for the successes of Calexico's schools, the author focuses on two of them. Why do you think he wrote more about those two reasons than about the other reason?
3. There are eight paragraphs in this selection. For each paragraph, write down one or two words (or at most a few words) that tell what its main topic is. Does each paragraph concentrate on one main point?

Topics for Discussion or Journal Writing

1. What is it like to grow up very poor? In what ways can poverty prevent students from learning, getting a high school education, and going on to college?
2. What are the advantages and disadvantages of growing up in a small town compared with living in or near a city?
3. Would you like to be a teacher? Why or why not?
4. Reread the last section, about Evangelina Bustamante Jones and Lori, the student teacher. Do you think you would enjoy being in a class taught by either of these women? Do they remind you of any teachers you have known?

Writing Topics for Paragraphs or Essays

1. Write about a particular class that you learned a lot from or about another learning situation that was important in your life.
2. What are your educational goals or dreams?
3. Investigate what kind of tutorial and small-group help is available to students at your college. Write a short report telling when, where, and how students can access these services.
4. Make a list of several classes in which you learned a lot and another list of classes in which you didn't learn as much. What did the more effective classes have in common that the other classes didn't?
5. Read all or part of a book by Mike Rose, such as *Lives on the Boundary* or *Possible Lives*. Then choose one of the following writing assignments.
    a. Imagine that you are one of the characters in the book. Then write about your educational experiences. What worked and what didn't?
    b. Write a short summary of the author's main points.

Breaking Through the Barriers

James M. Henslin

Jaime Escalante, a high school calculus teacher in East Los Angeles, is well known for his ability to motivate and inspire students. A popular 1987 movie, *Stand and Deliver,* brought Escalante's success story to the attention of the public. As you read the following selection from a college sociology textbook, consider why Jaime Escalante has been so effective in motivating students.

Prereading Questions

1. What qualities should a teacher have in order to motivate and inspire students?
2. What kinds of problems would you expect to find in an inner-city school?

Vocabulary

plagued with severely affected by
recruitment persuading people to join
motto a brief statement of someone's ideals or principles
tracked in this context, placed in certain kinds of classes, usually based on grades or standardized tests
barrio a Spanish-speaking area of a city, where most families have limited incomes
rigorous strict
binds obligates or requires
foundation an organization that provides money for special purposes
sociological about or related to society

SOURCE: "Breaking Through the Barriers" by James M. Henslin. From James M. Henslin, *Sociology, a Down-to-Earth Approach,* Fourth Edition, copyright © 1999 by Allyn & Bacon. Reprinted by permission.

Breaking Through the Barriers

Called "the best teacher in America," Jaime Escalante taught in an East Los Angeles inner-city school plagued with poverty, crime, drugs, gangs, and the usual miserably low student scores. In this self-defeating environment, he taught calculus. His students scored so highly on national tests that test officials, suspecting cheating, asked his students to retake the test. They did. Again they passed—this time with even higher scores.

2   Escalante's school ranks fourth in the nation in the number of students who have taken and passed the Advanced Placement S.A.T. Calculus examination. For students to even take the test, they must complete Algebra I, Geometry, Algebra II, Trigonometry or Math Analysis, and Calculus for first-year college and/or Calculus for second-year college.

3   How did Escalante overcome such odds? His success is not due to a recruitment of the brightest students. Students' poor academic performance does not stand in the way of being admitted to the math program. The *only* requirement is an interest in math. What did Escalante do right, and what can we learn from his approach?

4   "Success starts with attitude" could be Escalante's motto. Few Latino students were taking math. Most were tracked into craft classes and made jewelry and birdhouses. "Our kids are just as talented as anyone else. They just need the opportunity to show it. And for that they must be motivated," he said. "They just don't think about becoming scientists or engineers."

5   Here are the keys to what Escalante accomplished. First, teaching and learning can't take place unless there is discipline. For that the teachers, not gangs, must control the classroom. Second, the students must believe in themselves. The teacher must inspire students with the idea that they *can* learn (remember teacher expectations). Third, the students must be motivated to perform, in this case to see learning as a way out of the barrio, the path to good jobs.

6   Escalante uses a team approach. He has his students think of themselves as a team, of him as the coach, and the national exams as a sort of Olympics for which they are preparing. To stimulate team identity, the students wear team jackets, caps, and T-shirts with logos that identify them as part of the team. Before class, his students do "warm ups" (hand clapping and foot stomping to a rock song).

7   His team has practice schedules as rigorous as a championship football team. Students must sign a contract that binds them to participate in the summer program he has developed, to complete the daily home-

work, and to attend Saturday morning and after-school study sessions. To get in his class, even the student's parents have to sign the contract. To keep before his students the principle that self-discipline pays off, Escalante covers his room with posters of sports figures in action—Michael Jordan, Jerry West, Babe Ruth, and Tiger Woods.

8   "How have I been successful with students from such backgrounds?" he asks. "Very simple. I use a time-honored tradition—hard work, lots of it, for teacher and student alike."

9   The following statement helps us understand how Escalante challenges his students to think of what is possible in life, instead of problems that destroy the possible:

> The first day when these kids walk into my room, I have a bunch of names of schools and colleges on the chalkboard. I ask each student to memorize one. The next day I pick one kid and ask, "What school did you pick?" He says USC or UCLA or Stanford, MIT, Colgate, and so on. So I say, "Okay, keep that in mind. I'm going to bring in somebody who'll be talking about the schools."

10   Escalante then has a college adviser talk to the class. But more than this, he also has arranged foundation money to help the students get to the colleges of their choice.

11   The sociological point is that the problem was *not* the ability of the students. Their failure to do well in school was not due to something *within* them. The problem was the *system,* the way classroom instruction is arranged. When Escalante changed the system of instruction, both attitudes and performance changed. Escalante makes this very point—that student performance does not depend on the charismatic personality of a single person, but on how we structure the learning setting.

◆◆◆

Comprehension

1. What kinds of problems did Escalante encounter as a teacher in East Los Angeles?
2. What was Escalante's greatest achievement as a teacher?
3. According to the author, there are three key factors that account for the success of Escalante's program. What are they, and why is each one important?
4. What did Escalante do to get students interested in going to college?

Critical Thinking

1. Why do you think Jaime Escalante's approach has been so successful? Would this approach work well in other high schools? Why or why not?
2. What is the main point that the reading makes about our educational system?
3. What are some of the biggest challenges that teachers like Jaime Escalante face?
4. Why were only a few Latino students enrolled in math classes before Escalante's program began?

Language and Vocabulary

1. Were you familiar with the word *charismatic* before you read it in the last sentence of the reading? What do you think it means? Why does the author say, "Student performance does not depend on the charismatic personality of a single person"?
2. In paragraph 6, Escalante's "team approach" is compared to training for the Olympics. Does this comparison make sense? Why or why not?

Style, Structure, and Organization

1. How does the introductory paragraph (the first paragraph of the reading) capture readers' attention?
2. Look for three places in the reading where the author includes statements made by Jaime Escalante himself. How do these statements make the reading more interesting and effective?
3. Which paragraph expresses the author's main point about our educational system?

Topics for Discussion or Journal Writing

1. What do you think students liked best about Escalante's program?
2. Do you think that schools today are still experiencing the same kinds of problems that Escalante encountered in East Los Angeles?
3. Would you like to be a teacher? Why or why not? What grades or subjects would you like to teach?

4. Do you think that students should be "tracked," or placed in certain kinds of classes, on the basis of their grades and test scores? Why or why not?
5. Have you ever encountered ethnic stereotyping in school or elsewhere?

Writing Topics for Paragraphs or Essays

1. Write about a special teacher or someone else who inspired you to achieve something.
2. Compare and contrast Jaime Escalante's math program with the math classes at the high school you attended. In your paper, explain the most important similarities and differences.
3. Imagine that a friend of yours is thinking about dropping out of school. Using some ideas from the reading and some ideas of your own, persuade your friend to stay in school. Write either a personal letter to your friend or a persuasive paragraph.
4. Interview a favorite teacher or a person you admire. Use a tape recorder or take good notes, so that you can accurately quote some of the person's most interesting statements. Then write a paper about the person you interviewed, including at least two quotations.
5. Watch the movie *Stand and Deliver* to learn more about Jaime Escalante and some of his students. Then choose one of the following writing assignments:
   a. Write about Jaime Escalante. Explain why he is a good teacher.
   b. Write about one of the students featured in the movie. How did the experience of being in Escalante's class change this person's life?

The Rich Heritage of Public Speaking

Steven A. Beebe and Susan J. Beebe

The following reading selection, from a college textbook entitled *Public Speaking*, traces the history of public speaking from the time of the ancient Greeks and Romans through the twentieth century. Some of the well-known men and women who are mentioned in the reading affected the course of history through their influence as public speakers.

Prereading Questions

1. What qualities or skills do you think make some public speakers more effective than others?
2. Do you think that public speaking is more important or less important now than it was 100 years ago? Why?

Vocabulary

formulated in this case, created and stated as a method

orator someone who gives an eloquent formal speech

medieval related to or taking place during the Middle Ages

expound to explain in detail

town criers people who walked through a town shouting important news for everyone to hear

suffrage voting rights

circuits in this context, a series of towns or settlements where speakers made presentations

hand in hand used to describe things that are done together or belong together

prescriptions in this case, instructions

decry to condemn

SOURCE: "The Rich Heritage of Public Speaking" from Steven A. Beebe and Susan J. Beebe, *Public Speaking: An Audience-Centered Approach,* Fourth Edition, copyright © 2000 by Allyn & Bacon. Reprinted and adapted by permission.

infamy fame for something evil or criminal
medium in this case, a means or method of communication
eulogizing giving a memorial speech about someone who has recently died
via by means of

The Rich Heritage of Public Speaking

Even before people could read, they listened to public speakers. The fourth century B.C. was a golden age for rhetoric in the Greek Republic, where the philosopher Aristotle formulated guidelines for speakers that we still follow today. As politicians and poets attracted large followings in ancient Rome, Cicero and Quintilian sought to define the qualities of the "true" orator.

2   In medieval Europe, the clergy were the most polished public speakers. People gathered eagerly to hear Martin Luther expound his fourteen Articles of Faith. Later, citizens of the New World listened to the town criers and impassioned patriots of colonial America.

3   Vast nineteenth-century audiences heard speakers such as Henry Clay and Daniel Webster debate states' rights; they listened to Frederick Douglass, Angelina Grimke, and Sojourner Truth argue for the abolition of slavery, and to Lucretia Mott plead for women's suffrage; they gathered for an evening's entertainment as Mark Twain traveled the lecture circuits of the American frontier.

4   Students of nineteenth-century public speaking spent very little time developing their own speeches. Instead they practiced the art of **declamation**—the delivery of an already famous address. Favorite subjects for declamation included speeches by such Americans as Patrick Henry and William Jennings Bryan, and by the British orator Edmund Burke. Collections of speeches, such as Bryan's own ten-volume set of *The World's Famous Orations,* published in 1906, were extremely popular.

5   Hand in hand with declamation went the study and practice of **elocution,** the expression of emotion through posture, movement, gestures, facial expression, and voice. From the mid-nineteenth to early twentieth centuries, elocution manuals, providing elaborate and specific prescriptions for effective delivery, were standard references not only in schools, but also in nearly every middle-class home in America. Young children (including the mother of one of your authors) took elocution lessons, and elocution became an accepted means of literary study as well as a popular form of entertainment.

6   In the first half of the twentieth century, radio made it possible for people around the world to hear Franklin Delano Roosevelt decry December 7, 1941, as "a date which will live in infamy." In the last half of the century, television provided the medium through which audiences saw and heard the most stirring speeches: Martin Luther King Jr., declaring "I have a dream"; Gerald Ford assuring a nation reeling from Watergate that "Our long national nightmare is over"; George Bush affirming the American sense of community as "a thousand points of light"; and Earl Spencer of Britain eulogizing his sister, Princess Diana, as "the unique, the complex, the extraordinary and irreplaceable Diana."

7   As the twenty-first century dawns, so too does a new era of speechmaking—an era that will build on a rich heritage of providing information, influencing thought and action, entertaining, and paying tribute via the spoken word.

❖❖❖

Comprehension

1. In the history of public speaking, what is Aristotle well known for?
2. Name three of the most famous nineteenth-century speakers in America. What kinds of topics was each one known for?
3. What are *declamation* and *elocution?*
4. What major changes in communication took place during the twentieth century? What effects did these changes have on audiences who listened to public speakers?

Critical Thinking

1. Why are public speeches especially important in political campaigns?
2. How does speaking to a television audience differ from giving a speech in person? Are different qualities or skills important for a television speaker?
3. Have effective public speakers sometimes influenced the course of history? Give some examples.
4. Why is public speaking still taught in colleges and universities?
5. What is the authors' purpose in this selection—to inform, to persuade, or both?

Language and Vocabulary

1. Had you ever heard the expression "golden age" before you read it in the first paragraph of the reading? What do you think it means? Why did the authors use this term? If you were to describe the first decade of the twenty-first century as the "golden age" of something, what would it be?
2. The sixth paragraph quotes famous lines from five well-known twentieth-century speeches. Underline or highlight all five of the quotations. Then choose one that you think is especially effective and explain why.

Style, Structure, and Organization

1. How does the reading use chronological order (time order) as an organizational technique? What time periods does the reading mention?
2. Which paragraphs include examples of well-known and influential public speakers? Why did the authors provide so many examples?

Topics for Discussion or Journal Writing

1. Have you ever given a speech? How did you feel about the experience?
2. Have you ever taken a speech or communication class that included public speaking? If so, what did you learn about techniques for giving successful speeches?
3. How do you think people found out about current events and important issues before television existed? Which methods of getting information do you think were the most effective and the easiest to use?
4. In recent years, funerals of well-known people and public figures have often been broadcast on television, giving the public an opportunity to hear a type of speech known as a *eulogy* about the person who died. Have you ever watched one of these televised funerals? If so, did it leave you with a good feeling? Was the person who presented it an effective public speaker?
5. Do you agree with the authors that the twenty-first century will be "a new era of speechmaking"?

Writing Topics for Paragraphs or Essays

1. Listen to a public speaker at your school, such as a visiting writer, a guest speaker on any topic, someone making a presentation at a club meeting, or even a teacher giving a lecture. Then write a summary of the speaker's main points and your evaluation of the speech.

2. Listen to a speech by a political candidate and write a paper about it. Include a summary of the main points and your evaluation of the speech.

3. Write a short speech to give to your class about any topic that you think your audience would find interesting. Your purpose can be to entertain, to inform, or to persuade. Try to polish your words and phrases so that your speech will be effective. If you present it to the class, first practice the speech by reading it aloud several times.

4. Using library resources or the Internet, look up information about one of the well-known orators or speakers mentioned in the reading, such as Frederick Douglas, Sojourner Truth, William Jennings Bryan, Martin Luther King, Jr., Franklin Delano Roosevelt, or Earl Spencer. Write a paper about this person's life and accomplishments.

5. Write a paper about the history of radio, television, the telephone, the Internet, or any other form of communication. Research your topic at the library or online.

Emergency Medical Technicians

Joseph J. Mistovich, Brent Q. Hafen, and Keith J. Karren

This reading, taken from a textbook for paramedics called *Prehospital Emergency Care,* explains the differences between various levels of emergency medical technicians and paramedics. As you read this selection, focus on the training requirements and the responsibilities of each level of emergency medical personnel.

Prereading Questions

1. Are emergency medical services available in all communities?
2. What kind of training is required to become an emergency medical technician or a paramedic?

Vocabulary

EMTs emergency medical technicians
integral in this case, a necessary part of the system
trend movement
curriculum program of study, including classes and/or topics
assessment evaluation
airway the path that air takes to get into the lungs, including the mouth and throat
artificial ventilation assistance with breathing
shock a life-threatening condition caused by anything that reduces blood flow
dressing cleaning and medicating
splinting applying a rigid support for broken bones
extremities arms, legs, feet, hands, fingers, toes
colleagues co-workers

SOURCE: "Emergency Medical Technicians," by Joseph J. Mistovich, Brent Q. Hafen, and Keith J. Karren. From *Prehospital Emergency Care,* Sixth Edition, by Mistovich/Hafen/Karren, copyright © 2000. Reprinted by permission of Prentice-Hall, Inc., Upper Saddle River, NJ.

extrication techniques techniques for getting someone out of a dangerous situation, such as a wrecked car or collapsed building

coping with dealing with

intravenous into the veins

defibrillation applying an electric shock to the chest in order to reestablish a steady heartbeat

endotracheal intubation putting a tube into the throat in order to keep the airway passages open

cardiac related to the heart

interventions medically necessary procedures

electrocardiogram a test that shows how well the heart is working

cricothyroidotomy tracheotomy, opening a breathing hole in the throat

Emergency Medical Technicians

The Health Care System

First responders and EMTs are an integral part of a community's health care system—a network of medical care that begins in the field and extends to hospitals and other treatment centers. In essence, EMTs provide **prehospital care**—emergency medical treatment given to patients before they are transported to a hospital or other facility. (In some areas the term out-of-hospital care is preferred, reflecting a trend toward providing care on the scene with or without subsequent transport to a hospital.)

Levels of Training

2   There are four nationally accepted levels of prehospital emergency medical training: First Responder, EMT-Basic, EMT-Intermediate, and EMT-Paramedic.

First Responder

3   The **First Responder** is typically the first person on the scene with emergency care training. He may be a police officer, for example, or a firefighter, industrial health officer, truck driver, schoolteacher, or a volunteer associated with the community emergency care system. The U.S. Department of Transportation publishes a curriculum and guidelines for First Responder training, just as it does for EMTs.

4   First Responders can provide information valuable in patient care, including how the emergency came about, what was observed during patient assessment by the First Responder, and what emergency care they have provided before the ambulance arrived.

EMT-Basic

5   The **EMT-Basic** (EMT-B) level of certification is held by those who successfully complete a course based on the U.S. Department of Transportation curriculum and who have been certified as EMT-Basics by the state emergency medical services division.

6   The basic course prepares an EMT-Basic to function in three areas:

- Controlling life-threatening situations, including maintaining an open airway, providing artificial ventilation, controlling severe bleeding, and treating shock.
- Stabilizing non-life-threatening situations, including dressing and bandaging wounds, splinting injured extremities, delivering and caring for infants, and dealing with the psychological stress of the patient, family members, neighbors, and colleagues.
- Using nonmedical skills, such as driving, maintaining supplies and equipment in proper order, using good communication skills, keeping good records, knowing proper extrication techniques, and coping with related issues.

EMT-Intermediate

7   The **EMT-Intermediate** (EMT-I) is an EMT-Basic who completes additional training prescribed by the U.S. Department of Transportation EMT-Intermediate curriculum. This training includes emphasis on roles and responsibilities, EMS systems, medical/legal considerations, medical terminology, EMS communications, patient assessment, and initial assessment and management of shock. Additional skills include intravenous therapy, defibrillation, medication administration, endotracheal intubation, and ECG interpretation. In some states, advanced training qualifies EMT-Intermediates as cardiac technicians or cardiac rescue technicians.

EMT-Paramedic

8   The title **EMT-Paramedic** (EMT-P) is assigned to those who are trained in all aspects of prehospital emergency care, including or equal to the U.S. Department of Transportation paramedic curriculum, and who

have received the appropriate certification. Paramedics have a broad foundation of knowledge in emergency care. They also can provide advanced interventions including starting intravenous lines, administering medications, inserting endotracheal tubes (which some EMT-Basics may also be trained to do in some areas), decompressing the chest cavity, reading electrocardiograms, using manual defibrillators to restore heart rhythm, cardiac pacing, cricothyroidotomy, and advanced cardiac life support.

◆◆◆

Comprehension

1. What are the four levels of prehospital emergency medical training?
2. What does "first responder" mean?
3. What government agency sets the standards for training EMTs?
4. What are some differences between an EMT-Basic and an EMT-Paramedic?

Critical Thinking

1. What is the purpose of this textbook selection—to inform or to persuade?
2. Do you think the authors of this textbook have a good understanding of emergency medical procedures? Why do you think so?
3. Is this selection a good introduction to the field of EMTs? What further information on EMTs would you want to know next if you were thinking about studying in this field?
4. Will future EMTs have to be knowledgeable about technology? Why?

Language and Vocabulary

1. According to the reading, one of the functions of an EMT-Basic is "stabilizing non-life-threatening situations." What does "stabilizing non-life-threatening situations" mean?
2. The authors use many technical words to refer to the equipment and procedures that EMTs have to be familiar with. If any of these terms are unclear to you, look them up in a dictionary or on the Internet.

Style, Structure, and Organization

1. How does the organization of the selection help to make clear the differences in training between the various types of prehospital emergency medical personnel?
2. Count how many words are in each of the three sentences in the last paragraph of the reading. Does this mix of longer and shorter sentences work well in this paragraph? Why is one of the sentences so much shorter than the others?
3. This reading selection is organized as a *classification* with four specific categories. Find one sentence somewhere in the first two paragraphs that identifies these categories. Is this an effective *main idea sentence* for the whole selection?

Topics for Discussion or Journal Writing

1. How do you feel about medical procedures, such as getting your blood drawn or helping someone in a medical emergency? How well do you handle these kinds of situations?
2. Have you ever received first aid from someone, such as a paramedic or an EMT? What kind of experience was it?
3. After reading this selection, how confident do you feel about the amount of training that emergency services personnel receive?
4. In your opinion, will we need more EMTs and paramedics in the future? Why?
5. Do emergency medical personnel generally receive more respect than hospital workers, less respect, or about the same amount of respect? Why do you think that is?

Writing Topics for Paragraphs or Essays

1. Write about one time when you or someone you know received first aid from an EMT or a paramedic.
2. Would you like to be a paramedic or an emergency medical technician? Why or why not?

3. What organization runs the ambulance or paramedic service in your area? Is it staffed with EMTs, paramedics, or other personnel? Find out more about the service by telephone or by visiting the office in person, and then write a report about what you learn.
4. Interview a paramedic, an emergency room medical technician in a hospital, or a lifeguard. Ask what kind of training he or she received before being hired, what training was provided on the job, and how qualified he or she feels to perform the duties of the job.
5. Choose one of the following topics. Find out more about the topic by searching online or in a library; then write a short paper on the topic.
    a. What are the working conditions and salaries for EMTs and paramedics in your area, and what agencies hire them?
    b. What kind of technology is used in prehospital emergency services? Briefly mention several machines and describe at least one of them in more detail.

Internet Job Search

A. C. "Buddy" Krizan, Patricia Merrier,
Carol Larson Jones, and Jules Harcourt

More and more businesses are relying on the Internet, not only to sell products, offer services, and provide information to consumers, but also to attract well-qualified employees. Whether you are looking for your first job, thinking about changing careers, or just checking to see what's available, you may want to consider an Internet job search.

Prereading Questions

1. What are the best ways to find out about job opportunities?
2. How might a person begin a job search on the Internet?

Vocabulary

advent arrival

arena place or area

resume (or **résumé** or **resumé**) a written listing of a person's education, work experience, and job qualifications

cyberspace the virtual "space" where people share and access data via the Internet

URL Uniform Resource Locator, the address for a web site

internships opportunities for supervised training (usually open to recent graduates or advanced students)

recruiters company representatives who are actively seeking new employees

resources in this case, sources of information

banks in this case, databases containing many different items of information

diversity variety; in reference to the workplace, hiring people of different ethnicities, genders, ages, religions, and so on

SOURCE: "Internet Job Search," from *Business Communication,* Fourth Edition, by A. Krizan, P. Merrier, C. L. Jones, and J. Harcourt, copyright © 1999. Reprinted with permission of South-Western College Publishing, a division of Thomson Learning.

seekers searchers

hypertext links connections to other web sites that can be accessed simply by clicking on the title or the web address

home page the main page of an organization, a group, or a person, generally with links to other related pages

pitches in this case, ads or information designed to sell something

selective choosy, particular, careful in choosing

potential possible in the future

confidentiality keeping information private, not revealing it to others

Internet Job Search

With the advent of the Internet, you now have a new method for seeking your career position and making worthwhile connections. The Web has now opened up a new arena of job hunting for you. The Web can be used for accessing information on how to conduct a job search on the Web, how to develop an online resume, how to learn about the various companies, and which companies have openings in your field.

2   To begin the cyberspace job search you must first have a computer with access to the Web. A good place to start your job search is on your career center's home page, which will have links to the necessary resources. Your career center may be located through the Catapult Career Offices Home Pages: Index at **http://www.jobweb.org/catapult/homepage.htm** or through Jobtrak, which has partnered with over 500 college and university career centers nationwide. The URL for this Web site is **http://www.jobtrak.com/**. Jobtrak has job listings for full-time jobs, part-time jobs, temporary jobs, and internships. Jobtrak has information on career fairs, resume development, job searches, and top recruiters, too.

3   The Riley Guide Web site, which was developed by Worcester Polytechnic Institute's librarian Margaret F. Riley Dikel (the grandmother of resources for job seekers), is a site with information on employment opportunities and job resources on the Internet. This site, found at **http://www.dbm.com/jobguide**, has information ranging from the basic use of the Internet to incorporating the Internet into your job search to online job application procedures to recruiting online. This Web site includes all the current information on searching for positions on the Web.

4   Additional sites that can be accessed on the Web include the following:

   Career Magazine. **http://www.careermag.com**. This Web site is an online career magazine with information on job openings, employers, resume banks, job fairs, and various articles on current topics such as diversity in the workplace.

CareerMosaic. **http://careermosaic.com.** This Web site is popular with college students because it has a jobs database, a "usenet" to perform searches of jobs listed in regional and occupational newsgroups, an online job fair, career resource center, and an international gateway to link to *CareerMosaic* sites around the world. This Web site strives to be a valuable source to both the employer and the job seeker.

E-Span: Interactive Employment Network. **http://www.espan.com.** E-Span has as its motto "The Right Person for the Job and the Right Job for the Person." This site offers job-search information and job listings.

JobDirect. **http://www.jobdirect.com.** JobDirect connects entry-level job seekers with employers who want qualified applicants. This Web site will help students find summer jobs, internships, or career positions.

Monster Board. **http://www.monster.com.** One of the most popular Web sites for job seekers, the Monster Board offers a variety of hypertext links to job-search resources and connections to job listings.

Online Career Center. **http://www.occ.com.** Online is a nonprofit job-research home page sponsored by employer organizations and includes information on companies and job listings.

5   The U.S. Government's official Web site for jobs and employment information can be located at **http://www.usajobs.opm.gov/.** America's Job Bank, which will also list jobs that can be found in the 50 states, can be viewed at **http://www.ajb.dni.us**. The home page of the White House is another site for job openings in the United States; the address is **http://www.whitehouse.gov/wh/welcome.html**.

6   The above is a listing of just a few of the Web site addresses for job searching online. You may contact your career center staff or Internet directory indexes for additional sites since new ones are added regularly. As you surf the Internet and the many career-related sites, remember to select sites that are current, look out for sales pitches, check the fees for listing your resume, be selective in contacting that potential employer, and ask what type of confidentiality or privacy protection for your resume is offered. The job search on the Web is just another tool to assist you in locating your career position.

◆◆◆

Comprehension

1. What are the four main types of information that people who are seeking career positions can access on the Internet?

2. To begin a job search, how would you go about finding a career center on the Internet?
3. Choose two of the following sites and explain what each one offers: Career Magazine, CareerMosaic, E-Span: Interactive Employment Network, JobDirect, Monster Board, Online Career Center.
4. Where can you find the home page for the White House?

Critical Thinking

1. Why is the Internet an important tool in conducting a successful job search?
2. What is the authors' attitude toward the Internet? Do they seem to think that everyone can successfully use the Internet to search for jobs?
3. Which kinds of companies do you think would be most likely to list job opportunities on Internet sites? Which kinds of companies would not be likely to list job opportunities?
4. If your Internet search turned up one or more jobs that you were interested in, what additional steps would you expect to follow in order to apply for those jobs?

Language and Vocabulary

1. Had you heard the phrase "surf the Internet" before you read it in this selection? What do you think it means? Are there any ways in which surfing the Internet is similar to actual surfing—riding the waves on a surfboard?
2. In this reading selection, the authors used a number of technical terms related to the Internet, such as *cyberspace, hyperlink,* and *URL.* Make a list of all the technical terms in the reading, and try to figure out the meaning of each. If you don't know some of the terms, check a guide to Internet terminology or ask someone who is knowledgeable. (Since most of the terms have just been created in recent years, they are not likely to be listed in a dictionary.)

Style, Structure, and Organization

1. Some of the information in this reading is written in list form rather than paragraph form. Do you think the list form is a good choice? Why or why not? Does the list format make reading about various Internet sites easier or more difficult?

2. Underline or highlight the main idea statement (thesis statement) in the first paragraph of the reading selection. Is this the best place for a main idea statement? Why?

Topics for Discussion or Journal Writing

1. Would you be interested in doing an Internet job search? Why or why not?
2. Which of the web sites that the authors mentioned do you think would be most helpful? Why?
3. What is the most difficult part of finding a good job, whether using an Internet job search or other methods? Can you think of anything you could do to make the process easier?
4. Are you satisfied with your present job, or are you interested in finding a better job? Why? What do you like most about your present job?
5. If you could choose any type of career or profession (without being concerned about the years of schooling or the cost), what would be your first choice? Why does this career or profession appeal to you?

Writing Topics for Paragraphs or Essays

1. Access one of the web sites recommended in the reading and write a report about it. Include details about what types of information are available there, links to related sites (if any), and your evaluation of the usefulness of the site.
2. Write a résumé for yourself, either to meet your current job needs or to meet your future needs after you have finished college. Include your career goal, education and training, work experience, and anything else that may relate to your job qualifications. Some of the web sites listed in the reading have additional information about preparing an effective résumé.
3. Write at least five possible questions you might be asked in a job interview, and then compose a detailed answer to three of them.
4. Write an instructions paper on how to prepare for a job interview, how to write a résumé, how to use the career center at your college, or anything else that would be helpful for someone who is trying to find a job.
5. Write a comparison/contrast paper about two different jobs or careers. You may choose two careers that you are interested in, two jobs that you have held, your own present job and a different kind of job, or jobs that two of your friends or relatives have.

4

Media and Popular Culture

Taking Potluck Tom Bodett 98
Color TV Richard Breyer 103
Breaking the Habit Mike Duffy 109
Shoeless Joe W. P. Kinsella 116
Elvis Culture Erika Doss 122
Dressing Down John Brooks 127

Taking Potluck

Tom Bodett

Tom Bodett is well known as an American humorist. Although he grew up in Michigan, he lives in Homer, Alaska, and much of his humor is about life in Alaska. At one time, he hosted a radio variety show from Homer, and he has been a radio commentator. Listeners and readers alike have enjoyed his casual humor based on ordinary people and everyday situations.

Prereading Questions

1. Why do people enjoy potluck dinners and picnics?
2. Can you think of some foods that are popular in certain parts of the country but not in other areas?

Vocabulary

potluck a meal or party where each guest brings a food dish

staple a basic food

foodfest a feast; an event with lots of food

entrée the main course

splayed spread out

constitution in this context, the way something is made: structure or composition

cod a type of fish

hover remain nearby

slinks moves quietly, trying not to be noticed

trough in this case, a V-shaped feeding dish like those used for farm animals

lingering remaining

ravaged destroyed; in this context, meaning that most of the food has been partially eaten

dispirited without much spirit, lacking enthusiasm

Taking Potluck

Of all the wonderful distractions that summer has to offer, none is quite as wonderful as the potluck. I know it isn't strictly a summer event, but a potluck takes on much broader dimensions in the warmer months. It's held outdoors, usually accompanied by horseshoes or volleyball. The children run circles around each other, and the fish is fresh.

2   Fish is a staple of the Alaskan potluck, and I've never been to one that didn't have at least three species of it on hand in one form or another. Back in the Midwest where I first sat down to one, you could ruin a good potluck by bringing fish to it. People are suspicious of fish back there, and I'm sure the expression "smells fishy to me" originated at a community feed somewhere in northern Indiana. Fried chicken is the heart of the Great Plains foodfest, but outside the entrée, the ingredients of a good potluck are pretty universal.

3   Start with a large folding table on an uneven lawn and invite a bunch of people over. No matter what happens someone always brings too much fish, so there's no need to worry about the main course. Then wanders in a pot of beans and weenies and a relish tray with rolled-up cold cuts splayed around a radish-and-celery arrangement. Someone always brings marshmallows so the kids have something to get stuck in their hair, and a bachelor or two will show up with a six-pack and a bag of Doritos.

4   No fewer than five potato salads will appear in rapid succession. You have to like potato salad if you're going to like potlucks. In fact, I think the "pot" in "potluck" is an abbreviation for "potato salad," and the luck refers to those few fortunate individuals who can get through the meal and not wear some of it home.

5   Everything is served up on paper plates with the constitution of flour tortillas and eaten with little plastic forks that couldn't pry a bone from a cooked cod let alone penetrate your neighbor's lasagna.

6   Potlucks are hardest on those who do the cooking. They hover around the food table to see what's going over the best. "Now, no one has touched the three-bean salad. What's the matter with you people?" The builder of the salad turns the color of the red-cabbage clam dip and slinks toward the beer cooler. The hero of any potluck is the one who brings the deviled eggs. They are usually devoured before the other folks can even get the tin foil off their casseroles.

7   After one or two courses your plate has become something of a trough folded in the palm of one hand. An amazing blend of flavors is then inevitable. The juice from the fruit-and-nut salad seeps in under your uncle's world-famous beef-and-bean burritos, and the hot sauce from that makes an interesting topping for the fresh apple crumb cake you discovered while going back for one more bratwurst.

100 ◆ *Part 4 / Media and Popular Culture*

8   In a while most folks will have had their fill and will wander off sleepily in small groups to toss horseshoes or slap mosquitoes. There's always one or two guys who linger to graze at the table, but their picking has no real spirit behind it. A survey of the ravaged spread will reveal a half-dozen potato salads with one scoop out of each and a large basket of wholly untouched fruit.

9   I got an idea from this. You see, in this season of multiple potlucks it's not unusual to be invited to more than one on a single day. You can't make a different dish for each of them, so I recommend you make a potato salad and take the paprika shaker along with you. When you leave the first party, just smooth over your salad with a spoon and put some fresh paprika on top. No one will know the difference, and you'll be able to gracefully enter potluck after potluck.

10   To be prepared for the improbable—like if someone actually eats all your salad—keep a basket of plastic fruit in the car at all times. This will get you into the next party and it's perfectly safe, as no one ever eats the fruit. I glue them all together in case those lingering grazers get nosy and try to get them out of the basket. They usually give up after a few dispirited tugs and wander off to test the potato salads.

11   Of course, I don't recommend everyone follow my advice on this. *Somebody's* gotta bring the fish.

◆◆◆

Comprehension

1. How is an Alaskan potluck different from a Midwest or Great Plains potluck?
2. Which potluck menu items named by the author are universal (common at potlucks in all parts of the country)?
3. According to the author, which potluck food item is the most popular, judging by the fact that it is eaten first?
4. If a person is invited to more than one potluck on the same day, how does Tom Bodett suggest handling the situation?

Critical Thinking

1. Do you think the author really believes that "the 'pot' in 'potluck' is an abbreviation for 'potato salad' "? How can you tell whether or not he is serious?

2. Find at least four negative things that the author says about potlucks. Why does he mention these things? Do you think he is really being critical of potlucks, or is he trying to be humorous? How can you tell?
3. Do you think the author enjoys living in Alaska? Why or why not?
4. What do you think was the author's main purpose in writing this essay—to inform or to entertain?

Language and Vocabulary

1. Had you ever heard an expression like "graze at the table" to describe a style of eating at a potluck or buffet dinner? What do you think it means? Describe what a person does when he or she is *grazing*.
2. Find at least two statements that made you smile or laugh while you were reading this selection. What is there about the author's word choices that makes these statements humorous?

Style, Structure, and Organization

1. In some parts of the essay, the author seems to be giving instructions. For example, in paragraph 3, he says, "Start with a large folding table on an uneven lawn . . . ," as if he is telling readers how to organize a potluck. Find another place where the author tells readers what to do in a certain potluck situation. Does this part of the essay use a somewhat different style than other parts in order to give instructions to readers?
2. The author's style includes a lot of visual details, as well as some details that involve the senses of touch, smell, and taste. Highlight or underline at least five visual details that you think are especially effective and at least two details that use one of the other senses.

Topics for Discussion or Journal Writing

1. What are the advantages and disadvantages of a potluck, compared with other types of parties?
2. Would you feel comfortable at a potluck in Alaska like the one the author describes? Why or why not?
3. What kinds of difficulties might a person experience while adjusting to the customs and way of life in a different part of the country?

4. Plan a potluck that includes your favorite foods and activities. How is it different from the one described in the reading?
5. Would you enjoy listening to a radio show hosted by Tom Bodett? Why or why not?

Writing Topics for Paragraphs or Essays

1. Have you ever attended a potluck? Describe your experience. Include some humorous details if you would like to.
2. Write a humorous paper about an ordinary event, such as a birthday party, a date, a workout at the gym, or a visit to the dentist. Try to use some of the same kinds of techniques that Tom Bodett did in order to create humor.
3. Using library resources or the Internet, look up information about Homer, Alaska, or another town in Alaska. What are the most interesting things about that town? How is it different from the area where you live? Write a paper about that town aimed at persuading readers to visit the area or to move there.
4. Interview someone who has lived in another country or another state. Ask questions about the way of life there, including how people usually socialize and what types of food people prefer. Then write a paper comparing the way of life in that country or state with the lifestyle in your own area.
5. Find a magazine article, a newspaper column, a comic strip, or a web page that you think is humorous. (Be sure to select something in good taste that would be appropriate for everyone in your class to read.) Share the item with a workshop group or with the class to find out if others also appreciate the humor. Then write a paper explaining the author's purpose, how the author used humor, why it appeals to people, and anything else you would like to comment on.

Color TV

Richard Breyer

Richard Breyer is chair of the Television, Radio, and Film Department at the S.I. Newhouse School of Public Communications at Syracuse University. In this article, published in March 2000, he examines how the largest TV networks (Fox, NBC, CBS, and ABC) and cable TV studios portray minorities. As you read this article, use your own judgment to decide whether you agree or disagree with the author's main point.

Prereading Questions

1. How important is TV? How great an effect does it have on young people?
2. How many hours of TV do you think the average American watches every week?

Vocabulary

NAACP National Association for the Advancement of Colored People
CEO chief executive officer
prime-time the evening hours when the most people are watching TV
sitcoms situation comedies: light entertainment, such as *Friends* or *Frasier*
boycott refusal to participate (in this case, refusal to watch the network TV shows or to buy from their advertisers)
struck a chord with made sense to, was accepted by
struggling fighting against difficulties
bailiff an officer of the court who is responsible for security
casting choosing the right actors for the right TV characters
casts groups of actors who work together on a TV show
ensembles groups
demographic statistics that show information about the population
superficial shallow, not of major importance
arrogant stuck-up, thinking that they are better than all others
cracks me up makes me laugh

universal access availability for everyone (in this case, access to the Internet)

oversaturated in this case, produced an excessive amount

relevance connection, meaning

bland boring, plain

homogeneous alike, similar to each other

Color TV

Speaking at his organization's national convention in New York in July, Kweisi Mfume, the NAACP's president and CEO, criticized the four major networks (ABC, CBS, NBC, and Fox) for a lack of diversity in their fall prime-time programming. None of the 26 new shows planned for the fall season had a minority person in a leading or starring role.

2 "This," according to Mfume, "is an outrage and a shameful display by network executives who are either clueless, careless, or both."

3 In addition to the lack of diversity in front of the camera, there were few minority voices creating and producing this year's crop of programs. According to the Beverly Hills/Hollywood chapter of the NAACP, of the 839 writers who work on dramas and sitcoms, only 55 were black. And the majority of those 55 writers were working on UPN and WB shows. Only 15 were employed on shows airing on ABC, CBS, NBC, and Fox. NBC has only 1 black writer among its 189 staff writers, CBS has 2 out of 144, ABC 9 out of 171, and Fox 3 out of 160.

4 In addition, shows that featured black characters—such as *Spin City*, *Touched by an Angel*, and *Veronica's Closet*—had no black writers or writer-producers on staff, according to Bill Green, president of the Beverly Hills/Hollywood NAACP.

A Boycott Looms

5 Mfume found this to be such a disgrace that he threatened a boycott of the networks and their sponsors unless the leadership at ABC, CBS, NBC, and Fox demonstrated plans of action to change things by the end of last year.

6 Either the threat of boycott or Mfume's criticisms struck a chord with network executives and producers. By the third week of the new season, black characters began to appear in many of those "whitewashed" series as well as in some of the established programs like NBC's *E.R.*, where a black woman doctor was added to the cast. CBS's series *Judging Amy*, about a single mother from New York who becomes a judge in Hartford, Connecticut, added a black bailiff. *Family Ties*, another CBS series, about

a struggling law firm, added black and Hispanic law-school trainees. ABC's *Suddenly Susan* and *Wasteland* also added black actors to their casts.

7   After being criticized for the absence of minority characters in his NBC series pilot episode, Aaron Sorking, executive producer of *West Wing,* told the *New York Times,* "There'll be black faces, Asian faces, Latin faces, men, women all over the place. Are we a little late to the party? Yes we are."

8   Marcia Schulman, senior vice president for talent and casting at 20th Century Fox Television, which produces 22 shows for all four networks, shared her plans for next season: "I'm anticipating us putting together for next season casts that feature the kind of diversity that we have in real life."

9   The real life to which Schulman refers is an American "face" currently composed of 13 percent blacks, 11 percent Latinos, 5 percent Asians, and 1 percent Native Americans. And, given economic and demographic trends, in the future these minorities will represent an even larger percentage of the population and have even more buying power than today. This clearly is one of the reasons the networks responded as quickly as they did.

10   In the words of Scott Sassa, NBC's West Coast president, "It makes good business sense to try and reach these minority groups."

Network 'Arrogance'

11   However, this quick and, for many, superficial fix did not satisfy the NAACP and other critics of the networks. Nancy Miller, executive producer of *Any Day Now,* a series on the Lifetime cable channel about the friendship between a black woman and a white woman, calls the networks "incredibly arrogant." Miller believes that nothing substantial changes by simply adding minorities to the casts of existing series.

12   "It cracks me up that all these networks are scrambling to throw black and minority faces on these shows," she says. "That's not how you do it.

13   "It's got to come from the creators and the writers. And they don't seem to want stories about anyone but white people. How dare they! How incredibly arrogant!"

14   Lifetime is one of a number of cable channels offering the kind of opportunities for minority artists and executives Mfume finds lacking at ABC, NBC, CBS, and Fox. For example,

- There are stand-up comedy and talk shows about black issues on the Black Entertainment Network.

- Univision offers a wide variety of Spanish-language programs.

- WB's *The Steve Harvey Show*, about a 1970's rhythm and blues singer turned high school principal, won the NAACP's Image Award.
- *Resurrection Blvd.*, about a Latino family's quest for the American dream, and *Linc's*, a comedy set in a black-owned bar, appear on Showtime.

15   With cable doing a much better job than the broadcast networks of serving minority audiences, why, critics ask, focus on the four major networks' deficiencies? Wouldn't the NAACP better spend its time and energies lobbying for universal access to cable and the Internet? This would give more minority Americans, especially those on the lower end of the economic spectrum, access to shows like *Any Day Now* or *Resurrection Blvd.* This would also help minorities become part of the brave new World Wide Web, where they will have opportunities to do much more than watch prime-time television.

16   Commentator Earl Ofari Hutchinson, in an article in the *Los Angeles Times,* wonders if prime-time television is even worth fighting for. "TV executives [at the four major networks]," he claims, "have oversaturated the airways with a parade of goofball, sex-laced sitcoms, and action and gossipy talk shows that are deliberately designed to appeal to young, middle-class whites. Many blacks see absolutely no relevance in this programming to their needs and tastes."

A Call for Blacks to Read Books

17   Cynthia Tucker, editor of the *Atlanta Constitution*'s editorial page, argues that the NAACP should set its sights on loftier goals.

18   "He [Mfume] has got it exactly backward," she says. "Mfume ought to be using this controversy to warn black and brown Americans of the folly of spending countless hours in front of the television set—even if they're watching Bill Cosby, Martin Lawrence, and Oprah.

19   "Let prime-time TV keep its bland cast of homogeneous twenty-somethings," Tucker argues. "There are plenty of good books in which black youngsters can find themselves reflected."

♦♦♦

Comprehension

1. Why did the NAACP threaten a boycott of network television shows and their advertisers?
2. According to the NAACP, which shows that featured African-American actors had no African-American staff members?

3. Why is network TV adding more minority actors and staff?
4. According to the final paragraph of the reading, where can young African Americans find themselves reflected?

Critical Thinking

1. The author of this article has a definite point of view. What is the main point of the article?
2. Do you agree that minorities are underrepresented on network TV shows? Why or why not?
3. Based on this article, do you think the number of minority actors, writers, and directors in TV programs will increase, decrease, or stay the same?
4. Do you think this article is unbiased; that is, does it treat network TV as fairly as it treats cable TV?

Language and Vocabulary

1. What do you think "twentysomethings" means?
2. This article uses *acronyms*—strings of letters such as *NAACP* and *CEO*—to refer to certain people or groups. Underline or highlight three more acronyms in the reading, and look up any that you don't already know.

Style, Structure, and Organization

In the following sentences, identify the purpose of each underlined introductory expression: to state a time or place, to give a source, or to provide a smooth transition into the rest of the sentence.

Example: According to the Beverly Hills/Hollywood chapter of the NAACP, of the 839 writers who work on dramas and sitcoms, only 55 were black.
Purpose: *This introductory expression shows a source.*

1. By the third week of the new season, black characters began to appear in many of those "whitewashed" series. . . .
   Purpose: _____

2. With cable doing a much better job than the broadcast networks of serving minority audiences, why, critics ask, focus on the four major networks' deficiencies?
   Purpose: _____

3. In the words of Scott Sassa, NBC's West Coast president, "It makes good business sense to try and reach these minority groups."

Purpose: _____

Topics for Discussion or Journal Writing

1. What are the major ethnic groups in your area? Do you think that these ethnic groups are fairly represented on popular television programs?
2. Do you enjoy watching TV, or do you prefer other activities in your free time—reading a good book, talking with someone, or doing something active?
3. What TV programs have you seen that portray minority characters? Are there more minority actors on TV now than 10 years ago?
4. Is it important to see minority actors in a wide variety of roles on TV? Why?

Writing Topics for Paragraphs or Essays

1. Do you have any ideas for a new TV show that would show people of many different backgrounds as equals? Would it be a sitcom (a comedy), a drama, or something else? Try to come up with a place, a situation, and some characters for your idea, and write a story for one episode (one show).
2. What is your favorite TV show or movie of all time? Briefly describe the show, give some examples of what happens on the show, and tell why it appeals to you so much.
3. Why is it difficult for many people to talk or write about issues such as race and ethnic identity? Think of several possible reasons and then write about each one.
4. Have you ever watched a TV show that had a character you really identify with? Describe the character and tell how he or she is similar to you, how you are different, and the reasons you identify with that character.
5. Read a book or watch a TV show that includes people from different ethnic backgrounds. Then write a short critique of the show or book (include a short summary of the story, describe the characters, and give your reaction).

Breaking the Habit

Mike Duffy

Just before the sixth annual National TV-Turnoff Week began in April 2000, the following newspaper article appeared in the *Detroit Free Press*. To publicize TV-Turnoff Week, television critic Mike Duffy encouraged readers to think about their own television viewing habits.

Prereading Questions

1. Do you think that most people spend too much time watching television?
2. How would people spend their free time if they weren't watching television?

Vocabulary

carved out in this case, set aside time for
heresy a view that goes against accepted beliefs
media-saturated overly full of the media (television, movies, videos, etc.)
endorsed approved
Gutenberg Johann Gutenberg, fifteenth-century inventor of movable type for printing
affords provides
Red Wings Detroit hockey team
snooty stuck up, snobbish
elitism an attitude of superiority
underpinning support or rationale
sedentary sitting too much, not getting exercise
sensationalistic containing shocking or lurid details
degrading lowering
common denominator in this context, something that people have in common
effigy a lifelike model

misbegotten having an improper origin

samba a dance

oodles a lot

glutted flooded with an excess of something

Breaking the Habit

Once upon a time, Anne Trudeau had a TV life.

2   She watched "L.A. Law" and lots of PBS shows. She tuned in "ER" when it came on. And she carved out daily guilty pleasures with a favorite soap opera.

3   "I was hooked on 'General Hospital,' I'm embarrassed to say," recalls Trudeau, 42, a Ferndale resident.

4   But three years ago, Trudeau and her husband, Reilly Brian, kicked the TV habit; they dropped their cable subscription. Two years ago, they stored their one TV set on a cart in a closet.

5   Now they and their 3½-year-old daughter, Natalie, have virtually no TV life. And they love it.

6   "We're outdoors more. We go on walks. We go to the library three times a week," says Trudeau. "I don't even know what 'Ally McBeal' is about."

7   Heavens to Homer Simpson, that's heresy in a media-saturated American culture where a TV set is on 7 hours, 12 minutes a day in the average household.

8   But the next few days belong to the Trudeau family and others looking for alternatives to living in Couch Potato Nation.

9   The sixth annual National TV-Turnoff Week begins Monday.

10   Its observance has had little or no impact on the Nielsen TV ratings, but it has been growing ever so slowly, attracting an estimated six million participants last year. It's sponsored by TV-Turnoff Network, formerly TV-Free America, a Washington-based organization that "encourages children and adults to watch less television in order to promote healthier lives and communities," according to a recent press release.

11   "We've done an exceptional job of getting into schools," says Frank Vespe, executive director of TV-Turnoff Network. "If you go to school, you've probably heard of TV-Turnoff Week."

12   The unplugged TV week has the support of the U.S. Surgeon General and 61 national organizations, including the American Medical Association, the National Education Association, the American Pediatric Association, the Girl Scouts and the YMCA. The governors of 31 states, including Michigan, have endorsed the week.

13   Numerous schools in the Detroit area are participating.

14   "Our community is very TV-oriented," says Ernestina Iglesias, a teacher at Maybury Elementary School in southwest Detroit. "There are a lot of families from lower socioeconomic backgrounds. And TV is the baby-sitter in many homes. So it's going to be tough."

15   Maybury students are being asked to sign pledges not to watch television this week. And a letter being sent to parents asks for their participation.

16   Each day this week, Iglesias says, Maybury students will take home suggested family activities as possible replacements for TV watching: Read a book, take a walk with your parents, play a board game, bake cookies. And at the end of the week, students are to do a homework report on how they spent TV-Turnoff Week.

Results?

17   Does it work? Do kids change their relationship with the tube after turning it off for a week?

18   "I've had various levels of success," says Micki Sanders, a teacher for 20 years who has participated in TV-Turnoff Week at several independent and charter schools, including Waldorf Schools in Detroit and Southfield.

19   "Most kids can't have a real conversation anymore. They're so limited because their life experience is the television and movies they're watching," says Sanders, who teaches at Detroit Community High School and Kindergarten, a 3-year-old charter school on Detroit's west side.

20   Because her school is on spring break, Sanders isn't doing TV-Turnoff Week 2000. But she doesn't limit her philosophy about television to one week a year.

21   "I'm always telling them, 'Turn it off and wake up your brain. Mrs. Sanders doesn't like TV because it makes your brain go to sleep,' " she says. "The problem is that most of my parents are in their 20s and 30s and they're very addicted to TV themselves. It's a very addictive drug."

The Other Side

22   Of course, not everyone's wild about TV-Turnoff Week.

23   "Oh, what a stupid idea. That's like putting out your eyes if you had Gutenberg waiting in the lobby," says Jerry Herron, a pop culture scholar and head of the American studies program at Wayne State University.

24 "Turning off your TV set is like living in a house with a picture window and always having the shade drawn," adds Herron, a big fan of such smart, conversation-provoking television as "The West Wing" and "The Simpsons." He praises television as "a system of global literacy that Americans invented." Not watching it, Herron says, is like "refusing knowledge."

25 But the idea of National TV-Turnoff Week isn't to abolish television, says TV-Turnoff Network's Vespe.

26 "In general, most people are going to go back to watching TV. But this week affords them an opportunity to re-engage in activities that make life richer and fuller, whether it's reading a book, talking to your children or going to a city council meeting," says Vespe.

27 "And when people go back to TV, hopefully they'll watch smarter. Maybe they'll only turn on the TV for the specific shows they want to watch."

28 That's exactly what happened to Matt Likins, 31, a physical therapist who lives in St. Clair Shores. He learned about TV-Turnoff Week last year when the American Physical Therapy Association sent literature about the event to his Grosse Pointe Woods office.

29 "I was not completely successful. I ran afoul of the Red Wings playoff games last year," jokes Likins. "So I didn't go totally without TV. But the biggest difference for me is that after the week was over, I had a better awareness of how much I was actually watching each week.

30 "I was probably watching 20 or 25 hours of sports and movies every week. It's a habit I wasn't aware of because I'd just come home every night and pop on the TV."

31 Likins also found some positive marital vibrations to watching less television.

32 "My wife (Sharisse) was pretty pleased. She gets a lot more attention from me. And I'm doing more things around the house," says Likins, who still plans to watch Red Wings games during his modified TV-Turnoff Week.

Is It Television's Fault?

33 There is a faint tone of snooty elitism to some of TV-Turnoff Week's philosophical underpinning.

34 "The fundamental message of all TV is, 'You should consume,'" says Vespe. "That's not a message that encourages civic participation. It's a message that encourages going to the mall."

35 Television, of course, is always taking the blame for cultural ills.

36 Too fat and sedentary? It's TV's fault. Too much violence and too many gun killings? It's TV's fault. Too many sexually active teens? It's TV's fault.

37 "In the 19th Century, you could have found Victorians who felt Charles Dickens' writing was sensationalistic, degrading the popular taste and appealing to the lowest common denominator," says Wayne State's Herron.

38 Television, where Dickens' classic works now wind up on "Masterpiece Theatre," has become modern society's chosen pop culture effigy.

39 Liberals and conservatives alike love to take whacks at it. In the 1950s, it was comic books and rock 'n' roll that were ruining the nation's youth. Now it's television and its sitcoms, cartoons and misbegotten reality carnivals like "Who Wants to Marry a Multi-Millionaire?"

40 Except that even an intelligent television enthusiast like Herron knows too much of anything is not a good thing. "If you make your life a one-note samba, whether it's with TV or movies or drugs," he says, "you'll degrade your life."

41 And any temporary break from television that might get children and families walking, talking, baking cookies, interacting, playing games—how bad can that be?

42 "I don't think people who watch TV are bad," says former "General Hospital" fan Trudeau. "I just think the nature of media is addictive. I just think TV pulls you in and makes you slack-jawed."

43 Not that everyone who watches oodles of television and enjoys it is automatically transformed into a remote control zombie. But in a satellite-delivered, cable channel-glutted world of wall-to-wall channel-surfing, maybe less really is more. And smarter. Click.

◆◆◆

Comprehension

1. How many hours per day is a television set turned on in the average American household?
2. Who sponsors TV-Turnoff Week, and what is its purpose?
3. What does the other side say in defense of television?
4. What problems in society is TV often blamed for?

Critical Thinking

1. Do you agree with Anne Trudeau and teacher Micki Sanders, who are quoted in the article, that TV is addictive?
2. Do you think that participating in National TV-Turnoff Week is a good idea?
3. Why do Americans spend so much time watching television?

4. In what ways could family life be improved if people spent less time watching TV?
5. To what extent do you think that sex and violence shown on television have an effect on young viewers?

Language and Vocabulary

1. Jerry Herron, a pop culture scholar at Wayne State University, is quoted as saying, "Turning off your TV set is like living in a house with a picture window and always having the shade drawn." What does he mean by this comparison?
2. Had you heard the term *couch potato* before reading it in his article? What do you think it means? Would it be possible to be a couch potato without television?

Style, Structure, and Organization

1. Mike Duffy quotes several people in this article, including ordinary TV viewers. Choose one of the people whom he quotes and scan (look through) the reading to locate everything that person said. Which of this person's statements do you think is most effective?
2. Why does the author begin with "Once upon a time . . ."?
3. Why are most of the paragraphs in this article shorter than the paragraphs in an academic essay? (Hint: Consider the format in which the article originally appeared.)

Topics for Discussion or Journal Writing

1. If you didn't watch television for a week, how would you spend the time you saved?
2. Are there any television programs that you disapprove of or that you think are a waste of time? Why?
3. Are there any ways in which television can be a valuable learning resource?
4. Do you think that parents should supervise their children's television viewing? Why or why not?
5. Keep a journal of your television viewing for a week and rate each of the programs you watch by giving them one, two, three, or four stars. At the end of the week, evaluate your viewing habits. How many four-star pro-

grams did you see? Which programs rated only one or two stars? Do you think that you should consider eliminating some of those programs from your viewing schedule?

Writing Topics for Paragraphs or Essays

1. Defend one of your favorite TV programs. If possible, show that it offers some cultural or social value in addition to providing entertainment.
2. Write a cause and effect paper about the effects of TV violence on children. Be sure to mention some specific programs as examples. You may also want to look for articles about this topic at the library or on the Internet in order to add some factual information to your paper.
3. What real-life events have you watched on television that had an impact on you? Using some of these events as examples, write a paper about how television enables us to share important happenings.
4. Imagine that you are preparing a time capsule to be opened 50 years in the future, and you decide to include videotapes of two television programs that represent today's society. Write a paper that tells which two programs you would choose and why.
5. Do you think that families need to spend more quality time together? Why? How would you suggest that families improve the way they spend their time? Write a paper that answers these questions.

Shoeless Joe

W. P. Kinsella

This reading comes from W. P. Kinsella's fictional book about a man who builds a baseball diamond in his cornfield because he sees a vision of a baseball stadium and hears the message, "If you build it, he will come." "*He*" refers to Shoeless Joe Jackson, one of eight Chicago White Sox players who were involved in the biggest scandal in baseball history many years before this story takes place. Shoeless Joe and the others were accused of accepting money to intentionally lose the 1919 World Series to the Cincinnati Reds, but many loyal fans believed that Shoeless Joe was innocent.

Prereading Questions

1. Why are baseball fans so dedicated to the game?
2. What special qualities do dreamers and visionaries have?

Vocabulary

rashly foolishly, without thinking
vow promise
smock a long, loose shirt, generally worn over other clothes
surreptitiously secretly, trying not to be noticed
spinster a woman who has never been married
optimists people who always expect things to turn out well
dissolve in this case, to be overcome by
birthed in this case, created
bleacher a section of raised seats
deaden reduce the power or force of
cud a wad or lump of something held in the mouth and chewed
recalcitrant uncooperative
rutted having deep tracks from frequent use
curry in this case, groom or comb

deflect cause to turn in a different direction
hurled thrown, pitched
shutout a baseball game in which the opposing team scored no runs
beveled shaped to a certain angle
bunt a ball hit by tapping it lightly so that it won't roll past the infielders
aerated exposed to air
sheepishly with a feeling of embarrassment

Shoeless Joe

We have been trading promises like baseball cards, Shoeless Joe and I. First I had to keep my rashly given vow to finish the baseball field. As I did, Shoeless Joe, or whoever or whatever breathed this magic down onto my Iowa farm, provided me with another live baseball player each time I finished constructing a section of the field: another of the Unlucky Eight who were banished for life from organized baseball in 1920 for supposedly betraying the game they loved.

2   I completed the home-plate area first. In fact I was out there the very next morning digging and leveling, for besides being the easiest part to do, it was the most important to me. Home plate cost $14.95 at my friendly sporting-goods store in Iowa City. It surprised me that I could buy a mass-produced home plate, although I don't know why it should have, considering that one can custom-order a baby nowadays. But somehow I had pictured myself measuring and cutting a section from a piny-smelling plank, the sawdust clinging like gold to my jeans. I installed it carefully, securely, like a grave marker, then laid out a batter's box and baselines.

3   But nothing happened.

4   I continued to work on the rest of the field, but less enthusiastically. Bases cost $28.95 for a set of three, starched and glazed white as the smock of a fat baker. It was weeks before the stadium appeared again in the cornfield. Each evening I peered surreptitiously through the kitchen curtains, like a spinster keeping tab on her neighbors, waiting and hoping. All the while Annie kept reassuring me, and I would call her a Pollyanna and tell her how I hated optimists. But I find it all but impossible to be cross with Annie, and we would end up embracing at the kitchen window where I could smell the sunshine in her snow-and-lemon-drop curtains. Then Karin would drag a chair close to us, stand on it, and interrupt our love with hers, a little jealous of our attention to

each other. Annie and I would stare in awe at the wonder we had created, our daughter.

5   Karin is five going on sixty; the dreamer in me combined with the practicality and good humor of Annie. We would both kiss her soft cheeks and she would dissolve in laughter as my mustache tickled her.

6   "Daddy, the baseball man's outside," Karin said to me.

7   It was still daylight, the days longer now, the cornfield and baseball diamond soaked warm with summer. I stared through the curtains where Shoeless Joe softly patrolled the left field I had birthed.

8   I swept Karin into my arms and we hurried to the bleacher behind the left-field fence. I studied the situation carefully but nothing appeared to have changed from the last time. Shoeless Joe was the only player with any substance.

9   "What about the catcher?" I call down.

10 Joe smiles. "I said we'd look at him, remember?"

11 "I've finished home plate. What else do you need?"

12 "I said *we*," reminds Joe, "After the others are here, we'll give him a tryout. He'll have a fair chance to catch on."

13 "All the others?" I say.

14 "All the others," echoes Joe. "Get the bases down and sand and level that ground around first base. It'll deaden the hot grounders and make them easy for old Chick to field."

15 But I have more questions than a first grader on a field trip: "Why have you been away so long?"; "When will you come back again?"; and a dozen more, but Joe only shifts the cud of tobacco in his cheek and concentrates on the gray-uniformed batter 300 feet away.

16 I did sand the first-base area, sometimes cursing as the recalcitrant wheelbarrow twisted out of my hands as if it had a life of its own, spilling its contents on the rutted path leading to the baseball field. My back ached as if someone were holding a welding torch against my spine, turning the flame on and off at will. But I sanded. And raked. I combed the ground as I would curry a horse, until there wasn't a pebble or lump left to deflect the ball. And as I finished I ignored my throbbing back, triumphant as if I'd just hurled a shutout. I'd stand on my diamond, where just beyond the fence the summer corn listens like a field of swaying disciples, and I'd talk to the sky.

17 "I'm ready whenever you are," I say. "Chick Gandil, you've never played on so fine a field. I've beveled the ground along the baseline so that any bunt without divine guidance will roll foul. The earth around the base is aerated and soft as piecrust. Ground balls will die on the second bounce, as if they've been hit into an anthill. You'll feel like you're wearing a glove ten feet square." I wave my arms at the perfect blue Iowa sky, and then, as I realize what I'm doing, I turn sheepishly to look at the

house. Annie has been watching, and she flutters her fingers at me around the edge of the curtains.

18   The process is all so slow, as dreams are slow, as dreams suspend time like a balloon hung in midair. I want it all to happen now. I want that catcher to appear. I want whatever miracle I am party to, to prosper and grow: I want the dimensions of time that have been loosened from their foundations to entwine like a basketful of bright embroidery threads. But it seems that even for dreams, I have to work and wait. It hardly seems fair.

◆◆◆

Comprehension

1. Who were the "Unlucky Eight"? What happened to them?
2. What are the first three things that the narrator (the person telling the story) does to begin building the baseball field?
3. Where and when does the stadium appear?
4. When Shoeless Joe shows up, what instructions does he give about finishing the baseball field? What questions does he leave unanswered?

Critical Thinking

1. How does the man feel about building the baseball field? Do his feelings change at any points in the story?
2. How do his wife, Annie, and his daughter, Karin, feel about the project?
3. Why does the man talk to Chick Gandil? Who do you think Chick Gandil is?
4. Reread the last paragraph. Is the narrator thinking these words or saying them to someone? What does he mean by his final comment, "It hardly seems fair"?

Language and Vocabulary

1. Had you ever heard anyone called a "Pollyanna" before reading the word in this selection? What do you think it means? Look up *Pollyanna* in a dictionary to see if your guess is accurate. Also look for the origin of the term—who was the original Pollyanna?
2. Are you familiar with all of the baseball terms that the author uses, such as *home plate, batter's box, baselines, grounders,* and *bunt*? Make a list of all the baseball terms in the reading and look up the meanings of any that you don't know.

Style, Structure, and Organization

1. Why does the author include an actual conversation between the man building the baseball field and Shoeless Joe? How does this affect readers' view of the reality of the situation?
2. The author uses *personification*—giving human qualities or abilities to something nonhuman—when he writes, ". . . just beyond the fence the summer corn *listens* like a field of swaying disciples. . . ." Do you think this wording is effective? Why or why not?

Topics for Discussion or Journal Writing

1. Are you a baseball fan? If so, what do you especially like about the game, and who are your favorite players?
2. Which sports do you enjoy watching? Are there any special sports figures from the past that you would like to see in action?
3. Have you heard or read about any recent sports scandals or any accusations against a well-known sports figure? Based on what you know about the situation, do you think the accusations are true? Why or why not?
4. Have you ever had a dream or a vision that seemed real? If so, did it affect any of your actions in real life?
5. Do you believe that Shoeless Joe really appeared? Why or why not?

Writing Topics for Paragraphs or Essays

1. Why do you think sports heroes are so admired in our society? As you answer this question, mention at least two or three popular sports figures (past or present) as examples.
2. Watch the 1989 movie *Field of Dreams*, which is based on the book *Shoeless Joe* by W. P. Kinsella. Then write a review of the movie. Include a summary of what happens, your evaluation of the movie, and details about which parts you liked best.
3. Using library resources or the Internet, find out more about Shoeless Joe Jackson, his baseball career, and the part he may have played in the 1919 World Series scandal. Then write an informative paper about Shoeless Joe Jackson.
4. Write a paper about one of your favorite sports. In your paper, answer at least two of the following questions: Why do you like to watch or participate in this sport? What is unique and special about this sport? What qualities or skills does it take to be successful in this sport? Who are a

few of the most popular professional players? What is one of your most memorable experiences with this sport, either as a player or as a fan?

5. Write an imaginative story about meeting someone from the past—for example, a sports figure, a movie star, a legendary hero, or a political or religious leader. Describe the scene and include a conversation between the two of you.

Elvis Culture

Erika Doss

Although Elvis Presley died in 1977, his popularity continues. He is considered by many to be "The King," the most popular rock star in the history of American music. His first hit song, "Heartbreak Hotel," skyrocketed him to fame in 1956, and during the next few years almost all of his recordings made the "Top 10" list. Why do fans still adore and admire Elvis? In her book *Elvis Culture,* from which this reading is taken, Erika Doss examines this cultural phenomenon.

Prereading Questions

1. Why was Elvis Presley one of the most admired performers of the twentieth century?
2. Why do some people enjoy collecting special items, or memorabilia, related to a famous person, such as a sports figure or a movie star?

Vocabulary

sanctified considered sacred

quasi-religion resembling a religion

martyr a person who dies or suffers greatly for a cause or belief

icon symbol

J. F. K. John Fitzgerald Kennedy

mass-produced manufactured in large quantities

prevail dominate, have greater influence

pivotal of vital importance

rocket-fueled in this context, full of energy

rockabilly a combination of rock and roll and "hillbilly," or country, music

repertoire the range of music that a person performs

sensual involving the senses, seductive

captivating enchanting, capturing an audience's emotions

phenomenal exceptional, extraordinary

vibrato a vibrating or pulsating quality
conventions customary or usual ways of doing things
aura an intangible quality
flamboyant showy, elaborate, colorful
glitzy glamorous, flashy

Elvis Culture

Why Elvis? Why has Elvis Presley become sanctified as the central figure in what some are calling a quasi-religion? Why not some other popular culture martyr who died young, like John Lennon, Buddy Holly, Janis Joplin, Jimi Hendrix, or, more recently, Kurt Cobain or Selena? Why is Elvis—more so than Malcolm X, Martin Luther King, Jr., and J.F.K.—consistently held up as an "icon of the twentieth century"? Why is it Elvis's image that we see on the surface of every conceivable mass-produced consumer item, from black velvet paintings and ceramic statuettes to laminated clocks, liquor decanters, ashtrays, oven mitts, address books, earrings, checks, flags, key rings? Why does Elvis's image prevail in contemporary visual culture?

2 More to the point, why should any of this be taken seriously—why should any of us even bother with looking at and trying to make sense of Elvis Culture? The answer, quite simply, is that Elvis Presley occupies a big space in the daily lives of many Americans. For some, the space that he—or, more specifically, his image—occupies is not especially broad or deep. But for others, especially for fans, Elvis has sweeping significance in terms of personal, social, and even national identity: Elvis is who they want to be, who they most admire, who they mourn for; Elvis is their image of an ideal American. In a contemporary culture where images dominate (some estimate we receive three-quarters of our knowledge from visual sources), it is worth wondering why Elvis's image seems to dominate most of all.

3 Many fans were turned on to Elvis when they first saw him on television. Elvis turned up thirteen times on TV in 1956, each time drawing more viewers, more critical attention, more teenage fans. His first appearance on *The Ed Sullivan Show* in September drew the highest ratings in then-TV history, with over 82 percent of the American viewing public (54 million people) tuning in to watch Elvis sing "Don't Be Cruel" and "Love Me Tender." By the time of the second Sullivan show in October (the third aired in January 1957), Elvis's records were selling at the rate of $75,000 a day (accounting for more than half of RCA's profits). Fans mobbed his concerts (he performed live 161 times in 1956), followed him everywhere, ripped bits of upholstery from his pink and black Cadillacs, and organized "I Love Elvis" clubs.

4   Elvis's music was, of course, absolutely pivotal to his popularity. If he had been only a teen heartthrob and B-movie star, Elvis would never have attracted the adulation that continues unabated. From the start he courted a singing style that bound his fans and himself in an intensely emotional relationship. From the rocket-fueled and raw-voiced rockabilly energy of the 1950s performances to the gospel repertoire of his 1967 album *How Great Thou Art* and the slick pop of his 1970s arena acts, Elvis's music was always sensual (if not downright erotic) and utterly captivating.

5   Sight is the dominant sense in modern Western culture—how else can we explain the phenomenal popularity of television compared with radio?—and Elvis, perhaps more so than any other performer in the 1950s, recognized this. Just as he skillfully mixed black and white musical forms to create his own influential brand of rock and roll, Elvis consciously blended sound (the rhythm and pulse of his music, the vibrato of his voice) and sight (the look of his body, the style of his movements) into sensual and seductive spectacles.

6   Shattering musical and theatrical conventions, Elvis set the pace for the predominantly visual aura of contemporary popular culture: within a decade or so of his mid-1950s debut, flamboyant stage acts with Spectra-Color light shows and glitzy special effects became the norm for rock bands ranging from the Rolling Stones to the Grateful Dead. Today we talk about going to "see" Sting or Prince or Madonna, which tells us a lot about how profoundly visualized contemporary popular music has become.

◆◆◆

Comprehension

1. Why was Elvis Presley's music so appealing to fans?
2. According to the author, why is Elvis still very important in the lives of many Americans?
3. How did Elvis's style of performing influence other musicians during the last half of the twentieth century?

Critical Thinking

1. Why do fans do things that could be considered vandalism, such as ripping pieces of upholstery from Elvis's cars?
2. Why does the author describe the relationship between Elvis and his fans as "intensely emotional"? Do you think this type of relationship exists between all performers and their fans? Why or why not?

3. How important are visual elements to contemporary popular music? Give reasons for your answer.
4. Why do you think some people believe that Elvis is still alive?

Language and Vocabulary

1. This reading mentions several types of music, such as *pop* and *gospel*, as well as a few other musical terms, such as *vibrato*. Select at least three other musical terms that appear in the reading, and look up their meanings if you do not already know them.
2. In the last paragraph, the author calls readers' attention to our typical word choice of *see* rather than *hear* to refer to attending a live performance: "Today we talk about going to 'see' Sting or Prince or Madonna. . . ." Why do you think people tend to choose the visual verb *see* rather than *hear* or *listen to*?

Style, Structure, and Organization

1. Why does the first paragraph consist entirely of questions? Does the author answer all of these questions somewhere in the reading?
2. In informative and persuasive writing, body paragraphs often begin with a *topic sentence* that expresses the main idea of the paragraph. Choose paragraph 3, 4, or 5 of the reading and underline or highlight the main idea of the paragraph—either the first sentence or a portion of the first sentence.

Topics for Discussion or Journal Writing

1. Which performers of today do you think will still be enthusiastically admired 40 or 50 years from now? Why?
2. Do you think that Elvis might still be alive? Why or why not?
3. How do you think it would feel to sing in front of a live audience, with thousands of screaming fans captivated by your music?
4. What difficult challenges might a popular rock musician face?
5. Who is your favorite singer or musical group? What is special about that person's or that group's music?

Writing Topics for Paragraphs or Essays

1. Have you ever attended a live concert? If so, write about your experience, including details about the performance and the fans' reactions. How do you think this concert compared with one of Elvis's?

2. Write a paper about another popular musician who died young, such as Jimi Hendrix, Selena, Richie Valens, Rick Nelson, or Janis Joplin. (See the first paragraph of the reading for more suggestions.) In addition to writing about the person's life and accomplishments, include how fans reacted to the musician's death and how it affected his or her popularity. You will probably need to do some research at the library or on the Internet in order to find enough information.

3. Watch a movie about the life of a well-known musician or performer, such as *Selena, The Buddy Holly Story,* or *La Bamba* (Richie Valens). Then write a review of the movie. In your paper, include a summary of the main events, an evaluation of the movie, and your personal reactions.

4. Have you ever sung, danced, or played a musical instrument in front of an audience? If so, write about your experiences as a performer and how you felt about being on stage. If you have never performed in public, you may interview someone else who has and write about that person's experience instead.

5. Watch (and listen to) a music video. Which element of this video do you think is more important to the viewing audience, sight or sound? Are there any special visual effects that grab your attention? Write a review of the music video, including what you like and dislike about it.

Dressing Down

John Brooks

Most people don't know that when they put on a pair of Levi's they are wearing a style of clothing that is more than 100 years old. Although Levi Strauss first produced denim jeans in 1874, they did not achieve wide popularity until the mid-twentieth century. This article by John Brooks, which was originally published in *Atlantic Monthly* magazine, examines the amazing worldwide popularity of jeans.

Prereading Questions

1. Why do so many people like to wear jeans?
2. What types of situations or social occasions are jeans appropriate for?

Vocabulary

phenomenon something that is unusual or unexplainable
seismic startling, earthshaking (as if caused by an earthquake)
postwar after World War II
differentiation distinguishing one group from another, showing them to be different
Williams College a college in Williamstown, Massachusetts
chino-wearing wearing a type of pants made of a cotton twill material called chino
untrammeled not limited
banning prohibiting
ideological baggage an association with certain ideas and beliefs
propel cause something to move forward
dissent disagreement
emulate try to be like
indulgent lenient, tolerant
anomic lacking in purpose

posture in this case, attitude or point of view

post exchanges stores for service personnel on military "posts" or bases

ersatz fake, imitation

perennially again and again, continually

Benelux nations Belgium, the Netherlands, and Luxembourg

avidly eagerly

blatant obvious and offensive

saturation point the point at which the market is flooded because too many items are being produced

attire clothing

Dressing Down

Beyond doubt, the jeans phenomenon is a seismic event in the history of dress, and not only in the United States. Indeed, the habit of wearing jeans is—along with the computer, the copying machine, rock music, polio vaccine, and the hydrogen bomb—one of the major contributions of the United States to the postwar world at large.

2   Before the nineteen-fifties, jeans were worn, principally in the West and Southwest of the United States, by children, farmers, manual laborers when on the job, and, of course, cowboys. There were isolated exceptions—for example, artists of both sexes took to blue jeans in and around Santa Fe, New Mexico, in the nineteen-twenties and -thirties; around 1940, the male students at Williams College took them up as a mark of differentiation from the chino-wearing snobs of Yale and Princeton; and in the late forties the female students of Bennington College (not far from Williams) adopted them as a virtual uniform, though only for wear on campus—but it was not until the nineteen-fifties, when James Dean and Marlon Brando wore jeans in movies about youth in revolt against parents and society, when John Wayne wore them in movies about untrammeled heroes in a lawless Old West, and when many schools from coast to coast gave their new symbolism a boost by banning them as inappropriate for classrooms, that jeans acquired the ideological baggage necessary to propel them to national fame.

3   After that, though, fame came quickly, and it was not long before young Americans—whether to express social dissent, to enjoy comfort, or to emulate their peers—had become so attached to their jeans that some hardly ever took them off. According to a jeans authority, a young man in the North Bronx with a large and indulgent family attained some sort of record by continuously wearing the same pair of jeans, ever for bathing and sleeping, for over eight months. Eventually, as all the world

knows, the popularity of jeans spread from cowboys and anomic youths to adult Americans of virtually every age and sociopolitical posture, conspicuously including Jimmy Carter when he was a candidate for the presidency. Trucks containing jeans came to rank as one of the three leading targets of hijackers, along with those containing liquor and cigarettes. Estimates of jeans sales in the United States vary wildly, chiefly because the line between jeans and slacks has come to be a fuzzy one. According to the most conservative figures, put out by the leading jeans manufacturer, Levi Strauss & Company, of San Francisco, annual sales of jeans of all kinds in the United States by all manufacturers in 1957 stood at around a hundred and fifty million pairs, while for 1977 they came to over five hundred million, or considerably more than two pairs for every man, woman, and child in the country.

4   Overseas, jeans had to wait slightly longer for their time to come. American Western movies and the example of American servicemen from the West and Southwest stationed abroad who, as soon as the Second World War ended, changed directly from their service uniforms into blue jeans bought at post exchanges started a fad for them among Europeans in the late nineteen-forties. But the fad remained a small one, partly because of the unavailability of jeans in any quantity; in those days, European customers considered jeans ersatz unless they came from the United States, while United States jeans manufacturers were inclined to be satisfied with a reliable domestic market. Being perennially short of denim, the rough, durable, naturally shrink-and stretch cotton twill of which basic jeans are made, they were reluctant or unable to undertake overseas expansion.

5   Gradually, though, denim production in the United States increased, and meanwhile demand for American-made jeans became so overwhelming that in parts of Europe a black market for them developed. American jeans manufacturers began exporting their product in a serious way in the early nineteen-sixties. At first, the demand was greatest in Germany, France, England, and the Benelux nations; later it spread to Italy, Spain, and Scandinavia, and eventually to Latin America and the Far East. By 1967, jeans authorities estimate, a hundred and ninety million pairs of jeans were being sold annually outside the United States; of these, all but a small fraction were of local manufacture, and not imports from the United States, although American-made jeans were still so avidly sought after that some of the local products were blatant counterfeits of the leading American brands, complete with expertly faked labels. In the late nineteen-seventies, estimated jeans sales outside the United States had doubled in a decade, to three hundred and eighty million pairs, of which perhaps a quarter were now made by American firms in plants abroad; the markets in Europe, Mexico, Japan, Australia, and other places had come so close to the saturation point that the fastest-growing

jeans market was probably Brazil; Princess Anne of Great Britain, and Princess Caroline of Monaco, had been photographed wearing jeans, and King Hussein of Jordan was reported to wear them at home in his palace; the counterfeiting of American brands was a huge international undertaking, which the leading American manufacturers combated with world-ranging security operations. In Russia, authentic American Levis were a black-market item regularly commanding eighty or more dollars per pair. All in all, it is now beyond doubt that in size and scope the rapid global spread of the habit of wearing blue jeans, however it may be explained, is an event without precedent in the history of human attire.

◆◆◆

Comprehension

1. Before the 1950s, who wore jeans? in what parts of the country?
2. When did jeans first become popular in the United States? What factors helped make them popular?
3. What were the sales figures for jeans in 1957 and 1977? Why did sales of jeans increase so much during that time?
4. Where, when, and why were large numbers of counterfeit jeans produced and sold?

Critical Thinking

1. Do you think that the sales of jeans have increased or decreased since this article was written? Give reasons for your answer.
2. Are jeans still worn as a symbol of "revolt against parents and society"?
3. Why was the popularity of jeans slower to develop in Europe than in the United States?
4. Why were truckloads of jeans, liquor, and cigarettes the most common targets for hijackers at one time?
5. Why does the author give examples of several famous people who wore blue jeans in public? Which of these people do you think would have had the most influence on clothing trends in the United States? Why?

Language and Vocabulary

1. Had you ever heard the term *black market* before you read it in this article? What do you think it means? Look up the meaning if necessary. Can

you think of any other kinds of products besides jeans that have probably been sold on the black market?
2. What is a *fad*? Can other things besides clothing be fads? Look up the meaning of *fad* if necessary. Then write two or more sentences about certain styles of clothing or other things that you think are current fads.

Style, Structure, and Organization

1. Find two sentences that express the main idea of the article: one in the introduction and one at the end of the last paragraph.
2. To what extent does the author use *chronological order* (time order)? Is this an effective method of organization for this topic?

Topics for Discussion or Journal Writing

1. Do you think that jeans will continue to be as popular in the future as they are now? Why or why not?
2. How often do you wear jeans? Are there any situations for which you consider jeans inappropriate? What is the most formal occasion you have ever worn jeans for? How did you feel wearing jeans on that occasion?
3. Do people in your area and your age group tend to wear jeans frequently? Are jeans currently the most popular style of pants for men and/or women, or are other types of pants and slacks more popular now?
4. Should dress codes for public schools permit students to wear Levis and other types of jeans? Would school uniforms create a better educational environment?

Writing Topics for Paragraphs or Essays

1. Write about a current style of clothing that you like or dislike. Include a description of the style and why you like or dislike it. If possible, give some reasons for its current popularity. Also, predict whether this style will remain popular in the years to come.
2. Find out more about Levi Strauss, whose company produced the first denim jeans, and write about how he became successful.
3. Using library resources or the Internet, research the clothing styles of one particular decade of the twentieth century: 1920s, 1930s, 1940s, 1950s, 1960s, 1970s, 1980s, or 1990s. Write a report on what people were wearing during that decade.

4. Take a stand on the issue of dress codes or uniforms in public schools, and write a persuasive paper that explains and gives reasons for your viewpoint. You may choose to take a stand against dress codes in general, in favor of a specific dress code, or for or against school uniforms.
5. How many categories or types of clothing do most people need? Write a classification paper about the various types of clothing that should be an essential part of every man's or woman's wardrobe. Your classification should include at least three categories. Be sure to give each category a name, explain its purpose, and give some examples of types of clothes that belong in this category.

5

Fitness and Health

Strive to Be Fit, Not Fanatical Timothy Gower 134
Procrastination and Stress Lester A. Lefton 139
Managing Time Rebecca J. Donatelle and Lorraine G. Davis 144
Computer Addiction Is Coming Online William J. Cromie 148
Playing for Keeps Andy Steiner 154
Can You Afford to Get Sick? Helen Martineau 159

Strive to Be Fit, Not Fanatical

Timothy Gower

The author of this selection, Timothy Gower, is a newspaper columnist who writes on men's issues and men's health. He also writes for several magazines and has written a book, *Staying at the Top of Your Game.* As you read this column, identify the author's intended audience—who he is writing for.

Prereading Questions

1. How important is exercise?
2. How much exercise is enough to maintain good health?

Vocabulary

fitness Nazi a person who is fanatical about physical fitness
scold admonish, chastise, tell people about their bad points
biohazard a dangerous biological substance
beat in this case, the area a reporter covers
unabashedly unashamedly, without any shyness or apology
chinks in the armor vulnerabilities (in this case, potential health problems)
grueling long-lasting and difficult
malarkey nonsense
bum out make someone (or something) unhappy or depressed
palate in this case, one's sense of taste
retch vomit, throw up
ticker a slang word meaning the heart
crash weight-loss plans diets that promise rapid results
splurge a moment of going off a strict diet
blasé boring

Camel a brand of cigarette

to weasel to get what you want by being sneaky

orb circle

chromosomes tiny structures in body cells that determine what characteristics we inherit from our parents

Strive to Be Fit, Not Fanatical

I know what you're thinking. Who's this clown? Another fitness Nazi with a word processor who's going to scold and call me a girly-man if I don't do 150 chin-ups before breakfast? Or maybe he's one of those camera-hogging doctors who's always turning up on TV news shows, insisting that if I eat one more bacon cheeseburger my body will be declared a biohazard?

2   Nope. I'm just a reporter whose beat for much of the last decade has been health and medicine, with a particular focus on the care and feeding of the male animal. My interest is unabashedly personal: I just turned 38 and have begun to notice a few chinks in the armor. Chances are you have, too.

3   And if you're reading this column, maybe you've also picked up your share of health books and magazines that are targeted at men. Me, too, and you know what I've noticed? Some contain a lot of valuable information, but they all seem to have two things in common: 1) they avoid using big words, and 2) they take the old "no pain, no gain" philosophy very seriously. All that talk about "getting ripped" and "feeling the burn"—ouch!

4   Of course, "no pain, no gain" is hardly a new idea. Many men grew up hearing it from coaches who insisted that if you didn't collapse in a puddle of protoplasm at the end of practice, then you obviously weren't hustling. We've been led to believe that working out isn't supposed to be fun; it's supposed to leave your muscles aching and stomach rolling. Is it any wonder that only about one in five U.S. men exercises regularly?

5   The thing is, getting enough exercise and eating right aren't as hard as you might think. The idea that it takes long, grueling workouts to get in shape is malarkey. Believe it or not, more isn't always better when it comes to exercise. And if you're tired of diets that leave you with a fridge full of icky cabbage soup, then tuck in your napkin: Healthy eating doesn't have to bum out your palate.

6   Let's start with exercise. If you know that a little jogging is good for your heart, then you might assume that doing laps till you're dizzy and

ready to retch would make your ticker indestructible. But you would be incorrect. A 1997 Harvard study determined that the cardiovascular benefits of an intense aerobic workout peak at about 24 minutes; pound the pavement longer if you like, but your heart won't get any stronger.

7   Ditto for strength training. According to the gospel of the weight room, you must do a minimum of three sets of bench presses, curls, or any other strength-bulding exercise, to build up a muscle. But studies at the University of Florida show that's just not true; doing one set of an exercise produces more than three-quarters of the muscle you get from doing three. You gain a little less in the biceps department, maybe, but you get the heck out of that stinky, sweaty gym in one-third of the time. Sounds like a good deal to me.

8   Unless you are obese, forget about dieting. (And if you are dramatically overweight, see a doctor who specializes in obesity.) Nutrition experts say crash weight-loss plans that require you to stop eating certain foods don't work; you'll lose weight, but inevitably your willpower crumbles, and the pounds return. Instead, eat a balanced meal plan that includes lots of fruit, vegetables, whole grains and an occasional splurge. Add regular exercise, and eventually you'll attain a manageable, healthy weight.

9   Bottom line: Modest lifestyle changes can make a huge difference. Consider the evidence. Exhibit A: me. In high school my classmates gave me the nickname "Blaze." At first, I thought they were mispronouncing "blasé," but it turns out they were poking fun at me for being a slow and easily winded runner. During forced-jogging sessions in gym class, I'd bring up the rear, gasping like I was born sucking a Camel. Though I managed to weasel my way on to a few sports teams, few people mistook me for an athlete.

10 In the two decades that followed, I wasn't much of a Healthy Man. I'd go running occasionally, but only if it was getting close to 11 p.m. and the liquor stores were closing. Then, a few years ago, I began to notice a pale, flabby orb forming where my flat stomach used to be. It had to go. I started jogging for half an hour every other day and have never looked back.

11 Last winter I injured my back and went to the hospital. As a nurse took my heart rate, she suddenly arched her eyebrows.

12 "Are you an athlete?" she asked. It turns out my resting heart rate was 56 beats per minute. The average guy's heart rate is about 70, but with regular aerobic training, the cardiovascular system becomes more efficient, and the heart doesn't have to work as hard.

13 I lay back on the exam table and thought of that lonely teenager, huffing and puffing behind the pack during gym class, and how I could totally humiliate him in a race today. See ya, Blaze! If I can become a Healthy Man, anyone with the right chromosomes can, too.

Comprehension

1. According to the author, what kinds of food should people eat to be healthy?
2. How much exercise is necessary to improve our health?
3. What is one important benefit of regular exercise?
4. Is the author in better physical condition now, or was he in better shape in high school?

Critical Thinking

1. Who is the author's intended audience—in other words, who is he primarily writing this column for?
2. What is the main message (main idea) of this reading?
3. Do you think that the author's advice is reasonable for most people? Would his advice be useful for women as well as for men?
4. How do you think the author feels about fitness fanatics?

Language and Vocabulary

1. What does the word *cardiovascular* mean in the sentence "A 1997 Harvard study determined that the cardiovascular benefits of an intense aerobic workout peak at about 24 minutes; pound the pavement longer if you like, but your heart won't get any stronger"?
2. In this selection, the author uses several informal or slang expressions, such as *icky* and *see ya*. Find two or three more informal or slang expressions and highlight or underline them.

Style, Structure, and Organization

1. Does the informal style of this column work well for this topic?
2. How many sections does this newspaper column have, and how many paragraphs are in each section? Is this normal academic style, such as you would use in most college classes? If not, how is it different?
3. Where is the main idea of this reading stated—in the first paragraph, in the middle, or in the conclusion?

Topics for Discussion or Journal Writing

1. How would you describe your own level of health and physical fitness?
2. What physical activities do you enjoy doing?

3. If you wanted to take the author's advice, what would be your first step?
4. Why is it so difficult to change our lifestyles to become more fit or lose weight?
5. In your opinion, what is the most important single thing a person can do to be healthier?

Writing Topics for Paragraphs or Essays

1. Describe your own lifestyle, especially what kinds of food you eat and how much exercise you get.
2. This reading gives advice on physical fitness. Write a persuasive paper to convince people to follow this advice.
3. Interview a doctor, a nurse, a dietitian, a coach, a physical trainer, or another health or fitness professional. Ask for advice on improving your health, and write about it.
4. Compare your own fitness now and when you were in high school.
5. Choose one of the following topics. Find out more about the topic by searching online or in a library; then write about it.

   a. What are the best, proven ways to lose weight and keep it off?

   b. What are some of the best sports for life-long fitness, and why?

Procrastination and Stress

Lester A. Lefton

At the start of the twenty-first century, many people feel that there is a shortage of one extremely important resource: *time*. Procrastination—putting things off, waiting until the last minute to do something—sometimes seems as if it's the easy way out, but only temporarily. As you read this selection, compare the benefits of doing things on time to the shorter-term benefits of procrastinating.

Prereading Questions

1. Do you think that most people put things off until the last minute?
2. Which do you think is less stressful for most people in the long run—procrastinating or completing things on time?

Vocabulary

habitually usually, regularly

assert to insist

stress a feeling of emotional pressure, with physical effects

deadline date by which something must be finished, due date

assessed evaluated

ascertaining determining, deciding

hypothesized predicted

term paper a long paper based on information from several sources, a research paper

thus as a result

blind in this case, anonymous

negatively correlated in this case, two things moving in opposite directions: when one increases, the other decreases

SOURCE: "Procrastination and Stress" by Lester A. Lefton. From Lefton, Lester A. *Psychology*, Seventh Edition. Copyright © 2000 by Allyn & Bacon. Reprinted/adapted by permission.

impact effect

tardiness lateness

outweighed by in this case, not as important as

a causal effect a cause and effect relationship (one causes the other)

tendency inclination

impulsive emotional and spur-of-the-moment

postponement putting off, delaying

scant very little

adaptive useful, beneficial

Procrastination and Stress

Why do now what you can put off until tomorrow? The answer is that if you habitually put things off, your work will suffer and so may your health.

2   Getting work done on time is considered proper, rational adult behavior, especially in Western culture. But an awful lot of us procrastinate occasionally, and some people put off, delay, and make excuses for lateness very often. Critics of procrastinators call them lazy or self-indulgent and argue that their work performance suffers from the high stress levels they experience. Defenders—and many procrastinators themselves—assert that work performance is the same, sometimes better because of heightened pressure to get the job done. They'll argue, "I do my best work under pressure." But do they?

3   Diana Tice and Roy Baumeister investigated the effects of procrastination on performance, stress, and illness. Students were given an assignment with a deadline. Procrastinators were identified using a standard scale. The students' well-being was assessed with self-reports of stress and illness. Finally, task performance was checked by ascertaining whether students turned in assignments early, on time, or late.

4   The researchers hypothesized that procrastination might show poorer performance and health and higher stress levels. Alternatively, they acknowledged that there might indeed be benefits from intense, last-minute efforts.

Participants and Method

5   The participants were volunteers from a class of students taking a health psychology course. They were assigned a term paper and were told that if they could not turn the paper in on the due date they would auto-

matically be given an extension. Researchers recorded when students turned in their papers and then asked them to fill out questionnaires about health and stress. The instructor who graded the papers did not know who turned in which paper and when; the research design was thus blind.

Results

6   As expected, procrastinators (as identified at the beginning of the study) turned in their papers late; procrastinators also received lower grades than nonprocrastinators did. Interestingly, procrastinators' scores were negatively correlated with stress and reporting of symptoms—that is, the more of a procrastinator a student was, the fewer stress and wellness problems he or she reported. The procrastinators thus reported feeling better but had poorer grades.

Discussion

7   It appears that procrastination brings short-term health benefits. Procrastinators benefit from the carefree, casual situation they create for themselves—stress is lowered and illness is reduced. But when Tice and Baumeister did another study to assess whether these effects were the same at all points in the semester, they found that the procrastinators experienced much more stress late in the semester than the nonprocrastinators did. In fact, when the impact of procrastination is considered relative to the time (early or late in the semester), the effects are negative—total stress and illness are higher for procrastinators. As the researchers put it, the early benefits of tardiness were outweighed by the later costs of stress and ill health. Especially important is the finding that procrastinators wound up doing inferior work—postponing work seemed to lead to compromises and sacrifices in quality.

8   The researchers acknowledge that this study was not perfect. Participants were not randomly assigned. That stress, illness, and procrastination are related does not prove a causal effect. Further, some people wind up doing their work late for reasons other than procrastination, such as family emergencies. And, of course, university students are not representative of the general population.

Implications

9   The study suggests that procrastination should be considered a self-defeating behavior because it leads to stress, illness, and inferior performance. The tendency to prefer a short-term benefit *may* identify people who make other self-defeating mistakes such as abusing alcohol or

drugs or committing other impulsive acts. Of course, some procrastinators mistakenly believe that they can improve performance by postponement, but the evidence to support this view is scant. In the end, procrastination is not adaptive—procrastinators end up suffering more and performing worse than other people. Procrastinators of the world, organize now!

❖❖❖

Comprehension

1. Who were the participants in the study?
2. What short-term health benefits did procrastinators experience?
3. What bad results can procrastination lead to in the end?

Critical Thinking

1. What is the author's purpose in writing about this research study—to inform, to entertain, to persuade, or a combination of these?
2. How can procrastination reduce stress at some times?
3. Do you think the author is using clear logic, or does he seem biased?
4. Do you think the author is sometimes a procrastinator? Are there any clues in the reading that make you think so?

Language and Vocabulary

1. What are some *synonyms* (words with close to the same meaning) for *wound up* and *wind up* in the following phrases from the reading: "procrastinators wound up doing inferior work" and "some people wind up doing their work late"?
2. This selection contains many sentences written in the passive voice, such as "procrastination *should be considered* a self-defeating behavior" and "the early benefits of tardiness *were outweighed* by the later costs of stress and ill health." Does this technique make the paper feel somewhat formal and scientific?

Style, Structure, and Organization

1. Where is the main idea of this reading stated—in the introduction, the conclusion, or both?

2. Highlight or underline the heading of each of the sections of the reading. Are these types of headings common in readings, or are they mainly for certain kinds of reports about research?
3. Does the paper flow smoothly from one section to another, and does each section seem complete?

Topics for Discussion or Journal Writing

1. Are you a procrastinator (almost always, sometimes, almost never)?
2. Which is more stressful for you, to work hard and complete something on time or to put it off until later?
3. How do you feel about your use of time on a typical day? Do you usually have time to do everything you want or need to do?
4. Do you have any advice for people who are usually procrastinators? What do you recommend?

Writing Topics for Paragraphs or Essays

1. Describe a typical day in your life, from the time you get up to the time you go to sleep, and analyze how well you use your time.
2. Describe someone you know who has an extreme attitude toward time—either very rigid or very relaxed. Would you like to be able to treat time the way that person does?
3. Write about a time when you were late turning something in or arriving somewhere. How did it make you feel to be late? What can you do to avoid being late in the future?
4. Make a list of people you know who are successful in school, at work, or in their personal lives, and interview one of them. Ask if he or she has any advice on the subject of managing time and avoiding procrastination, and write a report of the interview, together with your own opinion or reaction.
5. Choose one of the following topics. Look up information on the topic online or in a library; then write a short report on what you find out.
   a. Various personality types and how each type manages stress differently
   b. Attitudes toward time in various cultures. (For example, compare Swiss or Japanese ideas of time with Arabic or Latin American ideas of time.)

144 ◆ Part 5 / Fitness and Health

◆◆◆

Managing Time

Rebecca J. Donatelle and Lorraine G. Davis

Time, the subject of both this reading and the previous one ("Procrastination and Stress"), is an important topic because people are busier now than ever before. The Internet, cell phones, pagers, and hand-held computers keep us connected with work, information, and people around the clock. As you read the following practical instructions for making the most of your time, look for tips that you think would be helpful.

Prereading Questions

1. Do you think that most people are good at managing their time and balancing their lives?
2. Do you think that time management can be learned, or are some people just born with the gift of managing time well?

Vocabulary

stress management program a plan for reducing the negative effects of stress

obligations necessary duties or responsibilities

toss in this case, throw away

prioritize put in order of importance

categorize put into categories of related items

post put up (a notice or sign)

energize fill with energy

precious extremely valuable

potential possibilities

restorative strength-building

assess judge, evaluate

Managing Time

Time. Everybody needs more of it, especially students trying to balance the demands of classes, social life, earning money for school, family obligations, and time needed for relaxation. The following tips regarding time management should become a part of your stress management program:

- *Clean off your desk.* According to Jeffrey Mayer, author of *Winning the Fight Between You and Your Desk,* most of us spend many stressful minutes each day looking for things that are lost on our desks or in our homes. Go through the things on your desk, toss the unnecessary papers, and put papers for tasks that you must do in folders.
- *Never handle papers more than once.* When bills and other papers come in, take care of them immediately. Write out a check and hold it for mailing. Get rid of the envelopes. Read your mail and file it or toss it. If you haven't looked at something in over a year, toss it.
- *Prioritize your tasks.* Make a daily "to do" list and try to stick to it. Categorize the things you must do today, the things that you have to do but not immediately, and the things that it would be nice to do. Prioritize the Must Do Now and Have to Do Later items and put deadlines next to each. Only consider the Nice to Do items if you finish the others or if the Nice to Do list includes something fun for you. Give yourself a reward as you finish each task.
- *Avoid interruptions.* When you've got a project that requires your total concentration, schedule uninterrupted time. Unplug the phone or let your answering machine get it. Close your door and post a Do Not Disturb sign. Go to a quiet room in the library or student union where no one will find you. Guard your time and don't weaken.
- *Reward yourself for being efficient.* If you've planned to take a certain amount of time to finish a task and you finish early, take some time for yourself. Go for a walk. Start reading something you've wanted to read but haven't had time for.
- *Reduce your awareness of time.* Rather than being a slave to the clock, try to ignore it. Get rid of your watch, and try to listen more to your body when deciding whether you need to eat, sleep, and so on. When you feel awake, do something productive. When you are too tired to work, take time out to sleep or to relax to try to energize yourself.
- *Remember that time is precious.* Try to value each day. Time spent not enjoying life is a tremendous waste of potential.
- *Become aware of your own time patterns.* For many of us, minutes and hours drift by without our even noticing them. Chart your daily

schedule, hour by hour, for one week. Note the time that was wasted and the time spent in productive work or restorative pleasure. Assess how you could be more productive and make more time for yourself.

Comprehension

1. What are some of the many demands on a student's time?
2. What are the three levels of priorities listed in the reading selection?
3. How can people become more aware of their own time patterns?

Critical Thinking

1. Who is the authors' intended audience—in other words, who are the writers primarily directing this reading selection to?
2. How can good time management affect a person's health and mental attitude?
3. Do you think that time management is more important today than it was in the past? Why?
4. How well do you think the authors manage time themselves? Does knowing these time management techniques guarantee that a person will always be good at managing time?

Language and Vocabulary

1. What do the authors mean when they write, "reduce your awareness of time"?
2. In this selection, the authors give many instructions on how to manage time better. Some of them are to *categorize, prioritize, schedule* and *assess*. Find three or four more of the authors' instructions. If you are unsure of the meaning of any of the words in these instructions, look them up in a dictionary.

Style, Structure, and Organization

1. Does the introductory paragraph give the reader a clear idea that the rest of the reading selection will include instructions and advice to help people manage their time better?

2. Highlight or underline the heading of each of the eight body paragraphs. Do the headings provide a good indication of the information in each paragraph?
3. Is there a conclusion? Would the selection be more effective if it had one?

Topics for Discussion or Journal Writing

1. Describe your own time management skills and how you feel about them.
2. What are some things you would do if you had more free time?
3. If you wanted to take the authors' advice, which one or two time management tips would you try first?
4. Why is it especially challenging to manage projects that involve many people, such as planning a wedding, building a highway, or starting up a new business?
5. In your opinion, are people going to have more free time in the future or less free time? Why?

Writing Topics for Paragraphs or Essays

1. Compare this reading selection with the previous one, "Procrastination and Stress." How are they similar and how are they different?
2. Choose three of the tips in the reading, and make an effort to use them for several days. Then write a report about your experience, and evaluate the techniques you chose. Which techniques seem to work best for you?
3. Go to an office supply store or a college bookstore, or find an office supplies site online. Investigate three to five time management tools, such as organizers or calendars, and write about the benefits and possible drawbacks of using each of them.
4. Choose one of the following instructions topics. Find out more about the topic by searching online or in a library; then write a short instructions paper on how a person can improve one of these important areas of his or her life.
    a. What are some of the most important steps people can take to improve their health?
    b. What are some useful tips on how to relate well with other people in a specific situation, such as at work, in a social situation, or in a relationship?

Computer Addiction Is Coming Online

William J. Cromie

With computers improving every year and video games becoming more exciting, many people are spending excessive amounts of time in front of their video screens. In this article, author and physician William J. Cromie examines the effects of being a computer addict.

Prereading Questions

1. What attracts people to spend a lot of time surfing the Internet or playing video games?
2. How can people tell the difference between a healthy pastime and an unhealthy addiction?

Vocabulary

absorbing interesting, capable of holding someone's full attention
the Web, the Internet the network linking millions of computers together
aberrant not normal
pathological harmful
addicted to something unable to control your desire for something or to function without it
anecdotal evidence other people's stories, not scientifically validated
self-esteem how a person feels about himself or herself
incorrigible unable to reform or behave well
therapist in this context, a psychologist, counselor, or other professional who can help patients work through an addiction
relapses recurrences of the addictive behavior

Computer Addiction Is Coming Online

Luci could not wait to get in front of her computer. It took the divorced mother away from two demanding children and the drudgery of housework. She could play absorbing games, chat with appealing people, "travel," gamble, even have fantasy sex.

2   When her ex-husband visited their children, he saw that they were being neglected. He discovered that Luci (not her real name) spent 10 or more hours a day on the Web.

3   The husband sued for custody of the children. The court agreed with his claim that Luci's excessive use of the computer was abnormal. She lost custody of the children.

4   Maressa Hecht Orzack, a Harvard University psychologist, cites this true case as an example that computer addiction is real and a growing problem. As founder and director of Computer Addiction Services at McLean Hospital, a Harvard-affiliated teaching hospital in Belmont, Mass., she receives messages every day from people who ask for help or want information about the signs of computer addiction. "It's an emerging disorder," Orzack says, "suffered by people who find the virtual reality on computer screens more attractive than everyday reality. Healthcare specialists, school counselors, corporate executives, and families have begun to notice the aberrant behavior and mental health problems of computer addicts. They feel unhappy when they are away from the machine. Some try unsuccessfully to stop using it. Many of them spend constantly-increasing amounts of time and money on computers, often neglecting their families and work. Then they compound the problem by denying it."

5   "It's a new and serious addiction not too many people know about," says Carol Steinman of Harvard University's Faculty and Staff Assistance Program. "In the past year and a half, we have seen this problem among people of all ages."

Symptoms and Surveys

6   Orzack herself knows how easy it can be to become addicted. A few years ago, she was trying to teach herself to use a new software program. When frustrated with trying to understand the manuals, Orzack escaped to playing solitaire on the machine.

7   "I've always liked the game and I started spending more and more time with it," she recalls.

8   Soon, Orzack avoided her primary reason for being on the machine. She started staying up late and spending less time at work.

9 "I have a lot of experience with impulse control problems, like gambling and eating disorders, so I realized what I was getting into," she admits.

10 Orzack started treating herself by placing limits on the amount of time she played, rather than staying at a game until rewarded by winning. "It's one of the strategies I use with patients," she notes.

11 At first, people thought Orzack was crazy when she talked about people becoming addicted to computers. But several articles in scientific journals and newspapers, as well as anecdotal evidence, convinced her that other professionals were concerned about the problem. Recently, a new scientific journal devoted to this subject, called *Cyber Psychology and Behavior,* was started.

12 No one knows how big the problem is. Several research groups have tried to measure it but without notable results. "Many addicts don't admit it," notes Orzack, "or they're not aware of it. There isn't a good definition of what is normal and what is pathological use."

13 Here is Orzack's list of the signs and symptoms:

- Using the computer for pleasure, gratification, or relief from stress.
- Feeling irritable and out of control or depressed when not using it.
- Spending increasing amounts of time and money on hardware, software, magazines, and computer-related activities.
- Neglecting work, school, or family obligations
- Lying about the amount of time spent on computer activities.
- Risking loss of career goals, educational objectives, and personal relationships.
- Failing at repeated efforts to control computer use.

14 In addition, addicts often have problems such as skipping meals, repetitive stress injuries, backaches, dry eyes, headaches, and loss of sleep.

15 One 14-year-old boy e-mailed Orzack begging her for help. "I have been a computer addict since I was 11," he wrote. He said his grades went from 3.8, when he wasn't using the computer much, to 1.3. He told her he missed meals, suffered backaches, lost track of time, went to bed late, and fell asleep in school.

16 "I'm afraid that I will run away if my parents take my computer away," he continued. "It is almost like the computer owns me."

17 One of the few studies done on admitted addicts found they had other problems such as loneliness, shyness, depression, and low self-esteem. Orzack's observations agree with these findings, and she adds "lousy marriages, incorrigible kids, and boredom at school, home, and work."

18 Linda Welsh surveyed 810 college students at Northeastern University in Boston and found that 62 of them (almost 8 percent) fit the profile of those she labels "Internet dependent."

19   "That's consistent with other research I'm familiar with, most of which was done with college students," Welsh says. "These studies come up with a number between 6 and 10 for the percentage of people who are computer-addicted."

Treatment

20   Treatment is tricky, according to Orzack. "Like an eating disorder, you can't expect people to give it up completely," she says. "Tempting 'food' is all around at work, at school, and in their homes. You have to limit the time spent in front of a machine the way you limit the time spent at the table. Moderation is important, especially for the new generation of kids who begin to use computers in the first grade, or even before then."

21   One of the hardest things is to get people to come in and talk face-to-face with a therapist. They want to do it all on the Internet.

22   Orzack describes one man who spent all night on the Internet. He couldn't get up to go to work or keep appointments. She kept contacting him by Internet to remind him of his obligations until he finally came to see her.

23   Orzack and other therapists use the same treatment methods as they do with gambling, alcohol, or eating addictions. In one technique, known as cognitive-behavioral therapy, people are taught to monitor their thoughts and identify those that trigger addictive feelings and actions. At the same time, they learn new skills to cope with the addiction and ways to prevent, or handle, relapses.

24   In another technique, motivational interviewing, patient and therapist work together to set goals such as learning to recognize the difference between healthy and addictive computer use. "The efforts of patients are constantly reaffirmed, and they are not scolded for slips or failures," Orzack explains.

25   She uses a combination of both techniques, making "contracts" with people to specify how much time they will spend in front of a computer screen. As an example, she encourages them to set an alarm, or two alarms if needed, to signal when to turn to other activities. Orzack tries to get them to devote more time to other pursuits, such as exercising, talking with family and friends, and developing new recreational or social interests.

26   The average treatment takes three months of regular sessions and telephone (not e-mail) checkups. But, Orzack acknowledges, some people require a year or more to deal with their bad habits.

27   "Nobody's ever cured," she says. "You just learn to deal with the problem."

◆◆◆

Comprehension

1. What are some indications that someone might be a computer addict?
2. What are some of the methods of treating computer addiction?
3. How long is the average treatment time for computer addiction? Is anybody ever really cured, according to the article?

Critical Thinking

1. What is the author's purpose in writing this article?
2. What is the main idea of this article?
3. Do the examples in the article provide good support for the main idea? Which examples do you think are most effective?
4. What should you do if you think you are addicted to computers, video games, or the Internet?
5. Do you think that in the future the number of computer addicts is going to increase or decrease? Why?

Language and Vocabulary

1. Had you ever read or heard the expression *repetitive stress injuries* before? What is your best guess as to its meaning? What kinds of repetitive stress injuries do you think are likely to occur as a result of computer addiction?
2. In this article, the author includes quite a few technical words and expressions that health professionals use to describe addictions and other mental health problems, such as *abnormal* and *impulse control problems*. Find three or four more of these mental health terms and look up the meaning of any that you do not understand. Does using technical vocabulary make this article clearer and more specific?

Style, Structure, and Organization

1. Find the part of the reading where the author uses *narration*—the experiences that people have had with computer addiction. Mark it by running a marker or pen down the side of the reading.
2. Now find where the *definition* of computer addiction is given, and use a different color marker to highlight it.
3. Finally, mark all the sections that show the *effects* that computer addiction can have on people. Do you think that this combination of narration, definition, and cause-and-effect writing is effective for this article?

Topics for Discussion or Journal Writing

1. Do you spend a lot of time in front of a computer screen? Do you think you spend too much time online or at the computer?
2. What do you think it feels like to be addicted to something?
3. What is the first place or who is the first person you would go to for help if you thought you were addicted to something?
4. Would you like to be a counselor, psychologist, or therapist who helps people with their addictions? Why or why not?

Writing Topics for Paragraphs or Essays

1. Write about someone you know who might be addicted to computers or who may have another type of addiction. What would you recommend for that person?
2. Describe some of your favorite computer activities, software, or web sites.
3. Tell the story of computer addiction from the addict's point of view.
4. Research the career of psychologist or therapist. What are the job duties, working conditions, pay ranges, and required education for this career?
5. Choose one of the following topics and find out more about it by searching online or in a library; then write about it. If possible, use a combination of types of writing in your paper.
    a. What are some of the most common addictions in our country today, and how do they affect individuals and our society?
    b. What are the best and most successful treatments or strategies for overcoming an addiction?
    c. Write about one type of addiction. What are the effects of this addiction? How can a person overcome it?

Playing for Keeps

Andy Steiner

Linda Mastandrea has succeeded in ways that no one thought she could, not even Linda herself. Most people do not expect a person with cerebral palsy to play basketball, to compete in track and field events, or to serve on the United States Olympic Committee. Andy Steiner, senior editor for the magazine *Utne Reader*, tells the story of this amazing woman.

Prereading Questions

1. Why do many people enjoy participating in college or high school athletics?
2. What kinds of sports are available for athletes with disabilities to participate in?

Vocabulary

sprinter a runner, a competitor in short races at top speed

cerebral palsy a disorder characterized by impairment of muscles and coordination

sidelines (on the) watching rather than participating

profile in this context, image or public awareness

perception a point of view or way of perceiving something

marketable salable, capable of bringing in money

attest to give testimony or affirm that something is true

squad team

pale in this case, to be of lesser importance or value

perks extra benefits

dished out handed out, given

Playing for Keeps

Sprinter Linda Mastandrea holds two Olympic medals, but she didn't start racing until she was in her 20s. In fact, for the first part of her life, no one, including herself, thought she could ever be athletic.

2   "As a kid growing up with cerebral palsy, I couldn't run, I couldn't jump, I couldn't even walk very well." Mastandrea, 35, says. "So I spent a lot of time on the sidelines. People assumed sports were out of the picture for me."

3   Today, she's leading a campaign to raise the profile—and funding—of Paralympic athletics. An attorney and advocate in the Chicago office of the nonprofit America's Athletes with Disabilities, Mastandrea has been a member of the United States Olympic Committee (USOC) board of directors since 1998, and is using her position to be a "thorn in the side" of the other members, pushing and prodding them to provide equal funding and recognition for Paralympic athletes.

4   Her goals are numerous, but she's convinced they're attainable. They include securing funding and training facilities for disabled athletes, providing Paralympians with the option of joining the health insurance plan provided to able-bodied Olympians, and encouraging media attention and exposure for Paralympic events, which are currently held immediately following the closing ceremonies of the "real" Olympic Games.

5   "Paralympic athletes have struggled under the USOC leadership for years," Mastandrea says. "In many ways, it comes down to money. There's a perception that athletes with disabilities are not marketable, and therefore supporting us is a charity thing. But I think a lot of people—able-bodied or not—identify with people with disabilities. An athlete is an athlete is an athlete. If you love sports, you love sports. I'm here to attest that the thrill of the game can change your life. It doesn't matter if you're in a wheelchair or if you are standing."

6   Her own life changed when the coach of her university's wheelchair basketball team encouraged her to join the squad. On wheels, Mastandrea discovered that she was an athlete. "Before college, sports was something for everybody else," she says. "But once I got in a chair and on the basketball court, it was like, 'Wow. I've never felt this great before. I'm playing basketball even though my legs don't work very well.' Once I realized I could be an athlete, I never looked back."

7   Track and field was next, and soon Mastandrea was competing—and winning—in 100-, 200-, and 400-meter races against other disabled athletes. In 1992 she joined the U.S. Paralympic team, traveling to the summer games in Barcelona, and later to Atlanta (where she earned her gold and silver medals) in 1996.

8   The Paralympic experience was exciting, but it was also expensive. Mastandrea, like her teammates, had to pay for her own coaches, rent her own training facilities, and find her own health insurance. Since 1994 the USOC has provided travel, housing, and uniforms for Paralympic athletes, but those benefits pale in comparison to the perks dished out to able-bodied competitors.

9   "It's a lot like where the women's sports movement was 25 years ago," Mastandrea says. "Disabled athletes are up against a lack of recognition, a lack of funding, a lack of opportunity."

❖❖❖

Comprehension

1. When Linda Mastandrea was growing up, why did everyone assume that she could not participate in sports?
2. How did Mastandrea first become involved in athletics?
3. What athletic awards has Mastandrea won?
4. What are Mastandrea's goals as a member of the United States Olympic Committee (USOC)?

Critical Thinking

1. Why do you think the Paralympics receive less publicity and public attention than the regular Olympics?
2. What does Mastandrea mean when she says, "An athlete is an athlete is an athlete"?
3. What makes the Olympics special and unlike any other type of athletic competition?
4. Do you think the Olympics have become too commercialized in recent years? Give reasons for your answer.

Language and Vocabulary

1. The word *Paralympic* is not defined in the reading. What do you think it means? What two other words do you think were combined to create the word *Paralympics*?
2. Notice the expression *thorn in the side,* which is used in the third paragraph. Based on the *context* (other information in the same paragraph),

what do you think this expression means? (Hint: To help figure out the meaning, think about how annoying an actual thorn stuck in someone's side would be.)

Style, Structure, and Organization

1. How does the introduction (the first paragraph) capture readers' attention? What were you curious about when you first read the introduction?
2. In writing this profile of Linda Mastandrea, why did author Andy Steiner include several statements from Mastandrea herself? Choose one of Linda Mastandrea's statements that you especially like and explain why you like it. What does it add to the reading?

Topics for Discussion or Journal Writing

1. Do you admire Linda Mastandrea? Why?
2. What are some of the biggest challenges that people with disabilities face?
3. Have you ever seriously competed in basketball, track and field, or another sport? In what way was the experience rewarding for you?
4. Can you think of any ways in which your school or local community could do more to provide equal opportunities for people with disabilities?
5. Do you know anyone who has either a physical disability or a learning disability? What are some of the obstacles that person has had to overcome?

Writing Topics for Paragraphs or Essays

1. Interview someone you admire and write a paper about that person. Use "Playing for Keeps" as a model for your writing.
2. Write about someone with a disability who has had to overcome many obstacles. How has that person succeeded in meeting challenges and coping with problems? Are there certain obstacles that remain? You may interview someone you know personally, or you may write about a well-known person.
3. Using library resources or the Internet, look up information about how the Olympics began and the history of the Olympic games. Write an informative paper about the most interesting information you find.

4. Using library resources or the Internet, look up information about the Paralympics or the Special Olympics, including how these special Olympic games began and their history. Write a paper about your findings.
5. Write a paper about a time in your life when you overcame an obstacle, a time when you proved yourself to be more capable than someone else thought you were, or a time when competing for an award made you feel good about yourself. Tell the story with interesting details, and include some of your feelings.

Can You Afford to Get Sick?

Helen Martineau

With medical costs rising faster than incomes, the topic of medical insurance is an important one. The author of this article writes partly from personal experience. She herself received insurance through COBRA, a law that requires insurers to continue coverage at the same rate for 18 months after an employee leaves a job.

Prereading Questions

1. Are most people in this country worried about paying their medical bills? Why?
2. Does the health care system in this country provide good medical care to everyone?

Vocabulary

mishap problem or accident

forgo do without

unemployment rate the percentage of people who cannot find work

the working poor people who work at very low-paying jobs

freelance independent

(neck) brace a piece of equipment designed to support the neck

splint a piece of equipment designed to keep broken bones from moving around

fractured broken

neurological having to do with the nervous system

no-fault insurance insurance that pays no matter who caused the accident

coverage insurance

eligibility in this case, the right to keep the insurance coverage

SOURCE: "Can You Afford to Get Sick?" by Helen Martineau. Reprinted with permission from the October 1999, *American Health.* Copyright © 1999 by The Reader's Digest Assn., Inc.

premiums the cost of the insurance policy

wherein in which

pharmaceutical . . . industry businesses that manufacture and sell prescription drugs and medicines

lobbyists people paid to convince government officials to pass laws favorable to the lobbyists' employers

group rates lower-cost insurance plans sold only to large groups

to further to advance

former previous

Can You Afford to Get Sick?

What would you do if you had no insurance and suffered a major medical mishap? Would you forgo treatment or risk debt to get the proper care? If you're one of the 43.4 million uninsured Americans, these, unfortunately, are your options.

2   Though the U.S. currently has the strongest economy and lowest unemployment rate in decades, the number of uninsured Americans is rising by an estimated one million a year. While most uninsured people are between the ages of 21 and 44 and among the working poor, the Census Bureau reports that nearly five million Americans without insurance have family incomes in excess of $75,000.

3   Blair Breard, 37, a freelance film producer in New York City, learned the consequences of not having health insurance the hard way. While crossing a Manhattan street in March 1992, she was struck by a car, thrown 20 feet into the air and knocked unconscious when she hit the ground. When the ambulance arrived, emergency workers cut off her coat, put her neck in a brace and placed her twisted left arm in a splint before rushing her to the hospital. Not only was her arm broken in four places and a big toe fractured, but the skin on the left side of her face was scraped off as she landed on the pavement. Uninsured, she was instructed to sign a document at the hospital stating that she would be responsible for all payments for her care. Breard returned home from the hospital without having had any neurological exams and with only a prescription for pain medication in her pocket.

4   Three weeks later Breard got the first bill for her treatment: the ambulance alone cost $200. Luckily, New York State requires drivers to carry no-fault insurance, so the bill for the initial treatment of her injuries on the day of the accident was completely covered.

5   But the money she received from the driver's insurance policy could go only so far. Without coverage for her bills and subsequent physical

therapy (she was unable to work for five months because of her injuries), Breard had to borrow $10,000 from her family to pay her rent and utilities. She simply couldn't afford to get sick.

6   Clearly, a healthy economy doesn't guarantee a healthy community. Why? For starters, most of the more than six million Americans who have gone off public assistance (and thus off Medicaid) in the past five years have moved into low-paying jobs that offer no benefits. Those that do often pay only a portion of the insurance bill, forcing employees to pick up the rest. With the price tags on prescription drugs creeping up almost 10% a year, advances in technology boosting the cost of testing, insurance premiums rising 20% this year alone, and the increasing expense of hospital stays and doctors' visits, it's no surprise that the Employee Benefit Research Institute in Washington reports that the cost of health care is rising at a faster pace than wages.

The Politics of Coverage

7   Remedying the situation has proved to be a difficult task. Though Congress passed the Health Insurance Portability Act in 1996 to maintain workers' insurance eligibility when they switch jobs, the law doesn't prevent insurance companies from increasing premiums. And it still doesn't provide for self-employed persons or those working for small firms.

8   In 1992 President Clinton tried to make universal health care one of the cornerstones of his election platform, wherein private companies would offer coverage for their employees, as they do now, and the government would kick in for the unemployed or self-employed. Despite the fact that the U.S. is the only industrialized democracy without universal health coverage, Clinton's plan died by the fall of 1994. According to John Stauber, executive director of the Center for Media and Democracy in Madison, WI, the bill fell victim to the efforts of the pharmaceutical and insurance industry lobbyists, who convinced legislators that the American public didn't want universal health care. (Remember those TV commercials with Harry and Louise?)

9   "It's a basic philosophical difference," says Rachel DeGolia, associate director of Universal Health Care Network, a national advocacy group based in Cleveland, OH. "We believe that health coverage is a right, while those who oppose universal health care believe it's a privilege."

The Future of Benefits

10 Many advocates think a total overhaul of the system is the only way we'll get coverage for everyone. "If anything is going to happen," says Quentin Young, M.D., national coordinator of the Physicians for a National Health

Care Program in Chicago, "it's going to be on a state level, because the insurance industry has such a hold on the purses of the congressmen inside Washington's beltway."

11   A number of state representatives have already started to take action. In the spring of 1998, Congressmen David Obey (D.-WI) and Robert T. Matsui (D.-CA) introduced the American Health Security Partnership Act, which would allow a state to determine how its citizens are covered. This year, the Bernardin Amendment was proposed in Illinois; it would require the state legislature to guarantee health care to all citizens by 2002. And Rep. Jim McDermott (D.-WA) recently proposed the American Health Security Act of 1999, which would provide universal health insurance for all Americans as of January 1, 2001.

Getting Covered Now

12   If you're self-employed or your employer doesn't offer insurance, the key is to benefit from group rates. Here are a few options:

Join a business organization. Group insurers exist for nearly every profession. Working Today (888-499-4669; www.workingtoday.org), an organization for independent workers, offers low insurance premiums. American Home Business Association (800-556-9150; www.homebusinessworks.com) offers discounts on major medical coverage and the National Association for the Self-Employed (800-232-6273; www.nase.org) provides access to health benefits.

Find a broker. Insurance brokers can find the lowest rate for small businesses and the self-employed. "There are actually a lot of programs offered by major insurers geared toward individuals, but the average person may have trouble finding them," says Michael Kristof, senior manager of Health Insurance Solutions, a brokerage in Stamford, CT (203-324-1313). Brokers can be found in the Yellow Pages under "Insurance."

Go back to school. Now may be the time to further your education. Taking one or two classes at a public university can get you a student rate on insurance.

Use COBRA. If you're leaving a job where you have health insurance, you're entitled by law to 18 months of the same coverage you've been getting. You may have to pick up the cost your former insurer paid for the insurance, but it will still be cheaper than most individual rates you might find on your own.

Comprehension

1. When this article was written, how many Americans did not have health insurance?
2. How did Blair Breard get the money to pay for her expenses after the accident?
3. What groups of people have fought against universal health insurance?
4. What are some of the ways that a person can get insurance coverage if it is not offered by his or her employer?

Critical Thinking

1. In your opinion, what is the author's purpose in writing this article?
2. Do you predict that in the future more or fewer people in the United States will have medical insurance? Why?
3. Is this article mostly fact or mostly opinion, and why do you think so?
4. How do you think the author feels about health insurance?

Language and Vocabulary

1. Based on the context—the rest of the article—what does *universal health coverage* mean?
2. In this selection, the author includes several words and expressions that are often used in discussing insurance. Some of them are *policy, premium, no-fault, coverage,* and *universal.* If you are unsure of the meaning of any of these words related to insurance, look them up in a dictionary.

Style, Structure, and Organization

1. In this article, does the author use facts to make her points? Does using facts make the reading seem more believable? Which facts are the most convincing?
2. In the third, fourth, and fifth paragraphs, the author tells about one person's personal experience. How does this make the reading more effective?
3. In the final section of the article, the author provides some tips for finding insurance coverage. Do you think this is an effective conclusion? Why?

Topics for Discussion or Journal Writing

1. Have you had medical insurance (a) all your life, (b) never, or (c) part of your life? Do you have medical insurance now? If not, does this reading give you some good ideas about how you could get inexpensive medical coverage?
2. Have you had any mostly good or mostly bad experiences with medical insurance and treatment?
3. Do you think it's okay for hospitals to treat people who have medical insurance differently than they treat people who don't?
4. Are most people you know happy with their medical insurance? Why or why not?
5. In your opinion, will the United States ever have universal health coverage? Why?

Writing Topics for Paragraphs or Essays

1. Write about one experience you have had with hospitals, doctors, or medical insurance.
2. If you don't have medical insurance, write instructions on how to get medical care for free or for very little money.
3. Go online or call some of the resources listed in the article and ask for information on the services they offer; write a short informative paper about what you discover.
4. Check some of the author's facts online or at a library. For example, is it true that the United States is the only industrialized country in the world without health coverage? Write a report, listing the facts that you checked and what you discovered.
5. Choose one of the following topics. Find out more about the topic by searching online or in a library or by interviewing people at homeless shelters; then write a short paper on the topic.
    a. Describe some typical medical problems of homeless people. What kind of medical care can they get in your area, and who provides it?
    b. Write a paper on what you would do if you were homeless and you or a family member needed medical attention.

6

Nature and the Outdoors

Journey of the Pink Dolphins Sy Montgomery 166
In the Shadow of Man Jane Goodall 171
Life in the Treetops Margaret D. Lowman 175
Nature's R$_x$ Joel L. Swerdlow 182
Monarchs' Migration: A Fragile Journey William K. Stevens 187
Heavy Traffic on the Everest Highway Geoffrey Tabin 193
Death Valley Doug and Bobbe Tatreau 199

Journey of the Pink Dolphins

Sy Montgomery

Searching for dolphins that live in the warm river waters of South America, Sy Montgomery explored the Amazon and other connecting waterways. In her book *Journey of the Pink Dolphins*, she wrote about her experiences, including some of the local legends about these elusive creatures. Sy Montgomery also writes a column about nature that appears in *The Boston Globe*.

Prereading Questions

1. Why do many people consider dolphins to be special?
2. Do you know of any fables or legends about animals?

Vocabulary

looking glass mirror
constellations formations of stars
boas large tropical snakes
sizzle a bubbling sensation (like drops of water dancing on the surface of a hot frying pan)
effusion an unrestrained outpouring
otherworldly from another world, mystical
eerily strangely, mysteriously
festas feasts, celebrations
ruddy reddish-colored
Shamans tribal religious leaders
twang a sharp vibrating sound, usually made by plucking strings on an instrument
pulses occurs at regular intervals
Shipibo a native South American tribe

traverses crosses or passes through
starboard the right side of a boat or ship (when facing toward the front)
port the left side of a boat or ship (when facing toward the front)
intangible not capable of being perceived by the senses
ballet a graceful classical dance

Journey of the Pink Dolphins

The river is the looking glass into another world. By day, the water is a perfect mirror of trees and sky—and yet its glassy surface moves so quickly that if you enter the water without a lifejacket, the current will sweep you under. The river people speak of the Encante, an enchanted city beneath the water, ruled by beings they call Encantados. Those who visit never want to leave, because everything is more beautiful there.

2   At night, even the stars seem brighter in the water than in the sky. The constellations shine above, their starry reflections below, and from the trees, the glowing eyes of wolf spiders, tree boas, tree frogs. In your canoe, you feel like you are traveling through the timeless starscape of space.

3   But if you stop and wait, the Encantados will come. At first you may feel a sizzle of bubbles rising beneath the craft, an effusion of pearls cast up from below like a net of enchantment. If the night is moonless, you will only know their breath. But if the moon is full, you may see a form rising from the water, gathering into the shape of a dolphin. Inches from your canoe, a face may break the surface—a face at once otherworldly and eerily familiar. The forehead is clearly defined, like a person's. The long beak sticks out like a nose. The skin is delicate, like ours. Sometimes it is grayish, or white—and sometimes dazzlingly, impossibly *pink*. The creature turns its neck and looks at you, and opening the top of its head, gasps, "Chaaahhhhh!"

4   In Brazil, they call this dolphin "boto." They say the boto can turn into a person, that it shows up at festas to seduce men and women. They say you must be careful, or it will take you away forever to the Encante, the enchanted city beneath the water. In Peru, they call the creature "bufeo colorado"—the ruddy dolphin. Shamans say its very breath has power, and that the sound it utters when it gasps can send poisoned darts flying, as from a blowgun. Scientists call it by the species name: *Inia geoffrensis*.

. . .

5   On the glass-smooth waters of Charro Lake, we wait for the moon.
6   A bat shoots by, a flying shadow. In the dark, frogs call in the clicking voices of bamboo chimes; others twang like rubber bands. Lightning pulses silently in the southern sky. But the moon hides behind dark billowing rain clouds, so we wait.

7   The Shipibo say that by moonlight, women are especially susceptible to spells cast by dolphins. The moon, it is said, is the sun of the underworld. It traverses the world of darkness, illuminating the Encante. That is why Dianne and I have come here now: with Moises and Graciella, with Jerry and Steve, we wait in our canoe for the moon to reveal the dolphins.

8   At 6:40, a glow pierces the clouds. By 6:45, it shines bright enough to write these words by. And still we wait.

9   Around us, bells, creaks, whistles, honks; the forest heaving and sighing, like a dream set to music. And then, at 7:04, we hear their breath: "Chaaahhhh!" A minute later, another gasp.

10   Another minute passes. And now, all around us, tiny bubbles begin to rise—behind us, in front of us, to starboard, then port. It is the expelled breath of dolphins—breath so close we can touch it.

11   I stop taking data. "This can't be happening," I say to Dianne. "Believe it—it's happening," she answers. I dip my hand in the water and feel the bubbles sizzle on my skin, intimate as a caress. It seems as unreal as a kiss from a ghost, and yet it continues: for four minutes, we touch the intangible and see the invisible, as the dolphins bless our canoe with their breath.

12   The bubbles disappear. In the seventeen minutes that follow, we can see, by moonlight, the glistening pink heads bobbing in the water. But still, more real than the visible are these breaths: a loud blow, a tail slap, a sigh; a gasp, a blow, a ballet of breath. And now the breaths grow fainter, more distant, as the dolphins move away.

◆◆◆

Comprehension

1. Who or what are the Encantados?
2. What other names does the pink dolphin have in Brazil and Peru? What special powers are the dolphins said to have in those countries?
3. What are the beliefs of the Shipibo about moonlight and the dolphins?
4. Before Sy Montgomery and her companions can actually see the dolphins, how do they first learn that the dolphins have arrived?

Critical Thinking

1. Why do you suppose some people believe in legends about the dolphins? Can you imagine how any of these legends might have begun?
2. Why did Sy Montgomery wait for the dolphins at night rather than look for them during the day? Do you think she believes any of the native legends?

3. How do you think the author felt about this experience? Why did she feel that way?

4. Based on what you learned about the pink river dolphins in this reading, in what ways do they seem similar to other dolphins that you have seen or read about?

Language and Vocabulary

1. In the first paragraph, the author uses the Portuguese name *Encantados*, which the river people have for beings that live under the water and appear at night in the form of dolphins. The name for the place where they live is also Portuguese: the *Encante*. What do you think these words mean in English? Look for clues that the author gives us. You may also want to ask someone who speaks Portuguese or look up the words in a Portuguese-English dictionary.

2. When the author describes being on the river at night in a canoe, she writes, "You feel like you are traveling through the timeless starscape of space." What do you think the word *starscape* means? You probably will not find *starscape* in a dictionary, so you will need to use clues in the reading. Also, think about similar words you may already know that use a combination of another word with-*scape*, such as *landscape* or *seascape*.

Style, Structure, and Organization

1. This reading has two distinct parts. What is the main topic of each part? Where does the second part begin?

2. At times, the author makes the dolphins seem almost human. At other times, they seem more like supernatural beings. Which descriptive details make them seem almost human? Which details make them seem supernatural?

3. Shortly before the dolphins appear in Charro Lake, what kind of mood (or *feeling*) does the author create through her description of the scene? Which details help establish that mood?

Topics for Discussion or Journal Writing

1. Would you enjoy going down the river and taking a canoe out on Charro Lake, as Sy Montgomery did? What do you think would be the best parts of the trip? Would anything seem scary or dangerous to you?

2. Have you ever seen a live dolphin or watched a movie in which trained dolphins played a significant part? Recall as many details as you can about the dolphins you saw.
3. If you could observe any animal that you wanted to anywhere in the world, which animal would you choose? Where would you go to see that animal, and what would the experience be like?
4. What legends, stories, superstitions, or religious beliefs can you think of in which animals are thought to have special powers?

Writing Topics for Paragraphs or Essays

1. Have you ever had an opportunity to go boating on a lake or river or to go river-rafting? If so, write about one or more of your experiences. Include descriptive details about the lake or river and any animals you observed.
2. Observe an animal at a zoo, an aquarium, or a marine park for at least half an hour. How would this animal's life be different in the wild? Write a paper from the animal's point of view, comparing life in captivity with life in the wild.
3. Find a newspaper column about nature, such as Sy Montgomery's column in *The Boston Globe,* or any other article about nature in a newspaper or magazine. Write a summary of the column or article, plus your own evaluation of it. Attach the column or article to your paper.
4. Write an informative paper about the Amazon River. Consult a good encyclopedia or other reference source to learn about the Amazon.
5. Use library resources or the Internet to find out more about dolphins. Then choose one of the following writing assignments:

   a. Compare and contrast marine dolphins with river dolphins.

   b. Identify and describe the four kinds of river dolphins and their habitats (where they live).

   c. Explain how dolphins communicate with each other.

   d. Report on how dolphins are trained and what they can be trained to do.

In the Shadow of Man

Jane Goodall

Since 1970, Jane Goodall has observed and interacted with chimpanzees in their native environment in Africa. As a result, she is the world's foremost expert on these amazing animals. She has written many books and articles and has produced several videos. The book that this reading comes from, *In the Shadow of Man,* tells the story of her fascinating observations of chimpanzees and of her interactions with them in the wild.

Prereading Questions

1. What qualities or abilities make human beings different from animals?
2. What can we learn from observing animals in their natural surroundings?

Vocabulary

weary tired, worn out
slight small
termite a hive insect that lives underground and builds mounds
casual observers in this context, people other than trained researchers
wandered moved around, not in a specific direction
swarm a moving mass of insects
discarded thrown away, rejected
mandibles in insects, similar to a jaw
a hide a small area screened off from view, also called a *blind*

In the Shadow of Man

I had had a frustrating morning, tramping up and down three valleys with never a sign or sound of a chimpanzee. Hauling myself up the steep slope of Mlinda Valley I headed for the peak, not only weary but soaking wet from crawling through dense undergrowth. Suddenly I stopped, for I saw a slight movement in the long grass about sixty yards away. Quickly focusing my binoculars I saw that it was a single chimpanzee, and just then he turned in my direction. I recognized David Graybeard.

2   Cautiously I moved around so that I could see what he was doing. He was squatting beside the red earth mound of a termite nest, and as I watched I saw him carefully push a long grass stem down into a hole in the mound. After a moment he withdrew it and picked something from the end with his mouth. I was too far away to make out what he was eating, but it was obvious that he was actually using a grass stem as a tool.

3   I knew that on two occasions casual observers in West Africa had seen chimpanzees using objects as tools: one had broken open palm-nut kernels by using a rock as a hammer, and a group of chimps had been observed pushing sticks into an underground bees' nest and licking off the honey. Somehow I had never dreamed of seeing anything so exciting myself.

4   For an hour David feasted at the termite mound and then he wandered slowly away. When I was sure he had gone I went over to examine the mound. I found a few crushed insects strewn about, and a swarm of worker termites sealing the entrances of the nest passages into which David had obviously been poking his stems. I picked up one of his discarded tools and carefully pushed it into a hole myself. Immediately I felt the pull of several termites as they seized the grass, and when I pulled it out there were a number of worker termites and a few soldiers, with big red heads, clinging on with their mandibles. There they remained, sticking out at right angles to the stem with their legs waving in the air.

5   Before I left I trampled down some of the tall dry grass and constructed a rough hide—just a few palm fronds leaned up against the low branch of a tree and tied together at the top. I planned to wait there the next day. But it was another week before I was able to watch a chimpanzee "fishing" for termites again.

. . .

6   On the eighth day of my watch David Graybeard arrived again together with Goliath, and the pair worked there for two hours. I could see much better: I observed how they scratched open the sealed-over passage entrances with a thumb or forefinger. I watched how they bit the ends off their tools when they became bent, or used the other end, or discarded them in favor of new ones. Goliath once moved at least fifteen yards from the heap to select a firm-looking piece of vine, and both males often picked three or four stems while they were collecting tools, and put the spares beside them on the ground until they wanted them.

7   Most exciting of all, on several occasions they picked small leafy twigs and prepared them for use by stripping off the leaves. This was the

first recorded example of a wild animal not merely *using* an object as a tool, but actually modifying an object and thus showing the crude beginnings of tool*making*.

◆◆◆

Comprehension

1. Who or what are David Graybeard and Goliath?
2. What did David Graybeard do with a long grass stem? Why were his actions surprising to the author?
3. In West Africa, how had observers seen chimpanzees using tools?
4. Why did Jane Goodall keep watch at the termite mound? How long did she have to wait?

Critical Thinking

1. What is the main idea or most important point of this selection?
2. What range of emotions did the author and researcher, Jane Goodall, probably experience during her research?
3. Does the reading include mostly opinion or mostly facts?
4. What qualities would a researcher need in order to be a successful observer of animal behavior in the wild?
5. Is *In the Shadow of Man* a good title for the book from which this selection is taken? Why do you think the author chose this title?

Language and Vocabulary

1. Had you ever read or heard the expression *strewn about* before you read it in the fourth paragraph of this selection? What do you think it means?
2. In this reading, the author uses many *-ing* words and phrases (present participles and participial phrases), such as "Quickly *focusing* my binoculars . . . ." Find six *-ing* words or phrases in the first paragraph. Do they make the reading more descriptive?

Style, Structure, and Organization

1. Jane Goodall uses a lot of descriptive details in this selection. Highlight or list four specific details in the second paragraph that help the reader

picture the scene. How does the author's use of descriptive details make this story interesting to read?
2. Where is the sentence that expresses the main idea of this selection—at the beginning, in the middle, or at the end? Is it effective where it is? Why?

Topics for Discussion or Journal Writing

1. Imagine the living conditions that Jane Goodall experienced while she studied the chimpanzees in the wild. What do you think it was like for her to spend so much time away from other humans?
2. What do think was the best thing about living in the wild and studying the chimpanzees?
3. Would you like to do this kind of research? Why or why not?
4. Do you think that many rare and endangered species of animals will become extinct in the near future? Why?

Writing Topics for Paragraphs or Essays

1. Write about a time when you had an adventure or witnessed something amazing.
2. Describe a wild place away from civilization that you have visited, heard of, read about, or seen on TV.
3. Use your imagination to describe the camp where Jane Goodall lived while she was doing her research with the chimpanzees. Include details about things you might see, hear, smell, or feel if you were there.
4. Tell the story of Jane Goodall's adventures and research from the chimpanzees' point of view.
5. Read more about Jane Goodall's research in one of her books, on the Internet at http://www.janegoodall.ca, or in *National Geographic* articles. Then choose one of the following writing assignments:
    a. Write about Jane Goodall's life. Include details about her research in Africa.
    b. Write a short summary of what Jane Goodall learned about chimpanzees in her lifetime of work.

Life in the Treetops

Margaret D. Lowman

Margaret D. Lowman writes about her experiences as chief scientist on a special expedition to the Blue Creek rain forest of Belize in 1994. This expedition was sponsored by the Jason Project for Education, which made it possible for Dr. Lowman and other researchers to share their discoveries with students in the United States, Canada, and several other countries by means of live broadcasts from their research sites. The author's two sons, Eddie and James, accompanied her on this expedition to Belize.

Prereading Questions

1. What types of plants and animals would you expect to find in a rain forest?
2. Why would learning firsthand about the rain forest be a valuable educational experience?

Vocabulary

donned put on
mode method or means
canopy in this usage, the dense upper area of the trees
shack a small, crudely constructed building
clambered climbed
commotion noisy disturbance
towheads people with very light blond hair
lavish excessive
traipsing walking about
preserve an area set aside for the protection and preservation of plants and/or animals
ecotourism tourism to places of ecological interest
venture a business
tract an area of land
neophytes beginners, those who are doing something for the first time

epiphyte a plant that does not need to have its roots in soil, absorbs moisture from the air, and is supported by a tree or another tall plant

emanating coming out of

reeling whirling, going round and round

spanning, spanned extending from one side across to the other

arborists tree specialists

agile able to move quickly and easily

jubilant very happy

emergent rising above the surroundings

sway a back-and-forth movement

awe amazement, wonder

reputedly supposedly

elation happiness, joy

Life in the Treetops

My children and I boarded a small six-seater plane with a simple propeller engine. Along its side the words *Maya Airways* were almost worn off. Our luggage was thrown casually into the back, and Eddie was invited to serve as copilot. He donned a pair of heavy headphones and we were off into the skies over Belize. I felt somewhat apprehensive about putting my precious children on this old propeller plane, but there was no other mode of transport to our field site. (Four years later both pilot and plane crashed into the Maya Mountains.)

2   My young sons were thrilled to be accompanying their mom on a tropical rain-forest expedition. Eddie was eight years old, James was six. (They had seen the Australian rain forest on numerous occasions as infants, but were too young then to remember any details.) Our destination was Blue Creek in southern Belize. Our mission was to set up the study site for the Jason Project, including the construction of a canopy walkway with several platforms upon which to conduct field research. I called this structure my green laboratory, but the boys called it their giant treehouse.

. . .

3   This was my second journey to the rain forests of Belize. Upon arriving at the Punta Gorda airport (one dirt runway and a small shack for shelter during rain or hot sun) we were met by an old truck with some of the Jason Project crew. We clambered into the truck bed and bumped along from the coastal town of Punta Gorda about 20 miles west, into the interior. At Blue Creek village Eddie and James caused quite a

commotion among the village children. The arrival of two towheads—probably almost of marriage age in their culture—aroused great curiosity. The girls brought samples of their bracelets and embroidery to show the boys. James (still in his antigirl stage) was horrified; Eddie (slightly older) was friendly, but did not know how to handle such lavish attention. They passed shyly into the forest, traipsing down the new trail built to access the canopy research station, future site of our giant treehouse.

. . .

4   Blue Creek was a leased preserve, operated by a small ecotourism venture back in Boston. The site offered little except an outhouse and one shed that served as kitchen, library, dining room, and sleeping area. But it had a superb tract of primary forest and a captivating limestone cave just 500 meters upstream from the "lodge."

. . .

5   We had reservations to stay at the Blue Creek "lodge" that night. Accommodations included the opportunity to lay out a sleeping bag on the floor of the open hut, or (in my fortunate situation) to tie a hammock between two posts. I had brought my faithful khaki hammock from the jungles of Cameroon, and the rest of the group was impressed. Everyone was in bed by 7:00 P.M. because there was no electricity and it was pouring rain. Sleeping in the rain forest was a new experience for most of our group. Several of the neophytes expressed concern about the risk of snakes while sleeping on the floor, and others looked about anxiously for bats. Only minutes after everyone had finally settled into his or her sleeping bag, we all leapt up at the sound of a loud explosion. A large fruit from the over-hanging bobo tree (similar in size to the cannonball tree, named for the obvious size and shape of its fruits) had fallen on the tin roof. Its fruits were slightly larger than coconuts, and weighed more. Everyone laughed nervously and settled back down for a relatively sleepless night.

. . .

6   After that first night in the Belizean jungle, we awoke to a glistening green world. Each leaf was dripping water from the evening storms, and every drip tip was functioning to funnel water off the leaf surface and onto the root system. I mapped trees at this site, examined the canopies with binoculars to estimate epiphyte diversity, and brainstormed with the crew about possible camera angles. We traveled back to Punta Gorda in the evening, slept in real beds, and absorbed the sounds of a tropical town—bicycles pedaling on bumpy streets, skinny dogs barking, frogs peeping, music and voices emanating from tiny open-air drinking huts, and a gentle drizzle cooling the sultry summer air.

7   I returned the next day to Belize City, and on to Miami and Sarasota. My brain was reeling with enthusiasm and ideas.

. . .

8   Three months flew by. By the time they were over, my walkway partner, Bart Bouricius, and I had designed and created a budget for our green laboratory. We had assembled a team of six experts for the erection of the walkway. Huts had been built that more than quadrupled the space of the field station, and foam mattresses and bunk-bed frames were flown in at great expense.

. . .

9   When my sons and I had settled into our camp site at the Blue Creek research station, we eagerly looked around us. The research station had changed dramatically since I had been there several weeks ago with Robin. Spanning the Blue Creek watercourse hung a stainless steel cable, and on either side a wooden platform had been built about 75 feet from the ground. Using our binoculars, we could observe the arborists, like a troupe of monkeys, "performing" overhead.

. . .

10   Eddie and James were eager to climb. They had been given children's harnesses for Christmas, so each had his own canopy gear. We had practiced at home, but this was the big time. Ironically, I was very anxious and not looking forward to having then ascend 75 feet into the sky. Even though I did this sort of thing virtually every day, it seemed more dangerous when I contemplated the ascent for my children. I knew, however, that they were probably more agile than I! My brother Ed, an expert woodworker who had helped build the platforms, was part of the construction crew. . . . Ed generously offered to accompany the boys to the top and promised to call me when they were on the bridge (so that I could open my eyes). In no time the three of them had ascended the ladder and reached the platform overlooking the creek. I hastily climbed up to join the jubilant crew.

. . .

11   A look at the tranquil stream below gave us a vivid respect for our height. The people at ground level looked like ants. We saw the glistening sun leaves and felt the winds gusting over the emergent flame tree adjacent to our platform.

. . .

12   The canopy was a whole new world for Eddie and James, and a whole new world for me to appreciate through their eyes. They cautiously crossed the bridge over the creek, which spanned approximately 72 feet and had a well-defined sway in the center. Once on the other side, they peered in awe at the white poisonwood tree (*Sebastiana* sp., family Euphorbiaceae), whose leaves reputedly inflict an irritating rash to human skin if touched.

13   After several exploratory hours in the canopy, the boys descended on the metal staples and ladders to the ground below. With elation they observed a hairy black tarantula on the tree trunk. It looked identical to our faithful pet spider, Harriet, at home. The day was a huge success. The boys did not even seem to mind their dinner of beans and rice, despite the fact that it was the fourth night of that menu.

◆◆◆

Comprehension

1. How did the village children at Blue Creek react to seeing Eddie and James? Why did they react this way?
2. Why was it difficult to get a good night's sleep at the Blue Creek "lodge"?
3. What changes did the author observe at the Blue Creek research station when she and her sons returned three months after their first visit?
4. How did the boys and the author get to the observation platform? What could they see from the platform?

Critical Thinking

1. How did the boys feel about their experience in the treetops?
2. What does the author mean when she writes that it was "a whole new world for me to appreciate through their eyes"?
3. Do you think Eddie and James were in any real danger? Why or why not?
4. How would you describe the relationship between Margaret Lowman and her sons?
5. How do you think the Jason Project could contribute to worldwide understanding of rain forests?

Language and Vocabulary

1. The author comments that, by using binoculars, they "could observe the arborists, like a troupe of monkeys, 'performing' overhead." When you read the author's comparison, what kind of scene did you picture in your mind? Can you figure out what the word *troupe* means? If not, look it up in a dictionary.

2. What do you think the term *rain forest* means? If necessary, look up *rain forest* in a dictionary or an encyclopedia to get a better understanding of the meaning.

Style, Structure, and Organization

1. Which of the following scenes can you picture most clearly in your mind: the "lodge" at Blue Creek, the tropical town of Punta Gorda, or the view from the platform? Which details do you think are most interesting and effective in the description of the scene you have selected?
2. In addition to using description, this reading also uses *narration*, or storytelling, to relate what happened. Make a list of all of the important events in the story, beginning with the author and her sons boarding a plane for Belize. Be sure to keep the events in chronological order (time order).

Topics for Discussion or Journal Writing

1. What do you think was the most exciting part of the trip for the author's sons, Eddie and James? Why?
2. Does Punta Gorda seem similar to any towns that you have ever visited? In what ways? Describe any similar town that you know about.
3. Based on what you learned in the reading, would you like to visit Belize? Why or why not?
4. Did you ever have an opportunity to go along with one of your parents and observe or participate in his or her job activities? If so, what did you learn from that experience?
5. What do you think would be most interesting and rewarding about conducting research in tree canopies? What would be the biggest challenges of the job?

Writing Topics for Paragraphs or Essays

1. Write about an interesting or exciting experience you had in the outdoors. Use both narration and description.
2. "Job shadow" someone for a day—that is, spend a full day with someone at his or her job. Then write about your experience.
3. Describe the expedition to Belize from the viewpoint of one of the author's sons.

4. Find out more about rain forests by using library resources or the Internet, and write a persuasive paper about why rain forests should be preserved.
5. Use information from the Jason Project web site at http://www.jasonproject.org/ to write a report about one of the following topics:
    a. The current Jason Project or one of the other expeditions in previous years
    b. One of the other research sites in Belize, such as the cave at Blue Creek or the Mayan city of Xunantunich
    c. The life of author and scientist Margaret D. Lowman (Hint: look for "Dr. Meg Lowman.")

Nature's R$_x$

Joel L. Swerdlow

Plants are something that we often take for granted, thinking of them merely as part of the landscape rather than as a source of medicines. Joel L. Swerdlow, an assistant editor for *National Geographic,* has investigated the effects of a number of medicinal plants from around the world, including the rosy periwinkle (scientific name *Catharanthus roseus*), which grows in Madagascar.

Prereading Questions

1. Do you know of any plants or herbal remedies that are used to treat illnesses?
2. How do you think new medicines are discovered and developed?

Vocabulary

chemotherapy a treatment for cancer that uses chemicals (drugs)

remission an inactive stage of a disease, disappearance of symptoms

chemotherapeutic used in chemotherapy

Hodgkin's disease a form of cancer affecting the lymph nodes, liver, and spleen

synthetic produced artificially, not from plant or animal sources

compounds combinations of two or more elements

chronic recurring or lasting for a long period of time

component an ingredient or a part

respiratory related to breathing

derived obtained or developed from a source

incentive a reward to create motivation

botanical related to plants

inconclusive not resulting in a definite conclusion

Nature's R_X

Party sounds float up from a swimming pool in Washington, D.C. Twenty children shout and splash, toss balls, and snack on sandwiches, cookies, chips, and sodas. The guest of honor is nine-year-old Audra Shapiro, who has just finished two years of chemotherapy and whose leukemia is in complete remission. Her recovery from this cancer depended on a plant that originated halfway around the world.

2   Until the early 1960s Audra's disease would have meant sure death. Now the long-term survival rate for childhood leukemia is above 90 percent, thanks in part to vincristine, a chemotherapeutic drug made from the Madagascar rosy periwinkle. Vinblastine, another drug made from the same plant, helps cure most cases of Hodgkin's disease.

3   Plants like the periwinkle have contributed to the development of 25 to 50 percent of all prescription drugs used in the United States, either directly or by providing biochemical models, or templates, used to make synthetic compounds. Digitalis, which is used to treat chronic heart failure, comes from the leaves of the foxglove plant, and ephedrine, a component of many commonly prescribed respiratory medicines, is derived from a chemical formula from the ephedra plant. But overall, in the past 40 years there has been little development of new plant-based pharmaceuticals. During that period the U.S. Food and Drug Administration (FDA) approved fewer than a dozen drugs derived from plants.

4   Part of the reason is simply bottom line. The development of a new FDA-approved drug costs as much as 500 million dollars. Manufacturers have found the route from plant to safe, reliable pill difficult and unpredictable, so there is limited incentive to base drug development on plants. Still, almost two-thirds of the Earth's 6.1 billion people rely on the healing power of plants; for them nothing else is affordable or available. And even in industrialized countries where scientifically formulated drugs are readily available—Americans spent 103 billion dollars on retail prescription drugs in 1998—use of nonprescription botanical drugs is rising dramatically. In 1990, 2.5 percent of Americans purchased herbal remedies; in 1997, 12.1 percent spent roughly five billion dollars on them.

5   What part of that money was spent wisely is a matter of some debate. While many plants have been the subject of extensive study and their effects well documented, data on others are inconclusive. Scientists are often unable to determine which chemical or combination of chemicals within a plant is responsible for relieving pain or stimulating blood flow or creating a feeling of increased well-being. Trying to find the part

of a plant that has a specific effect can be like disassembling a radio to search for the one part that makes the sound.

◆◆◆

Comprehension

1. Which diseases have been successfully treated with drugs made from the rosy periwinkle plant?
2. How do plants contribute to the development of prescription drugs?
3. According to the author, approximately how many people worldwide rely on plants for healing? Why?
4. Why do scientists' studies sometimes not result in useful and reliable data about the healing effects of plants?

Critical Thinking

1. How do you think the author feels about using plants as medicine?
2. Why do you think Americans' use of herbal remedies is increasing?
3. Do you think that herbal remedies are always reliable? Why or why not?
4. Does knowing about the potential healing qualities of plants affect your attitude toward preserving rain forests or natural wilderness areas? Explain your answer.

Language and Vocabulary

1. What does the symbol R_x, which is in the title of the reading, mean? How did you figure out the meaning? Have you seen this symbol anywhere before?
2. The last sentence of the reading includes a *simile*, a comparison using *like* or *as*, to explain how difficult it is to find the specific part of a plant that has a healing effect. What is examining a plant compared to? Does this simile create a clear picture of the situation? Give reasons for your answer.

Style, Structure, and Organization

1. Where in the reading does the author include a personal story about someone who has recovered from leukemia? Why does the author in-

clude this story? Is this the best place for it, or should it be in a different part of the article? Why?

2. At what points in the reading does the author include statistics? Why does he include these statistics? Do you think any of the statistics will surprise or shock readers? If so, why?

Topics for Discussion or Journal Writing

1. Do you believe in using herbal remedies? homeopathic medicines? vitamin or mineral supplements that are not endorsed by the Food and Drug Administration (FDA)? any other medicinal substances not prescribed by doctors? If so, discuss (or write about) why you believe these substances or remedies are effective.

2. Share a true story about the healing effect of anything other than traditional prescription or drug-store medicines. In addition to herbal remedies, you may want to consider such things as exercise, relaxation, meditation, prayer, or any form of alternative medicine.

3. In what other ways are plants important to us (besides their medicinal value)?

4. Is there a wilderness area or a forested area near where you live, or have you ever visited one? What kinds of interesting plants can be found there? Name as many native plants as you can and describe some of them.

5. Walk around your college campus and observe all the different kinds of plants, including trees. What are some of the most interesting plants? Try to identify them. (Hint: Check out a plant identification book from your library to help you.) This project can be done individually or collaboratively in groups.

Writing Topics for Paragraphs or Essays

1. Have you, or has anyone you know, used medicinal herbs or other plant remedies? If so, write a paper explaining which ones and how they have helped.

2. Using library resources or the Internet, look up information about poisonous plants, and find one that grows in your area. Write a paper about that plant, including information about how to identify it, what part of the plant is poisonous, and what to do if you accidentally come in contact with it.

3. Write a descriptive paper about any area that contains a variety of plants, either in their natural environment or in a landscaped area. Include plenty of visual details, as well as some details that use other senses, such as smell and touch.
4. Research more information about the rosy periwinkle, the foxglove plant, or another plant that is used medicinally, such as the Pacific yew, ginkgo, qing hao, aloe, or echinacea. Write a paper about your findings.
5. What disease or other health problem do you think is most threatening to the world's population in the twenty-first century? Why? What do you think should be done to find a cure or prevent the problem?

Monarchs' Migration: A Fragile Journey

William K. Stevens

One of the wonders of nature is the annual movement, or *migration,* of certain birds, butterflies, and other animals to find more favorable living conditions for the winter months. This reading tells about the fascinating journeys of monarch butterflies, with details about their lives that may come as a surprise to many readers.

Prereading Questions

1. Where do you think monarch butterflies spend the winter?
2. How do millions of butterflies get the message at the same time to travel someplace they have never been before?

Vocabulary

enclaves enclosed areas
cohort group
vigorous energetic
refuges places that offer protection
navigate plan and follow a certain course
retreats private and secure places
finery fine clothing (or something similar to fine clothing)
unerringly with no mistakes
mystique a mystical, almost spiritual quality
akin to similar to
quivering shaking or fluttering
reverence awe and respect
festooning decorating, hanging like streamers or garlands

SOURCE: "Monarchs' Migration: A Fragile Journey" by William K. Stevens. Excerpted from "Monarchs' Migration" by William K. Stevens, from *The Science Times Book of Insects* (The Lyons Press, 1998). Reprinted by special arrangement with the publisher.

climes climate areas

robust strong and healthy

chrysalis the pupa, enclosed in a protective shell, which later emerges as a butterfly

dormancy period of inactivity

on the deck almost on the ground

furious in this case, extremely active

dispersed scattered

Monarchs' Migration: A Fragile Journey

In the fir-covered mountains of southern Mexico, hundreds of millions of monarch butterflies packed in tight, brilliant clusters are now settling in for their winter rest after completing one of nature's most extraordinary feats. Each year, the insects migrate as far as 2,500 miles between their summer breeding grounds in the northern United States and Canada and their winter retreats in Mexico.

2   This splendid natural phenomenon can no longer be taken for granted. The butterfly's special wintering sites in 13 Mexican mountain enclaves—and in certain "monarch groves" in coastal California, where a smaller, separate cohort spends the winter—are threatened by logging and development. Vigorous conservation efforts in Mexico may have helped secure the monarch's refuges there. And voters in Pacific Grove, California, approved the $2 million purchase of a privately owned monarch grove to save it from development.

. . .

3   What makes the monarchs' migration so special is that the butterflies successfully navigate their path to wintering grounds they have never seen: The butterflies that leave the Mexican winter retreats to head back northward in the spring are the great-grandparents of those that return in the fall.

4   Catching rides from Canada to Mexico on winds and spiraling columns of warm air, these expert little gliders in orange and black finery set their course unerringly toward faraway destinations. Birds routinely migrate such long distances, but no other insects are known to do so. The returning monarchs, each born in the north, rely solely on navigational instructions programmed genetically into one of the tiniest of nervous systems.

. . .

5   . . . [T]he annual flight of the monarchs is part of an ecological relationship among the butterflies, their habitat and the climate that is as

fragile as the tissue-winged insects themselves. Conservationists wish to preserve the whole ecological framework because it is what makes possible the natural wonder of the migration. The monarch would disappear from almost all of North America if the migration ceased, although non-migrating populations would continue to exist in southern Florida and parts of the tropics.

6   Fortunately for the conservation effort, the monarch migration is beginning to acquire a mystique akin to that of the great whales and the African elephant. Growing numbers of tourists flock to marvel at the quivering masses of monarchs that festoon the trees in the wintering areas.

7   Residents of those areas invest the monarchs with a pride that sometimes borders on reverence. In Pacific Grove, they are the biggest thing in town. Motels are named for them. Children dressed in monarch costumes parade through the town each fall, when the butterflies appear.

8   In Mexico, the insects' arrival at the beginning of November coincides with a religious observance in which the butterflies, according to a mythology going back to pre-Columbian days, are seen as the returning souls of the dead. And in the United States, the monarch is a front-runner, along with the honeybee, in a continuing campaign to name a national insect.

9   The monarch's glamour, in the view of some conservationists, makes it an ideal test of the willingness of North Americans to care for an ecological treasure.

. . .

10   The United States enjoys two different populations of monarchs, one to the east of the Rockies and one to the west. The western monarchs spend the winter in the groves of California. Monarchs east of the Rockies are the offspring of butterflies that overwintered in Mexico.

11   The winter refuge in Mexico, discovered in 1974, consists of 13 compact wintering sites scattered in a small 75-by-35-mile area in the mountains 75 miles west of Mexico City.

12   The wintering area is just south of the Tropic of Cancer and its temperature is relatively stable. The butterflies roost in mountainside fir trees within a narrow altitude band ranging from 9,500 to 11,000 feet, their gaudy bodies sometimes festooning a tree so thickly that neither branch nor needle can be seen.

13   At the end of their autumn flight from colder climes, the monarchs arrive in Mexico robust and unmated, their brilliance as fresh as if they had just emerged from the chrysalis. They are superbutterflies with a nine-month life span, living longer than any others. In the spring, they awaken from their winter dormancy rushing pellmell to where the first milkweeds are coming up along the United States Gulf Coast.

14   "We don't know too much about their flight north, but we do know one thing—they're in more of a hurry" than on the fall return flight, said

Dr. David Gibo, a biologist at the University of Toronto who has studied the monarchs' flight habits. "It's a race to the milkweed."

15   Because of their haste, he said, the butterflies appear to use up much of their energy in flight so high-powered that although millions leave Mexico, relatively few reach the United States. Those that do arrive come in low, almost on the deck, males searching for females and both sexes searching for milkweeds.

16   This furious expenditure of energy drains the parent butterflies of life. Their offspring fly off northward, following the milkweed as it appears, and by summer have dispersed across the northern half of the United States east of the Rockies, ranging as far north as North Dakota, southern Ontario and Maine.

◆◆◆

Comprehension

1. What two areas do monarch butterflies travel to for the winter?
2. How do the monarch butterflies know where to go when they migrate?
3. What would happen to the monarch butterfly population in North America if the migrations no longer occurred?
4. What is different about the butterflies' behavior during their flight north in the spring?
5. How many generations of butterflies are involved in the southward migration and the return flight to the north? Which generation lives the longest?

Critical Thinking

1. Why are conservationists concerned about protecting the areas where monarch butterflies spend the winter?
2. Why is the monarchs' migration described in the title of this article as "a fragile journey"?
3. What effects do logging and development have on the habitats of insects such as the monarch butterfly? Can these activities threaten the survival of some species?
4. Why does the author refer to the monarch as "an ecological treasure"?
5. Why have the wintering areas of the monarchs become popular with tourists?

Language and Vocabulary

1. What does the word *navigate* usually refer to? Is this an effective word choice to refer to the monarchs' way of following a certain course? What does the author mean by "navigational instructions" in the fourth paragraph?
2. Were you familiar with the words *conservation* and *conservationists* before reading them in this article? What do these words mean? What are the primary concerns of conservationists?

Style, Structure, and Organization

1. Many newspaper and magazine articles begin with key information about the story: *Who? What? Where? When?* and *Why?* How many of these questions are answered in the first two paragraphs of this reading? What are the answers? (Hint: Although *who* normally refers to people, in this case it can refer to butterflies.)
2. Is the writer's purpose merely to inform readers, or is he also trying to persuade readers? How does the writer's purpose affect his style of writing?

Topics for Discussion or Journal Writing

1. How do you feel about butterflies and other types of insects? How do you feel about spiders? Why?
2. If the United States decides to select a national insect, do you think the monarch butterfly would be a good choice? Why or why not?
3. What other insects do you think are interesting or special in some way?
4. Did you ever watch a caterpillar spin a cocoon? Share your experience with the class, or write about it in your journal.

Writing Topics for Paragraphs or Essays

1. Write about a fascinating, scary, educational, or otherwise memorable experience you had involving a type of insect.
2. Find out more about monarchs and other types of butterflies by using library resources or the Internet. Then choose one of the following writing assignments:
   a. Compare and contrast butterflies and moths. Be sure to include a definition of each one.
   b. Describe one or more migration routes of the monarchs.

3. Over a period of two or three days, observe one type of insect or spider that lives in your area and write a descriptive paper about your observations.

4. Do some research and write a paper about a bird, fish, or mammal that migrates to a warmer climate or to a special breeding area to reproduce. You may want to use one of the following as your topic: swallows, Canadian geese, robins, bobolinks, salmon, gray whales, humpback whales, bats, sea turtles, or seals.

5. Select a topic that would be of special interest to conservationists, such as an animal species that is endangered or a unique forested area that is threatened by excessive logging or development. Write a paper that is both informative and persuasive.

Heavy Traffic on the Everest Highway

Geoffrey Tabin

Mount Everest, located between Nepal and Tibet, is part of the massive mountain system known as the Himalaya. Rising to an altitude of 29,028 feet, Everest is the world's highest mountain and presents special challenges for climbers. Geoffrey Tabin, who is well known as a mountain climber and a travel writer, describes the last part of the ascent in this excerpt from his book *Blind Corners*.

Prereading Questions

1. Why are some people attracted to sports that are physically demanding and dangerous, such as mountain climbing?
2. Do you think there are still places on the earth that no one has ever seen? Where might they be?

Vocabulary

sheer almost vertical, straight up or down

Hillary Step a steep notch in the ridge about 200 feet below the top of Everest

crampon a set of spikes that clamps onto a climber's boots for walking or climbing on ice

adrenaline a natural chemical that the body releases into the bloodstream in response to sudden stress; it raises blood pressure and speeds up the heartbeat

ambient surrounding

summit the top or peak of a mountain

cliché an expression that has been repeated so many times that it has become commonplace

vistas broad, sweeping views

SOURCE: Reprinted from *Blind Corners* © 1998 by Geoffrey Tabin with permission from *The Globe Pequot Press,* Guilford, CT, 1-800-962-0973, www.globe-pequot.com.

plateau a large, relatively flat area that rises higher than some other nearby areas

savor enjoy

solo alone, by one person

to commemorate to honor the memory of, in honor of

post-monsoon season after the season of heavy winds and rain

siege tactics specific strategies for a well-planned, long-range attack

sponsorship financial support

bidding in this case, stating one's intention or proposing to do something

foray attempt or venture

ardent extremely enthusiastic and serious

synonymous with equivalent to, having the same meaning

Heavy Traffic on the Everest Highway

The ridge I am climbing is barely two feet wide. To the east is a sheer drop of twelve thousand feet into Tibet. Westward it is eight thousand feet down to the next landing, in Nepal. The angle increases from seventy degrees to vertical at the Hillary Step. Climbing unroped, I delicately balance the crampon points on my right foot on an edge of rock. I swing my left foot, with all my remaining strength, into the adjoining ice. Precariously balanced on quarter-inch spikes attached to my boots, I gasp for breath. Forty feet higher the angle eases. Adrenaline mixed with joy surges through me. After eight hours of intense concentration, I know I will make it. The seventy-mile-an-hour wind threatens to blow me off the ridge. The ambient temperature is far below zero. Yet, I feel flushed with warmth. Ahead stretches a five-foot-wide walkway angled upward at less than ten degrees. Thirty minutes later, just after ten o'clock in the morning, the path ends in a platform of ice the size of a small desk. Everything is below me. I am the two hundred and ninth person to stand on the summit of Mount Everest.

2   The sky is deep blue and cloudless. The cliché is true, the vistas do seem to stretch infinitely in all directions. I look down over Lhotse, the world's fourth highest peak, upon the endless chain of mountains in Nepal. The Tibetan plateau on the other side extends to the horizon, where I can see the curve of the world dropping away. For fifteen minutes I savor the view as the highest person on earth. Then the crowds start to arrive.

3   Within an hour climbers from three countries are taking turns being photographed on the summit of Mount Everest. An American woman arrives on top. A Korean makes the climb solo to commemorate the October 2 closing ceremony of the Seoul Olympics. On the way down the woman, Peggy Luce, becomes snow-blind and then takes a near fatal fall before being rescued by the heroism of Dawa Tsering Sherpa. And this is one of the dullest days of the season.

4   Thirteen teams from ten countries made at least one attempt on every face and ridge on Mount Everest during the post-monsoon season of 1988. It was the first time that the Nepalese and Chinese gave out multiple permits for a mountain. Climbing styles ranged from siege tactics utilizing fixed camps, Sherpa porters, and supplemental oxygen to a solo, oxygenless, nonstop attempt from base camp. Everyone was out to set a record or do something new. Without a "first" it is nearly impossible to obtain sponsorship.

5   I was with the Northwest American Everest Expedition. Our team of eleven climbers, led by Seattle attorney Jim Frush, included three women bidding to become the first American woman to climb Mount Everest. The media played up this angle, as did our sponsors. Having been there before gave me a realistic perspective on the task ahead. Any success would have to be a team effort. Diana Dailey, Peggy Luce, and Stacy Allison were all selected for their climbing ability, strength, and personal qualities. They just happened to be women. On the mountain we would all be equal.

6   Chomolungma treats everyone equally. The Sherpa people and Tibetans, who live in her shadow, call the Goddess Mother of the Earth Chomolungma. They believe she resides in the mountain bearing her name. In 1842 the British survey of India calculated the height of Chomolungma to be 29,002 feet above sea level (it is actually 29,028 by modern measurements), and proclaimed it the highest mountain in the world. In 1863 the English renamed her Mount Everest, after Sir George Everest, a former Surveyor General of India, and proposed that she should be climbed. They brought Sherpa people along on their initial foray and were amazed by their strength at altitude and natural mountaineering talent. Moreover, as ardent followers of Mahayana Buddhism who believe that true Nirvana should be delayed until everyone on earth finds happiness, they are a delight to be with. They have accompanied so many expeditions that the name "Sherpa" has become synonymous with the job of high-altitude porter. Thirty Sherpas accompanied our expedition.

♦♦♦

Comprehension

1. What is the Sherpa name for Mount Everest, and what does it mean?
2. Based on what you learned in the reading, what are some of the challenges and difficulties involved in climbing Mount Everest?
3. How many other climbers besides the author were members of the same expedition, and how many Sherpas accompanied the expedition? What do we learn about some of the climbers on this team?
4. How many countries, nationalities, or ethnic groups are listed in this selection? List them and briefly explain what people of each country or nationality accomplished, or their connection with Mount Everest.

Critical Thinking

1. Scan the selection (quickly glance over it) for the words *Sherpa* and *Sherpas*. What did you learn about Sherpas from the reading?
2. Based on the reading, what kind of physical conditioning do you think Everest climbers and explorers need in order to reach the top and return alive?
3. Besides physical conditioning, what other qualities would be important for a climber to have in order to reach such a difficult goal?
4. How did Geoffrey Tabin feel about standing on top of Mount Everest? Do you think that his feelings changed when other climbers started to arrive?
5. Is the author trying to convey a message to the reader? If so, what is the message?

Language and Vocabulary

1. In the first four paragraphs of the reading, the author uses several terms that refer to land or rock formations, such as *ridge, drop, summit, plateau,* and *face*. Do you know what all of these terms mean? If not, try to guess at the meaning, and look up any terms you don't know. Then write a definition or draw a picture to illustrate each of these five terms.
2. Had you heard the term *base camp* before reading it in "Heavy Traffic on the Everest Highway"? What do you think the term means? Why do you think Everest climbers would need a base camp?

Style, Structure, and Organization

1. What point of view does the author have—is he a mountain climber, a reporter, or someone else? How does this point of view affect the way he writes?
2. Two of the writing techniques Geoffrey Tabin uses in this reading are *narration* (telling a story) and *description*. Highlight or underline at least two narrative sentences or passages and two descriptive sentences or passages. Which one of the four sentences or passages that you have marked do you like the best? Why?
3. Why do you think most of the sentences in the reading use present tense verbs? Find two places where the author changed to past tense verbs, and explain the reason for these changes.

Topics for Discussion or Journal Writing

1. What is the most adventurous thing you have ever done?
2. Would you like to climb Mount Everest someday? Why or why not?
3. Modern technology and the sheer number of people on earth mean that many special places will soon be overcrowded, if they aren't already. What is the most special outdoor place you have visited? Were a lot of people there? What was the most exciting or most rewarding part of your experience?
4. Have you ever experienced extreme weather conditions or an extreme physical challenge? If so, share your experience with the class or write about it in your journal.

Writing Topics for Paragraphs or Essays

1. Take a short hike, a bicycle ride, or a leisurely walk in an outdoor area near where you live. Describe what you saw, and include narrative details about anything interesting that happened.
2. Write about a place you visited where there was a crowd of people, but you would have preferred being alone.
3. Look up *global warming* on the Internet or in a library and write a cause and effect paper about it. Include either the causes of global warming or the results of global warming.

4. Read more about Mount Everest on the Internet or at a library. Then choose one of the following writing assignments:
    a. Write about the Sherpa people. Who are they, and what makes them special?
    b. Compare an early Everest expedition with a modern one.
5. Watch the IMAX film *Everest* about events on Mount Everest in 1996, when several experienced climbers lost their lives, or the movie *K2*, which is about an ascent of the world's second highest mountain, also located in the Himalaya. Then write a review that includes three sections: (1) a summary of the events; (2) details about the part you found most exciting, most shocking, or most interesting; and (3) your reaction and opinion.

♦♦♦

Death Valley

Doug and Bobbe Tatreau

Doug and Bobbe Tatreau spent many of their vacations in national parks, monuments, and recreation areas, taking pictures and doing research for their travel books. One of these books is *Parks of the Pacific Coast,* which this reading is taken from.

Death Valley was first designated as a national monument in 1933, and in 1994 the Desert Protection Act officially made the area a national park. Death Valley National Park contains more than 3 million acres of wilderness and includes many spectacular rock formations.

Prereading Questions

1. How do we benefit from having National Parks?
2. What kinds of natural settings are most appealing to campers, hikers, and other outdoor enthusiasts?

Vocabulary

ominous threatening or suggestive of something negative
blistering extremely hot
austere severe or somber in appearance
stark bare
pastel light-colored
meager sparse, small in quantity
alkaline containing various mineral salts
paradoxes things that seem to contradict each other yet are both true
pinyon a variety of pine trees with edible seeds (also spelled *piñon*)
pinnacles tall, pointed formations
torrential swiftly flowing water, a heavy downpour
treacherous dangerous, hazardous
lavishly abundantly
phenomena remarkable or amazing occurrences (plural of *phenomenon*)

remnants remains

potpourri mixture, variety

inserted put into something

plaque a sign or marker

arrowweed a desert plant

shocks in this case, stacks of corn or grain in an upright position for drying

vulnerable exposed or susceptible to possible injury

Death Valley

Death Valley—the name is ominous. the weather blistering, the land deceptively austere. Nevertheless, most visitors love this stark, majestic landscape, returning frequently to study the curious splendor of pastel mudhills, salt flats and the meager vegetation surviving despite the rocky, alkaline soil. Others complain the region is ugly—an unrelieved, barren panorama of grays and browns without the green usually associated with natural beauty. The decision is split. But whether you love Death Valley or hate it, you will remember it.

2   A terrain of paradoxes, Death Valley is more than a valley and it is certainly not dead. Though 20 percent of its land is below sea level (the lowest is 282 feet below), several mountain ranges parallel this 120-mile-long valley. The 11,049-foot Telescope Peak often wears a snowy cap even in late April. Pinyon and juniper forests crowd these higher reaches which remain cool in summer when the valley floor is sizzling.

3   In the center of the valley, little grows naturally. The salt creates attractive, humped pinnacles, but leaves the soil poisoned. The infrequent, sometimes torrential rain can be treacherous but, at the same time, it scrubs off the gray/brown surface to reveal the pinks, greens and purples of the hillside called Artist's Palette; if the timing is right, the moisture produces delicate spring blooms that lavishly decorate the valley floor.

4   There is another side of Death Valley to explore—the mining-boomtown phase during which man and sometimes his machines invaded the valley to reap its mineral riches. The unique natural phenomena and the remnants of the civilized invasion provide a potpourri of pursuits for the visitor. There is always much to see and do.

. . .

5   **Central Valley Region:** Between Stovepipe Wells and Badwater are the park's most popular features. Two miles east of Stovepipe Wells Village are the sand dunes, an unbroken display of sand hills that brings

out the child in all of us. The dunes are for walking but only during the cooler morning hours or at sundown, as the sand can be very warm.

6   Just north of the picnic area is the old stovepipe well and a historical plaque explaining that, when the dunes began to cover these valuable water sources, stovepipes were inserted to mark their locations.

7   In the same area, on the south side of Highway 190 is the Devil's Cornfield where clumps of arrowweed look like fat, stumpy corn shocks only a devil might cultivate.

8   Another popular feature is the Devil's Golf Course. The Golf Course is formed by sodium chloride (similar to table salt) which forms a crust over the mudfloor of what was once the ancient Manly Lake. The pinnacled artistry of salt and mud is intriguing but makes difficult walking as the salt can scratch vulnerable ankles. Five miles south of the Golf Course is Badwater, approximately 282 feet below sea level, the lowest point in the United States. It is actually a large salt pool tucked into the curve of the road bordering the valley.

◆◆◆

Comprehension

1. Why do visitors have differing opinions about Death Valley?
2. Why is there little vegetation in most parts of the park?
3. What are four of the most popular features in the Central Valley region of Death Valley?
4. What is the lowest point in the United States? What is its elevation?

Critical Thinking

1. As the authors point out, "Death Valley is more than a valley and it is certainly not dead." Why, then, do you think the area is called Death Valley? Do you think the name is appropriate? Why or why not?
2. Could camping or hiking in some parts of Death Valley National Park be dangerous? If so, what precautions should visitors observe?
3. Based on what you learned in this reading, why do you think Death Valley was selected to be a national park?
4. Why is it important to preserve wilderness areas and places of special geological interest, such as Death Valley? Give reasons for your answer.
5. What do you think was the authors' purpose in writing "Death Valley?" Did the authors' purpose affect the way they wrote this selection?

Language and Vocabulary

1. What do you think a "mining boomtown" is? Take a guess at the meaning, and then look up *boomtown* in a dictionary if necessary. How do you suppose being a mining boomtown at one time affected the Death Valley area?
2. Although readers may not be familiar with some of the terms used to identify features of the Death Valley area, such as *mudhills, salt flats, valley floor, pinnacles,* and *sand dunes,* in most cases it is possible to figure out the meaning. Choose two of these terms and explain what you think they mean. (Consult a dictionary if you need to check your answers.)

Style, Structure, and Organization

1. How does the introductory paragraph capture readers' attention? What part of the introduction makes you interested in finding out more about Death Valley?
2. Notice that each paragraph of this reading (after the introduction) focuses on one topic or one aspect of Death Valley. Make a list of the main topics covered in paragraphs 2–8. Which one of these paragraphs do you like best? Why?

Topics for Discussion or Journal Writing

1. In what ways is Death Valley different from other areas you have visited or read about?
2. After reading about Death Valley, do you think you would enjoy visiting the area? Why or why not?
3. Have you ever visited any national parks, national monuments, or national historic sites? If so, share your experiences with the class, or write about them in your journal.
4. If you could go anywhere in the United States for a vacation, where would you choose to go? What would you like to see there? What kinds of activities would you find most appealing?
5. If the United States government did not set aside park lands to preserve and protect them, what do you think would happen to unique areas, such as Death Valley (California), Mesa Verde (Colorado), the Grand Canyon (Arizona), Carlsbad Caverns (New Mexico), Mammoth Cave (Kentucky), or the Everglades (Florida)?

Writing Topics for Paragraphs or Essays

1. Write a descriptive paper about a place you have visited, including vivid details that will give readers a clear picture of the most interesting sights in the area. Use the Death Valley reading as a model for your writing.
2. Access a web site that offers information about Death Valley National Park, such as http://www.death.valley.national-park.com/info.htm. Look for additional information about the history, geology, climate, and/or wildlife of the Death Valley area that was not included in the reading selection, and write a paper about what you learn. (If you do not have Internet access, try consulting encyclopedias, travel brochures, magazine articles, or any other available sources of information.)
3. Create a travel brochure for a park or recreation area that you are interested in. Your brochure should feature information that would attract people to the park, such as special things to see and activities for visitors. If possible, include a few pictures.
4. Write an instructional paper about hiking, camping, mountain biking, rock climbing, or any other outdoor activity you know how to do. Include the reasons people enjoy the activity, the equipment that is needed, and precautions that people should be aware of.
5. Using a library or Internet resources, locate information about a national park in the United States or Canada, and write a paper that is informative as well as descriptive. The following are just a few of the parks you may want to consider for your topic: Rocky Mountain National Park (Colorado), Denali National Park (Alaska), Mesa Verde National Park (Colorado), Carlsbad Caverns (New Mexico), the Everglades (Florida), Acadia National Park (Maine), Banff National Park (Alberta, Canada), Pacific Rim National Park (British Columbia, Canada).

7

Technology and the Future

What'll They Think of Next? Melissa Melton and Barbra Murray 206

The 10-Minute Tech Inspection Peter Bohr 211

Tourist Trap James Hebert 217

Indistinguishable from Magic Robert L. Forward 222

The Mars Direct Plan Robert Zubrin 227

The World After Cloning Wray Herbert, Jeffrey L. Sheler, and Traci Watson 233

◆◆◆

What'll They Think of Next?

Melissa Melton and Barbra Murray

The pace of life is changing faster than it ever has before. Cutting-edge discoveries and inventions in electronics, computers, biotechnology, and other fields promise us a different lifestyle in the future, with new benefits as well as new challenges. As you read this article about future technology, consider which of these innovations will be most useful.

Prereading Questions

1. Why is it important for people, governments, and businesses to be able to predict the future?
2. How do people generally react to new inventions?

Vocabulary

innovations new inventions, new ways of doing things
corpuscles blood cells
implanting inserting
hemoglobin the main part of red blood cells
gene part of each cell that determines characteristics of a plant or an animal
fetch bring
mph miles per hour
depot central station
sensors sensing instruments
transmit send
guru teacher, leader in the field
virtual memos electronic memos (similar to e-mail)
thugs criminals, robbers

SOURCE: "What'll They Think of Next?" by Melissa Melton and Barbra Murray. Copyright January 3, 2000, *U.S. News & World Report*. Visit us at our Web site at www.usnews.com for additional information.

surfing the Net using the Internet
computer peripheral a device used with a computer, such as a printer
whiff a sniff or smell

What'll They Think of Next?

The eighteenth century produced the steam engine. The nineteenth yielded the light bulb. The twentieth gave us television and the Internet. So what's ahead in the twenty-first? Here are a few upcoming innovations that historians may—or may not—notice 100 years from now.

- *Crops of corpuscles.* You can't get blood from a turnip, but how about from corn? Tests at the French National Institute of Health and Medical Research indicate that artificial blood for human use can be made by implanting the hemoglobin-making gene into stalks of corn or leaves of tobacco. *Due date: 2003.*

- *Bionic nurse.* Space travel is just one of the roles envisioned for a robot that scientist Joseph Engelberger is helping NASA develop. Engelberger, who sold General Motors its first industrial robot for assembly-line work in 1961, wants the space agency's two-armed, voice-controlled machine to serve also as a health aide to the elderly. It would fetch sundries, assist with walking, and communicate with doctors. Engelberger even hopes it will detect changes in a depressed person's voice. "Talk to me about it," the robot would say. *Due date: 2005.*

- *Drive the friendly skies.* Highway traffic won't go down, so the only way to go is up. Moller International of Davis, Calif., expects its M400 Skycar to take off and land like a helicopter and cruise at 350 mph like an airplane. It would get 15 miles per gallon of fuel and, at $100,000, cost not a great deal more than some luxury automobiles. *Due date: 2010.*

- *Veinprints.* The patterns of veins on the backs of people's hands are as different as their fingerprints. The University of Pennsylvania has been testing a system, Veincheck, that opens dormitory doors once the back of a hand is scanned. The product, from England's Neuscience, likely will be used in coming years not just on doors but also on ATMs, helping curb the use of stolen bank cards. *Due date: 2000.*

- *Dr. Loo.* In 1910, at the Pennsylvania Railroad depot in Terre Haute, Ind., the first pay toilet was installed. It took your money. Now in the works is a high-tech toilet. It will take your temperature. Sensors on the health johnny also will monitor body weight and blood pressure and check the levels of sugar and protein in the urine of kidney disease and diabetes patients. The toilet, from Japanese electronics giant Matsushita, then will transmit the data to a physician. *Due date: 2003.*

- **Virtual Dilbert.** Virtual reality guru Jaron Lanier is leading a four-campus effort to create "telecubicles," work spaces that can be linked electronically. Cubicle walls become screens onto which distant colleagues are projected, and the worker's desk becomes part of a shared worktable across which virtual memos may be passed. *Due date: 2005.*

- **Smog cutter.** Auto mechanics of the future likely will be raising the hood to look at the "plasmatron." That's what MIT researchers call a device aimed at dramatically cutting emissions of nitrogen oxide, the main component in smog. Their invention, the size of a wine bottle, uses a mix of electronically charged particles, called "plasma," to help turn gasoline into a more efficient fuel, one that's rich in hydrogen. *Due date: 2005.*

- **Stiffing thugs.** A device being developed in San Diego gives new meaning to the police command "Freeze!" HSV Technologies Inc. says its "phaser weapon" emits a laser beam that painlessly and harmlessly immobilizes a suspect by causing his muscles to contract. The challenge now is to make the briefcase-size device as small as a handgun. *Due date: undetermined.*

- **The AOL smell.** Imagine an Italian restaurant ad in which the prospective customer, surfing the Net, not only sees the pasta but gets a whiff of garlic and oregano. DigiScents of Oakland, Calif., is developing a $200 hand-size computer peripheral that emits scents to match on-screen images. *Due date: 2000.*

◆◆◆

Comprehension

1. What institute is predicting that artificial blood will be produced by corn or tobacco plants?
2. According to predictions, when will the M400 Skycar be ready? What will it be able to do?
3. How could veinprints be used in the future?
4. Which items mentioned in the article could improve health care?

Critical Thinking

1. What is the authors' purpose in writing this article?
2. Which of the predicted inventions do you think will be most useful and most successful? Why?
3. Do you think that veinprints and other technology will reduce people's privacy in the future?
4. Can you think of any other areas where we will see major changes in the next 100 years?

Language and Vocabulary

1. What does the word *bionic* mean? If you are not sure, take a guess. Then try to find the word in a dictionary.
2. The word *telecubicles* is defined by the words that follow it as "work spaces that can be linked electronically." Find two other words in the reading that are defined by the words that follow them. Highlight the words and their definitions.

Style, Structure, and Organization

1. How would you describe the style of this article (direct, poetic, dramatic, formal, complex, etc.)?
2. This article is written in small chunks, each about a single topic, with no transitions between them. Does this pattern of organization work well for an article in a news magazine? Would it work well for an essay for a class?
3. Which sentence in the first paragraph states the main idea of this article?

Topics for Discussion or Journal Writing

1. If you knew what was going to happen in the future, what steps could you take to prepare?
2. What is one invention *not* listed in the article that you would like to see developed in the future?
3. Two of the innovations in the article have a *due date* of 2000. Do you think these items were actually ready for use in 2000? How could you find out?
4. How will technology change the way that people learn?
5. In your opinion, what is the single scariest thing about new technology, and why?

Writing Topics for Paragraphs or Essays

1. Write about a day in the life of an average person 100 years from now. Use your imagination, as well as what you know about recent advances in technology.
2. If you could invent one new machine, what would it be? Describe what it would do and how it would benefit people.
3. Write a scary or suspenseful story about a future where technology controls people's lives, instead of the other way around.
4. Using the Internet or a library, find some sources that try to predict the direction of future technology. Write a review of one book, one magazine article, or one web site. Include the author, title, date, page numbers, and other information about the source, such as the publisher (for a book) or the URL (web address). Begin with a short description of the source, and tell how interesting or useful it was to you.
5. Choose one of the following topics and find out more about it by searching online or in a library; then write about it.
    a. What is one of the most serious problems facing the world today, and how will it affect people's lives in the future?
    b. What is one of the most interesting or valuable areas of research today that will improve people's lives in the future? Consider some of the major discoveries that are being made, as well as some predictions.

The 10-Minute Tech Inspection

Peter Bohr

The automobile has played a huge part in American culture, starting with the Ford Model T and Model A in the early 1900s. Today's automobiles are safer and more economical than those of previous decades, and they don't require as much maintenance. However, there are some important checks that drivers should make on a regular basis.

Prereading Questions

1. Do you think that most people know how to take good care of their cars?
2. What are some problems that can happen if an automobile is not well maintained?

Vocabulary

teeth-gnashing grinding one's teeth together (in this case, showing extreme annoyance)

tune-ups adjustments that help the car run better

odds chances

stranded stuck without transportation

a host a large number

microprocessors microcomputers

melts down breaks down completely

avert avoid, prevent

paraphernalia miscellaneous equipment

gizmo gadget, device

translucent allowing light to come through

frayed somewhat shredded on the edges

(battery) terminals the positive and negative contacts

lodged stuck

fifty-fifty half and half

car-savvy friend a friend who knows a lot about cars

The 10-Minute Tech Inspection

Want to see a mechanic have an eye-bulging, teeth-gnashing fit? Just suggest that your new Super Whizmobile is "maintenance-free" because its maker advertises that it can go 100,000 miles between tune-ups.

2   "Hi-tech advances in cars have greatly reduced the frequency of maintenance intervals," says Auto Club automotive expert Steve Mazor. "But ignoring basic maintenance greatly increases the odds of being stranded with car trouble."

3   Your car's engine may be controlled by a host of microprocessors but they won't keep it running if the engine melts down because you failed to notice that the radiator ran out of coolant. Such problems do occur. In fact, nearly three-quarters of the roadside assistance calls made by the Auto Club's contracted tow-truck operators involve troubles—flat tires and starting problems, for example—that could have been avoided if the cars' owners had done a little preventive poking around.

4   So roll up your sleeves, because I'm going to acquaint you with your car's vital checkpoints. Taking the time to perform a few simple procedures might just help you avert a costly, irritating, and possibly dangerous breakdown.

5   Make sure the car is on a level surface with the engine off. Pop open the hood. Can you find the engine? Good. Actually, that's quite an accomplishment, what with sideways-mounting engines and all the complex paraphernalia automakers hang on them these days.

6   Find the oil dipstick; it's usually located alongside the engine (A good rule of thumb is to check your owner's manual if you have any doubt about what some gizmo might be, especially if you're going to add fluid. The Pennzoil–Quaker State oil folks did a survey and discovered that car owners put fluids in the strangest places—motor oil in the radiator, transmission fluid in the crankcase, and water just about everywhere. Not good.)

7   Next, pull out the dipstick, wipe it off, stick it all the way back in, and pull it out again. Can you see an oil mark between the hatch marks? If not, add some oil (your owner's manual will tell you what kind) and recheck the level. If you need to add more than a quart, take the car to your repair shop and find out why it's losing so much oil.

8   Make sure the engine is cold, and then find the plastic radiator-overflow tank. If it's translucent, can you see colorful liquid inside that

looks like Kool-Aid? If you can't see through the side, remove the cap and look in. If there's no fluid, pour in some radiator coolant. Many overflow tanks have fluid-level indicators on the side that make it easy to tell how much to add. Otherwise, check your owner's manual for the amount and type of coolant (you can add water in a pinch).

9   If the radiator needs more than a half quart to fill it, better have your mechanic take a look at it. Also, the color of the coolant should be vivid; if it looks like dirty dishwater, it's time to have it changed.

10   While you're checking out the radiator, examine the hoses. Are they cracked or brittle-looking? Do they have any bulges, or are they squishy-soft? If so, have them replaced. You probably won't find the right size in a small-town gas station if a hose bursts on your next trip out of town.

11   Find the belts that run the alternator, air-conditioning compressor, and perhaps the radiator cooling fan. Inspect them to make sure they're not cracked or frayed. Find the automatic transmission-fluid dipstick; follow the procedure outlined in your owner's manual to check the level. Uncontaminated fluid should be red or pinkish. If the fluid looks black or smells burned, better have it changed. Find the brake-fluid reservoir and check to see that it's filled to the proper level.

12   Now locate the battery. Be sure the cables are tightly secured to the terminals. If the terminals look like they've grown moss, gently scrub them with an old toothbrush and a fifty-fifty mix of baking soda and water. If the battery's a refillable type, take off the caps and check all six cells to see that water reaches up to about an eighth of an inch from the top. If not, add distilled water. If there's corrosion in the pan (the shelf where the battery sits), have your mechanic check the battery case for leaks. (And by the way, when you're inspecting a battery, always wear eye protection and never smoke.)

13   Next, start the engine. Look under the hood (be sure to keep your fingers, hair, and clothing away from moving parts). Do you see a fan whirring near the radiator? Does the engine settle into a smooth idle after it warms up, or does it run unevenly? Do you hear any ominous sounds? If something sounds odd, have your mechanic check it out.

14   Get down on your hands and knees and look under the vehicle. Your car may hold nearly a dozen fluids of one sort or another; all of them should be in the car, not on the driveway. Note any rusty holes in the exhaust system. If your car has front-wheel drive, look just behind the front wheels. If you see a greasy mess, the rubber boots covering the constant velocity (CV) joints might be torn. Have your mechanic take a look before the CV joints become ruined from grit getting into the bearings.

15   Next, turn on all the lights and walk around the car to see that they work (have a friend help you check the brake lights). Look at the windshield wipers; make sure they're not deteriorated, or you may wind up

with a scratched windshield. Be sure the windshield-washer reservoir is filled with wiper fluid.

16   Now look at the tires. Do they have plenty of tread? Are the sidewalls cracking? Look for nails or screws lodged in the tread, which could cause a slow leak. Inspect the front tires closely for signs of uneven wear. If they're scalloped or worn excessively on one side, either the suspension is worn or your car has an alignment problem. Buy a tire gauge and check your tire pressures, including the spare.

17   If all this sounds intimidating, ask your mechanic or a car-savvy friend to show you what's under the hood. Then perform this inspection every couple of weeks, and you can rest secure in the knowledge that you've done all you can to avoid problems down the road.

◆◆◆

Comprehension

1. Who is Steve Mazor?
2. Why should people perform a quick inspection every few weeks?
3. What things should you check under the hood while the engine is off? (List at least six things.)
4. What things should you look for underneath the car?

Critical Thinking

1. What is the main idea of this reading selection?
2. Does regular maintenance cost money or save money in the short run? What about in the long run?
3. By checking your car regularly, can you guarantee that it will never have any mechanical problems?
4. Do you think the author practices what he preaches?

Language and Vocabulary

1. What does *whirring* mean? If you aren't sure of the meaning of a word, try to guess the meaning from the way it is used in the reading before looking it up in a dictionary.
2. In this selection, the author uses a lot of terms that refer to specific parts of a car. Some of them are *engine, tires, CV joints,* and *suspension.* Find five or six other terms that refer to parts of a car. If you are unsure of the

meaning of any of these words, look them up in a dictionary or ask someone who knows a lot about cars.

Style, Structure, and Organization

1. Where is the main idea of this reading stated—near the beginning, at the end, or both? Is this an effective way to begin or end a short essay?
2. In some paragraphs, the author uses words such as *next* and *while* as transitions that lead from one set of instructions to the next. Find two more words that the author uses as transitions. Do they sound natural in the reading?
3. This selection has 17 short paragraphs. Does each paragraph have its own unique topic? Choose 6 paragraphs and list the topic for each one. For example, paragraph 14 could be listed as "Under the car."

Topics for Discussion or Journal Writing

1. What kind of transportation do you use on a daily basis? Do you ever use other types of transportation? How do you feel about each type of transportation you use?
2. Are you good about performing preventive maintenance on your vehicles and other equipment? Why or why not?
3. Have you ever been in a car when it broke down? How did you feel about the experience?
4. How do you feel about these instructions? Do you think you could follow these steps and possibly prevent a mechanical breakdown?
5. In your opinion, will more people drive cars in the future, or fewer? Why?

Writing Topics for Paragraphs or Essays

1. Write about one time when you worked on a car, even if it was just helping someone else. If you have never worked on a car, imagine what the experience would be like.
2. On your own car (or on another person's car after getting permission), perform the steps listed in the reading, and make a note of what you find at each step. Then write a narrative paragraph telling what you found, including an introduction and a conclusion.
3. Write about one time you were in a car or another vehicle and it broke down. How did the story end?

4. Go online or to a library and find ratings for various cars. (Consumer's Union or *Consumer Reports* might be a good place to start.) Then choose one car and write a paper that tells its advantages and disadvantages.

5. Choose one of the following topics and write a short instructions paper about it.

   a. What are some useful tips that can help students learn effectively and earn good grades?

   b. What are some useful tips on how to manage money?

   c. What are some useful tips for taking care of a dog, a cat, a bird, or another type of pet?

Tourist Trap

James Hebert

The idea of time travel is amazingly attractive, partly because it offers the possibility of living another life, in another time. Although "real" time travel remains a physical impossibility today, the mind accepts no such barriers. As you read this newspaper feature article, look for the connection between time travel, history, and great literature.

Prereading Questions

1. If people could travel in time, do you think that most people would choose to travel into the past or into the future? Why?
2. Why are great novels so popular? How do they make people feel?

Vocabulary

traversing crossing or going through
mere unimportant
to chill to visit, to hang out (slang)
fiddle with make some small changes or adjustments
long-vanquished diseases diseases that have been eliminated for a long time
thus therefore, for that reason
void empty space
notions ideas, impressions
spawned gave birth to, originated
genre type of writing
a vividly realized past a past time that seems very much alive and real
elucidates explains in detail
bonds in this case, connections
gizmos gadgets, devices
shackles of the finite in this context, the limitations of mortality

Tourist Trap

It's difficult to contemplate the concept of time travel without getting into some very serious weirdness.

An example: If you hitch a ride into the past on a time machine and prevent your parents from meeting, does that mean you won't be born? And if you weren't born, how could you have gone back in time in the first place?

3   Those who study the idea of time travel have a word for these little hang-ups: paradoxes.

4   There are many of them—not the least of which is that if time travel will ever exist, then it must, in a sense, exist right now. (In fact, there could be time travelers from the future among us at this moment.)

5   But no mere paradox has ever kept people from dreaming about traversing time, about going back 400 years to chill with Bill Shakespeare or journeying forward a century or so to play catch with one's own great-grandkids.

6   Ideas about the mechanics of time travel may have changed greatly between, say 1895, when H. G. Wells wrote *The Time Machine*, and 1985, when Hollywood made *Back to the Future*.

7   But the motivations are no different: To break free from the tyranny of time, to race ahead and see splendors to come, or go back and relive historic events. And maybe, just maybe, even fiddle with a few things.

8   So: Is it possible? Is there a chance that humans will ever travel through time?

9   Well, don't book your vacation for Renaissance Italy just yet. For one thing, you'll need *a lot* of vaccinations, lest you come back and infect the 20th Century with long-vanquished diseases.

10   For another, no one on Earth is anywhere near ready to build a working time machine right now (a few highly suspect claims on the Internet notwithstanding).

11   But—and this is a very qualified "but"—some physicists believe there is a theoretical basis for the possibility of time travel through wormholes—tunnels that, according to quantum physics, could act as "shortcuts" between points in space and time.

12   One problem: No one has ever actually seen a wormhole, although tiny ones are believed to lurk in something called "quantum foam," strange stuff that is believed to exist at the subatomic level—in other words, it's very, very tiny.

13   Another problem: Even if wormholes are real, no one has any idea how one would go about enlarging them or harnessing them for use in time travel.

14   A more straightforward, if as yet unattainable, method of traveling into the future would be simply to hop on a spaceship and accelerate to near the speed of light. Moving at this speed actually slows down time, at least relative to a stationary observer.

15   Thus, when you returned home after a couple of years, time (at least for earthlings) could have advanced by centuries. And everyone here would have forgotten you. Except, of course, for the Internal Revenue Service.

16   With the time-travel theories of scientists either too hard to grasp or just too darned dry, science fiction has leapt into the void, offering its own notions of how to fool Father Time.

17   Many of the stories and movies on the subject fall into the Barcalounger School of Time Travel: Basically, you plop into a chair attached to a time machine (or car, or spacecraft) of mysterious construction, and—boom!—24th Century, here we come. Think of Wells' *The Time Machine,* or the movies *Back to the Future* and *Twelve Monkeys.*

18   Other stories have offered more romantic notions of time travel. In both the novel *Time and Again* and the movie *Somewhere in Time* (adapted from a novel), the main characters journey back in time through little but sheer willpower.

19   Both happen to be love stories. *Time and Again* was produced as a musical at San Diego's Old Globe Theatre three years ago. *Somewhere in Time,* released in 1981, has amassed such a cult following that its fans hold regular conventions and its Web site offers a range of movie-themed collectibles.

20   Some writers, turning away from the idea of physically traveling through time, have jumped straight ahead to deal with the possible consequences of changing the past. They've spawned a highly popular genre, the alternative history.

21   What if John F. Kennedy had survived his wounds? What if Hitler could have been stopped before Germany invaded Poland?

22   Alternative historians start with such ideas, and then construct whole new worlds around them—traveling through time into universes that might have been.

23   And in a sense, great literature offers a kind of time travel, too. Not only can it transport a reader back to a vividly realized past, but it also can carry the writer forward into our own time, so that he or she speaks to us as if sitting in the same room.

24   No one knew this better than the American poet Walt Whitman. In "Crossing Brooklyn Ferry," one of his most affecting works, Whitman

addresses the reader directly, as if to dismiss the very notion of a barrier between his time and ours.

25   He elucidates the bonds between our worldly experiences and his—*Just as you feel when you look on the river and sky, so I felt*—and then says:

> What is it then between us?
> What is the count of the scores of hundreds of years between us?
> Whatever it is, it avails not—distance avails not, and place avails not.

26   Without wormholes or gizmos or strange devices of any kind—with nothing but words on a page—the poet has broken the shackles of the finite and leaped straight into the present.

27   Human imagination. Now *there's* a time machine.

◆◆◆

Comprehension

1. Who wrote *The Time Machine?* When was it published?
2. Are there really "wormholes" in time?
3. What kind of stories are *Somewhere in Time* and *Time and Again*? How do they relate to time travel?
4. Which Whitman poem does the author quote from?

Critical Thinking

1. What is one paradox that might be associated with actual time travel?
2. What do you think is the author's main point about time travel?
3. How does the author feel about science fiction, literature, and poetry?
4. In what way can great literature be a sort of time machine?
5. Why do you think this article was called "Tourist Trap"?

Language and Vocabulary

1. What is a *paradox*? If you don't know, find it in the reading and make your best guess. Then look it up in a dictionary. Was your guess close to the actual meaning?
2. What is an *alternative history*? Come up with an example of your own.

Style, Structure, and Organization

1. This article is divided roughly into three parts: "real" time travel, science fiction, and great literature. Which parts are the most—or the least—interesting to you? How are all three parts related?
2. As a newspaper article, this selection includes 27 short but effective paragraphs. Would you expect to see a similar organization in a paper written for a college class (other than journalism)? How would an academic-style essay be different?

Topics for Discussion or Journal Writing

1. Do you think people will ever travel in time?
2. If you had the choice, would you choose to travel in time or would you live your life out in the present? Why?
3. What do you think the greatest benefit of time travel might be?
4. Have you ever read any books or watched any television shows or movies that featured time travel? What were their titles? How did they portray time travel?

Writing Topics for Paragraphs or Essays

1. Use your imagination to describe how life will be different 20, 40, or 100 years from now. Tell how technology might have advanced, and describe some of the things that you might see around you.
2. If you could travel back in time, what time period would you choose? Why are you interested in that time period? Is there something in particular that you would like to learn about that period of history?
3. Write a short alternative history telling what the world would be like today if history had taken a different turn. For example, how would our lives be different today if Native Americans had "discovered" Europe, instead of the other way around?
4. Have you ever read a book or story that made another time seem very real? Write a short critique of the book or story. Give the author, title, number of pages, publisher, year, and type of story. Then write a short summary of the story. Include your reactions and opinions. (For example, did the author use vivid description? Could you identify with one of the characters?)
5. Write a short summary of "Tourist Trap" and tell your reaction to it—does the topic interest you? Why or why not?

222   ◆   Part 7 / Technology and the Future

◆◆◆

Indistinguishable from Magic

Robert L. Forward

Robert L. Forward holds a Ph.D. in gravitational physics, and that's just the beginning of his qualifications to write on interstellar travel. He has written more than 150 technical articles, holds 20 patents, and owns a company that has been awarded millions of dollars in contracts for space technology. As you read this selection, look for two possible ways that humans might travel to the stars.

Prereading Questions

1. Is the topic of space travel popular today? Do most people think that humans will ever reach the stars?
2. What books, videos, or TV shows on space travel are popular today?

Vocabulary

puny small and weak
the human race earth people
evoked in this case, imagined
space warps possible shortcuts through space
benevolent good
folly foolishness
gulf a huge gap or empty space
resign (oneself) sadly accept
interstellar between stars
robotic probes unmanned spacecraft with instrument packages
amenities luxuries, extras
squadron group
suspended animation a condition of minimal or no body functions, with the objective of extending a human life span

Indistinguishable from Magic

It was only a few centuries ago that the human race realized those bright lights in the night sky were suns, like our Sun. We then realized that those other suns probably had worlds orbiting around them, some possibly like our world. Since that time, one of the dreams of the human race has been to visit those other worlds in ships that travel between the stars. But as we began to realize the immensity of the distances that separate our star from the other stars, we began to despair of ever building a starship using the puny technology that the human race controls.

2   Science fiction writers, in an attempt to get their storybook heroes to the stars before the readers got bored, evoked starships with faster-than-light drives, space warps, and other forms of future technology that were indistinguishable from magic. At the same time, the general public evoked fantasy starships in the form of flying saucers flown *to* the Earth *from* other stars. These starships were propelled by antigravity or magnetism, and were piloted by benevolent little green men who would save the world from its folly.

3   If little green men can cross the great gulf, can we?

4   Yes. It is difficult to go to the stars, but it is not impossible. The stars are far away, and the speed of light limits us to a slow crawl along the starlanes. To travel to the stars will take years of time, gigawatts of power, kilograms of energy, and billions (if not trillions) of dollars. Yet it can be done—if we wish to. And if we decide to go, what kind of starships can we build?

5   It turns out that there are many types of starships possible, each using a different technology. There are some starships that we can build now. For these technologies we know the basic physical principles and have demonstrated the ability to achieve the desired reactions on a laboratory scale. All that is needed is the application of large amounts of money, material, and manpower. There are also some promising starship designs that use future technology that is barely distinguishable from magic. Here we know the basic physical principles, but we have not yet controlled the future technology in the laboratory. Once we have turned that future technology from magic into reality, we can then proceed with starship designs based on those technologies.

6   No matter how fast we can make a starship go, we must resign ourselves to the fact that interstellar travel will always take a long time. Even if we had a starship that traveled at the speed of light, it would take over 4.3 years to travel to the nearest star system, then another 4.3 years before a message (or the starship) returns. We don't have speed-of-light starships yet, and won't for a long time.

7   The first travelers to the stars will be our robotic probes. They will be small and won't require all the amenities like food, air, and water that humans seem to find necessary. The power levels to send the first squadron of robotic probes out to the stars are within the present reach of the human race. If we wanted to, we could have the first interstellar probe on the way to the nearest star system early in the next millennium.[1]

. . .

8   Scientists studying hibernating animals have found the hormone that initiates hibernation and have used the drug to induce hibernation in other animals. Whether this drug will induce hibernation in humans without causing serious side effects is unknown. Also, it is unknown whether hibernation actually increases lifespan, or just makes living possible when there is insufficient food. Still, there is enough biological research on suspended animation that one of these days we may use that method of keeping a crew alive long enough to carry out century-long exploration missions.

9   Even if these particular biological techniques do not turn into a real suspended animation capability, there is another method to carry out a slowship mission: let the people die, but allow their children to carry on. A slowship journey to the stars will send a colony of people off in a generation starship. Although only the first generation would be true volunteers, with enough thought and planning we could turn the slow-moving starship into a truly acceptable worldship, with all the amenities and few of the problems of living on Earth.

10   The important thing to realize is that our present technology can take us to the stars. To be sure, our first robotic interstellar probes will be slow, will consume a lot of power and money, and will return small amounts of data.

11   It is difficult to go to the stars. But it is not impossible. There are not one, but many, many future technologies, all under intense development for other purposes, that, if suitably modified and redirected, can give the human race a magic starship that will take us to the stars.

12   And go we will.

❖❖❖

Comprehension

1. What fantasies does the general public have about "little green men"?
2. According to the author, who or what will be the first travelers to the stars?

---

[1][*Indistinguishable from Magic* was published in 1995, so we are already in the "next" millennium.]

3. Do speed-of-light starships exist yet? How long would it take a starship traveling at the speed of light to reach the nearest star system?
4. What are two possible ways that humans might reach the stars?

Critical Thinking

1. Who is the author's intended audience—is the author primarily writing to other scientists or to the general public?
2. What would be some possible benefits of traveling to the stars?
3. Based on this reading selection, how do you think the author feels about space travel?
4. This selection is taken from the book *Indistinguishable from Magic*. Why do you think the author chose this title? Is it a good title for this topic?

Language and Vocabulary

1. What does *hibernation* mean? Try to figure out the meaning of the word from the way it is used in the reading, and then check a dictionary if necessary.
2. What do you think the author means by the terms *generation starship* and *worldship*?

Style, Structure, and Organization

1. Do you think the author's technical articles would be written in the same style as this reading selection or in a different style? Why?
2. The concluding paragraph of this selection consists of just four words: "And go we will." Are conclusions usually this short? Is the conclusion effective?
3. Find another paragraph that consists of just one short sentence. Why do you think the author chose to use such short paragraphs? Which have a more dramatic feel, short sentences or long sentences?

Topics for Discussion or Journal Writing

1. Do you think that humans will ever travel to the stars? If so, do you think it will happen in your lifetime?
2. Would you like to go to the stars someday? Why?

3. Which of the technologies mentioned in the reading seems the most likely to succeed?
4. What are some reasons *not* to travel to the stars?
5. In your opinion, will governments ever invest the huge amounts of money necessary to develop star travel?

Writing Topics for Paragraphs or Essays

1. Imagine that you are a traveler on a generation starship. Write about a typical day on the starship.
2. Think of a new technology that would seem like magic. Describe the technology and how people might react to it.
3. Have you ever had a comical or frustrating experience with technology? Write about what happened and how you felt at the time.
4. Go online or to a library and look up information about Robert L. Forward. A good place to start might be http://www.forwardunlimited.com/index.html. Write a short biography of his life.
5. Read a science fiction story by Robert L. Forward or another author. Then choose one of the following topics:

    a. What new technology was in the story? Write about each type of new technology and whether you think it will ever be invented.

    b. In the story, how has technology affected people? Write about the effects of the story's future technology on individuals or on the society.

The Mars Direct Plan

Robert Zubrin

The author of this article, Robert Zubrin, has written more than 100 articles on space travel and Mars exploration. Although traditional space programs are extremely expensive, in this article the author proposes a practical way to send a manned mission to Mars only a few years from now. As you read the article, consider if this proposal might become a reality in your lifetime.

Prereading Questions

1. What are some of the possible benefits of sending a scientific exploration team to Mars?
2. What are some major obstacles that might prevent or delay a successful manned mission to Mars?

Vocabulary

coherent organized, complete

embodying representing or including

booster rockets rockets that help boost the spacecraft into orbit

stage the section of the rocket that falls off when it has used up its fuel, or one part of a larger project

unmanned without any people on board

payload the most important part of the spacecraft: the people and/or equipment needed to complete the mission

trajectory a path or course through space

compressors machines that compress gases (in order to refuel the rockets)

cargo the equipment and supplies being carried

retrorockets rockets that fire forward in order to slow the spacecraft

deploys starts and begins to use

cryogenic frozen

propellant the fuel that moves or propels the rocket

SOURCE: From "The Mars Direct Plan" by Robert Zubrin. Copyright © March 2000 by *Scientific American, Inc.* All rights reserved.

feedstock the raw materials from which a larger quantity of materials can be produced

inaugural first, original

hurl throw, propel

ground rover a vehicle for getting around on Mars

cherish treasure, hold dear

put our stamp on the future influence future generations

beyond reckoning impossible to measure adequately

The Mars Direct Plan

"Space is there, and we are going to climb it." These words from President John F. Kennedy in 1962 set forth the goal of sending an American to the moon within the decade. But for most of the 30 years since the Apollo moon landing, the U.S. space program has lacked a coherent vision of what its next target should be. The answer is simple: the human exploration and settlement of Mars.

2   This goal is not beyond our reach. No giant spaceship built with exotic equipment is required. Indeed, all the technologies needed for sending humans to Mars are available today. We can reach the Red Planet with relatively small spacecraft launched directly to Mars by booster rockets embodying the same technology that carried astronauts to the moon more than a quarter of a century ago. The key to success lies with the same strategy that served the earliest explorers of our own planet: travel light and live off the land. The first piloted mission to Mars could reach the planet within a decade. Here is how the proposed plan—what I call the Mars Direct project—would work.

3   At a not too distant date—perhaps as soon as 2005—a single, heavy-lift booster rocket with a capability equal to that of the Saturn 5 rockets from the Apollo era is launched from Cape Canaveral, Fla. When the ship is high enough in Earth's atmosphere, the upper stage of the rocket detaches from the spent booster, fires its engine and throws a 45-metric-ton, unmanned payload on a trajectory to Mars.

4   This payload is the Earth Return Vehicle, or ERV, which, as the name implies, is built to bring astronauts back to Earth from Mars. But on this voyage no humans are on board; instead the ERV carries six tons of liquid-hydrogen cargo, a set of compressors, an automated chemical-processing unit, a few modestly sized scientific rovers, and a small 100-kilowatt nuclear reactor mounted on the back of a larger rover powered by a mixture of methane and oxygen. The ERV's own methane-oxygen tanks, which will be used during the return trip, are unfueled.

5   Arriving at Mars eight months after takeoff, the ERV slows itself down with the help of friction between its heat shield and the planet's atmosphere—a technique known as aerobraking. The vehicle eases into orbit around Mars and then lands on the surface using a parachute and retrorockets. Once the ship has touched down, scientists back at mission control on Earth telerobotically drive the large rover off the ERV and move it a few hundred meters away. Mission control then deploys the nuclear reactor, which will provide power for the compressors and the chemical-processing unit.

6   Inside this unit, the hydrogen brought from Earth reacts with the Martian atmosphere—which is 95 percent carbon dioxide (CO_2)—to produce water and methane (CH_4). This process, called methanation, eliminates the need for long-term storage of cryogenic liquid-hydrogen fuel, a difficult task. The methane is liquefied and stored, and the water molecules are electrolyzed—broken apart into hydrogen and oxygen. The oxygen is then reserved for later use; the hydrogen is recycled through the chemical-processing unit to generate more water and methane.

7   Ultimately, these two reactions, methanation and electrolysis, provide 48 tons of oxygen and 24 tons of methane, both of which will eventually be burned as rocket propellant for the astronauts' return voyage. To ensure that the mixture of methane and oxygen will burn efficiently, an additional 36 tons of oxygen must be generated by breaking apart the CO_2 in the Martian atmosphere. The entire process takes 10 months, at the end of which a total of 108 tons of methane-oxygen propellant has been generated—18 times more propellant for the return trip than the original feedstock needed to produce it.

8   The journey home will require 96 tons of propellant, leaving an extra 12 tons for the operation of the rovers. Additional stockpiles of oxygen can also be produced, both for breathing and for conversion into water by combining the oxygen with the hydrogen brought from Earth. The ability to produce oxygen and water on Mars greatly reduces the amount of life-supporting supplies that must be hauled from Earth.

9   With this inaugural site on Mars operating successfully, two more boosters lift off from Cape Canaveral in 2007 and again hurl their payloads toward Mars. One of these is an unmanned ERV just like the one launched in 2005. The other, however, consists of a manned vessel with a crew of four men and women with provisions to last three years. The ship also brings along a pressurized methane-oxygen-powered ground rover that will allow the astronauts to conduct long-distance explorations in a shirtsleeve environment.

. . .

10   Someday millions of people will live on Mars. What language will they speak? What values and traditions will they cherish as they move

from there to the solar system and beyond? When they look back on our time, will any of our other actions compare in importance with what we do now to bring their society into being? Today we have the opportunity to be the parents, the founders, the shapers of a new branch of the human family. By so doing, we will put our stamp on the future. It is a privilege beyond reckoning.

Comprehension

1. How soon could the first piloted mission actually reach Mars?
2. What is an ERV?
3. What kind of fuel would the returning spaceship use, and how would the astronauts get the fuel?
4. Does the author believe that humans will successfully colonize Mars someday?

Critical Thinking

1. What is the author's main point about the Mars Direct plan?
2. What is the advantage of this plan over a "regular" space trip, such as the moon landing in the 1960s?
3. Why would the Mars Direct plan be cheaper than a "regular" mission to Mars?
4. Do you think that this article was written for space scientists or for educated members of the general public? Why do you think so?
5. What is the author's tone—optimistic or pessimistic? Why do you think so?

Language and Vocabulary

1. In this article, the author includes some expressions that use the passive voice—for example, "No giant spaceship built with exotic equipment is required." Find two more sentences that have the passive voice. (Hint: Look for a form of the verb "to be" plus the past participle of another verb, like "is required.") Does the use of the passive voice make the reading seem technical?
2. What does the expression "put our stamp on the future" mean in the final paragraph? If you are not sure of the meaning, make a guess based on the other information you read in the article.

Style, Structure, and Organization

1. Do you think that most college students could understand this article? How would the style be different if it were written for middle school or high school students instead? How would it be different if it were written exclusively for scientists?
2. The body of the paper tells the reader the steps of the Mars Direct plan, and it is organized in chronological order—that is, one step after another, in the order that the steps would happen. Do you think this organizational style works well for this article?

Topics for Discussion or Journal Writing

1. Is space travel worth the cost when there are so many problems still to solve here on Earth? What would be some benefits of space travel?
2. Do you think that the first Mars explorers will discover life or maybe ruins of past civilizations? If there is life on Mars, how would it survive, and what might it look like?
3. Would there be interpersonal problems involved with four astronauts living in such a small environment for three years? Would you be able to put up with living in constant close contact with other people for that length of time?
4. The final paragraph of the reading discusses social issues associated with a Mars mission. Are you more interested in the science and engineering topics or in the social issues of a space voyage like this one?

Writing Topics for Paragraphs or Essays

1. If you were working on a Mars mission, would you prefer to work as part of the support crew on earth or to travel to Mars yourself? Why?
2. If there is life on other planets, what would they think of the human race? Write a short essay describing human society from an alien point of view.
3. Use your imagination to describe the first Mars colony. Write about the daily life of the people living there.
4. Read a science fiction story about people traveling to another planet and write a review of the book. Give the author, title, number of pages, publisher, and year it was published; then write a short summary of the story. Finally, explain what effect the book had on you and why.

5. Find out more about the topic of space travel by searching online or in a library, or read more about the Mars Direct Manned Mission on the Internet at http://www.nw.net/mars/marsdirect.html. Then choose one of the following writing assignments:

   a. Compare two different methods of space travel, either methods already in use or possible future technologies.

   b. Review at least three web sites about space travel. For each site include the title, the web address, a short summary of what the site includes, and your evaluation of each site (whether it is interesting, useful, confusing, etc.). Be sure to include an introduction and a conclusion for your review.

The World After Cloning

Wray Herbert, Jeffrey L. Sheler, and Traci Watson

This article originally appeared in *U.S. News & World Report*, not long after the widely publicized cloning of a sheep named Dolly. The authors ask and answer several questions about cloning that have been raised since Dolly first appeared, as well as considering some of the moral issues involved in cloning.

Prereading Questions

1. In the past few years, what kinds of animals have been cloned successfully?
2. Do you think it will be possible to clone human beings in the future?

Vocabulary

jaded cynical, having a negative view because of previous experiences
technophobe a person who is afraid of technology
in the wake of following directly afterward
scurried hurried
ethical moral
implications ideas that are suggested, implied, or closely connected
ramifications developments, consequences
debut first appearance
ethicists persons who specialize in ethics, or standards of morality
pales becomes or appears less important
DNA the part of a cell that carries genetic information
intact unbroken, undamaged
membrane a thin layer of tissue
embryos fertilized eggs in the early stages of development
ewes female sheep

SOURCE: "The World After Cloning" by Wray Herbert, Jeffrey L. Sheler, and Traci Watson. Copyright, March 10, 1997, *U.S. News & World Report*. Visit us at our Web site at www.usnews.com for additional information.

surrogate substitute

genes parts of each cell that are responsible for a person's characteristics

uterine referring to the uterus, the organ in the female body where embryos grow and develop

megalomaniac someone who is obsessed with power

unanimous in complete agreement

narcissistic focused on love of oneself

impoverished poor (in this case, without strength)

stigmatized marked as shameful or disgraceful, perceived as negative

apathetic uninterested

pedigree genetic inheritance

unscrupulous without moral principles

usurpation taking control of, taking over

from scratch from the beginning, using natural methods and/or ingredients

progeny offspring, other beings produced from one's genetic material

The World After Cloning

At first it was just plain startling. Word from Scotland that a scientist named Ian Wilmut had succeeded in cloning an adult mammal—a feat long thought impossible—caught the imagination of even the most jaded technophobe. The laboratory process that produced Dolly, an unremarkable-looking sheep, theoretically would work for humans as well. . . . It was science fiction come to life. And scary science fiction at that.

2   In the wake of Wilmut's shocker, governments scurried to formulate guidelines for the unknown, a future filled with mind-boggling possibilities. The Vatican called for a worldwide ban on human cloning. President Clinton ordered a national commission to study the legal and ethical implications. Leaders in Europe, where most nations already prohibit human cloning, began examining the moral ramifications of cloning other species.

3   Like the splitting of the atom, the first space flight, and the discovery of "life" on Mars, Dolly's debut has generated a long list of difficult puzzles for scientists and politicians, philosophers and theologians. And at dinner tables and office coolers, in bars and on street corners, the development of wild scenarios spun from the birth of a single sheep has only

just begun. U.S. News sought answers from experts to the most intriguing and frequently asked questions.

Why Would Anyone Want to Clone a Human Being in the First Place?

4   The human cloning scenarios that ethicists ponder most frequently fall into two broad categories: 1) parents who want to clone a child, either to provide transplants for a dying child or to replace that child, and 2) adults who for a variety of reasons might want to clone themselves.

5   Many ethicists, however, believe that after the initial period of uproar, there won't be much interest in cloning humans. Making copies, they say, pales next to the wonder of creating a unique human being the old-fashioned way.

Could a Human Being Be Cloned Today? What About Other Animals?

6   It would take years of trial and error before cloning could be applied successfully to other mammals. For example, scientists will need to find out if the donor egg is best used when it is resting quietly or when it is growing.

Will It Be Possible to Clone the Dead?

7   Perhaps, if the body is fresh, says Randall Prather, a cloning expert at the University of Missouri–Columbia. The cloning method used by Wilmut's lab requires fusing an egg cell with the cell containing the donor's DNA. And that means the donor cell must have an intact membrane around its DNA. The membrane starts to fall apart after death, as does DNA. But, yes, in theory at least it might be possible.

Can I Set Up My Own Cloning Lab?

8   Yes, but maybe you'd better think twice. All the necessary chemicals and equipment are easily available and relatively low-tech. But out-of-pocket costs would run $100,000 or more, and that doesn't cover the pay for a skilled developmental biologist. The lowest-priced of these scientists, straight out of graduate school, makes about $40,000 a year. If you tried to grow the cloned embryos to maturity, you'd encounter other difficulties. The Scottish team implanted 29 very young clones in 13 ewes,

but only one grew into a live lamb. So if you plan to clone Fluffy, buy enough cat food for a host of surrogate mothers.

Would a Cloned Human Be Identical to the Original?

9   Identical genes don't produce identical people, as anyone acquainted with identical twins can tell you. In fact, twins are more alike than clones would be, since they have at least shared the uterine environment, are usually raised in the same family, and so forth. Parents could clone a second child who eerily resembled their first in appearance, but all the evidence suggests the two would have very different personalities. . . .

10 Even biologically, a clone would not be identical to the "master copy." The clone's cells, for example, would have energy-processing machinery (mitochondria) that came from the egg donor, not from the nucleus donor. But most of the physical differences between originals and copies wouldn't be detectable without a molecular-biology lab. . . .

Wouldn't It Be Strange for a Cloned Twin to Be Several Years Younger Than His or Her Sibling?

11 When the National Advisory Board on Ethics in Reproduction studied a different kind of cloning a few years ago, its members split on the issue of cloned twins separated in time. Some thought the children's individuality might be threatened, while others argued that identical twins manage to keep their individuality intact.

12 John Robertson of the University of Texas raises several other issues worth pondering: What about the cloned child's sense of free will and parental expectations? Since the parents chose to duplicate their first child, will the clone feel obliged to follow in the older sibling's footsteps? Will the older child feel he has been duplicated because he was inadequate or because he is special? Will the two have a unique form of sibling rivalry, or a special bond? These are, of course, just special versions of questions that come up whenever a new child is introduced into a family.

Could a Megalomaniac Decide to Achieve Immortality by Cloning an "Heir"?

13 Sure, and there are other situations where adults might be tempted to clone themselves. . . . On adult cloning, ethicists are more united in their discomfort. In fact, the same commission that was divided on the issue of twins was unanimous in its conclusion that cloning an adult's twin is "bizarre . . . narcissistic and ethically impoverished." What's

more, the commission argued that the phenomenon would jeopardize our very sense of who's who in the world, especially in the family.

. . .

What Are the Other Implications of Cloning for Society?

14   The gravest concern about the misuse of genetics isn't related to cloning directly, but to genetic engineering—the deliberate manipulation of genes to enhance human talents and create human beings according to certain specifications. But some ethicists also are concerned about the creation of a new (and stigmatized) social class: "the clones." Albert Jonsen of the University of Washington believes the confrontation could be comparable to what occurred in the 16th century, when Europeans were perplexed by the unfamiliar inhabitants of the New World and endlessly debated their status as humans.

. . .

Could Cloning Be Criminally Misused?

15   If the technology to clone humans existed today, it would be almost impossible to prevent someone from cloning you without your knowledge or permission, says Philip Bereano, professor of technology and public policy at the University of Washington. Everyone gives off cells all the time—whenever we give a blood sample, for example, or visit the dentist—and those cells all contain one's full complement of DNA. What would be the goal of such "drive-by" cloning? Well, what if a woman were obsessed with having the child of an apathetic man? Or think of the commercial value of a dynasty-building athletic pedigree or a heavenly singing voice. Even though experience almost certainly shapes these talents as much as genetic gifts, the unscrupulous would be unlikely to be deterred.

. . .

Doesn't Cloning Encroach on the Judeo-Christian View of God as the Creator of Life? Would a Clone Be Considered a Creature of God or of Science?

16   Many theologians worry about this. Cloning, at first glance, seems to be a usurpation of God's role as creator of humans "in his own image." The scientist, rather than God or chance, determines the outcome. "Like Adam and Eve, we want to be like God, to be in control," says philosophy Prof. Kevin Wildes of Georgetown University. "The question is, what are the limits?"

17   But some theologians argue that cloning is not the same as creating life from scratch. The ingredients used are alive or contain the elements of life, says Fletcher of Wheaton College. It is still only God, he says, who creates life.

. . .

Would Cloning Upset Religious Views About Death, Immortality, and Even Resurrection?

18   Not really. Cloned or not, we all die. The clone that outlives its "parent"—or that is generated from the DNA of a dead person, if that were possible—would be a different person. It would not be a reincarnation or a resurrected version of the deceased. Cloning could be said to provide immortality, theologians say, only in the sense that, as in normal reproduction, one might be said to "live on" in the genetic traits passed to one's progeny.

◆◆◆

Comprehension

1. How did the world react to the news that a sheep had successfully been cloned?
2. Would a cloned human being be identical to the original in appearance and personality?
3. What are some of the problems that could arise for cloned individuals?
4. What are the two sides of the religious controversy about cloning?

Critical Thinking

1. Do you think the author is in favor of cloning humans or opposed to it? Find two or three statements in the reading that support your answer.
2. Why did the Vatican call for a worldwide ban on cloning?
3. Could cloning one day become a profitable illegal business?
4. Which possible uses of cloning seem useful and legitimate?
5. How do you think the clones would be treated by other members of society? Would they be considered a lower class of humans?

Language and Vocabulary

1. Had you ever heard the term *sibling rivalry* before reading it in this article? What do you think it means? If you use a dictionary to find the

meaning, try looking up the two words *sibling* and *rivalry* separately, and then put the meanings together.

2. This article uses a number of scientific terms, such as *DNA, molecular biology, cell, genes,* and *genetic engineering*. Make a list of six or more scientific terms from the reading, and find out the meaning of each. Then use two of these words in sentences of your own.

Style, Structure, and Organization

1. Unlike most academic essays, "The World After Cloning" is organized as a series of questions and answers. Is this an effective way to organize the article? Why or why not? Which questions do the best job of capturing readers' attention?
2. In several places, the authors present ideas from two different points of view. In the fourth paragraph, for example, the question "Why would anyone want to clone a human being in the first place?" is answered with reasons that sound good, but the next paragraph offers a contrasting viewpoint. Find at least one other section of the article that uses a similar pro-and-con technique. Do you think this technique is effective for writing about controversial topics? Why or why not?
3. Find at least two places in the reading where the authors quote or refer to experts to answer some of the questions about cloning. Does the information provided by experts make the answers clearer or more convincing? Why?

Topics for Discussion or Journal Writing

1. Would you ever want to clone yourself or someone else you know?
2. Do you think there should be a worldwide ban on the cloning of human beings? Why or why not?
3. How could cloning affect professional sports? Do you think these effects would be good or bad? Why?
4. In what ways could cloning be used for good purposes in the animal world? For example, what about cloning animal species that are endangered?

Writing Topics for Paragraphs or Essays

1. Imagine how you would feel about cloning if you were a clone. Write about cloning from the point of view of a clone.
2. Write an argumentative paper that takes a stand for or against cloning of human beings or in favor of cloning with certain restrictions. Consider

what restrictions (if any) you think should be placed on cloning and how cloning should be used. In your paper, show that you are open-minded by presenting a little bit about the beliefs of those who have an opposing viewpoint, but be sure that your own side is more persuasive.

3. Which potential use of cloning, either of humans or of animals, do you think would be most beneficial? Write a paper about the benefits of using cloning for that purpose. Give clear, logical reasons for your opinion.

4. Using library resources or the Internet, find out more about Ian Wilmut and his successful cloning of a sheep in 1997. Write an informative paper about what you learn.

5. Interview someone who is a twin (an identical twin, if possible). Ask questions about what it was like to grow up with a twin and whether or not he or she experienced any sibling rivalry. Write a paper about the twin you interviewed.

Text Acknowledgments

Strategies for Active Reading

"Humans and the Environment," excerpts from *Essentials of Physical Geography,* Sixth Edition, by Robert Gabler, Robert Sager, Daniel Wise, and James Petersen, copyright © 1999 by Harcourt Inc., reprinted by permission of the publisher.

Cultural and Social Issues

"American Fish" by R. A. Sasaki, from *The Loom and Other Stories* by R. A. Sasaki, copyright © 1991 by R. A. Sasaki. Reprinted by permission of Graywolf Press, St. Paul, Minnesota.

"Listen to Me Good" by Margaret Charles Smith and Linda Janet Holmes, from *Listen to Me Good: The Life Story of an Alabama Midwife,* copyright © 1996 by Margaret Charles Smith and Linda Janet Holmes. Reprinted by permission of the publisher.

"Boomer Parents" by Sandy Banks, from the *Los Angeles Times* online, August 15, 2000, originally titled "What Are Boomer Parents Teaching Kids?" Reprinted by permission of the Los Angeles Times Syndicate.

"Spanglish Spoken Here" by Janice Castro, from the July 11, 1988 issue of *Time,* copyright © 1988 Time Inc. Reprinted by permission.

"The Ambitious Generation" by Barbara Schneider and David Stevenson, from *The Ambitious Generation: America's Teenagers, Motivated but Directionless,* copyright © 1999, published by Yale University Press. Reprinted by permission.

"Saffron Sky" by Gelareh Asayesh, from *Saffron Sky* by Gelareh Asayesh, copyright © 1999 by Gelareh Asayesh. Reprinted by permission of Beacon Press, Boston.

"Suspect Policy" by Randall Kennedy, from the September 13 and 20 issues of *The New Republic.* Reprinted by permission.

Education and Career

"Stop!" by Sam Quinones, from *Ms. Magazine,* Vol. X, Num. 1. Reprinted by permission of *Ms. Magazine,* copyright © 1999–2000.

"How to Write with Style" by Kurt Vonnegut, Jr., from the *Power of the Printed Word* series, copyright © 1982 by International Paper Company. Reprinted by permission of International Paper.

"The Reading Debate" from Laura E. Berk, *Child Development,* Fifth Edition, copyright © 2000 by Allyn & Bacon. Reprinted by permission.

"Possible Lives" by Mike Rose, excerpt from *Possible Lives: The Promise of Public Education in America,* copyright © 1995 by Mike Rose. Reprinted by permission of Houghton Mifflin Company. All rights reserved.

"Breaking Through the Barriers" by James M. Henslin, from James M. Henslin, *Sociology: A Down-to-Earth Approach,* Fourth Edition, copyright © 1999 by Allyn & Bacon. Reprinted by permission.

"The Rich Heritage of Public Speaking" by Steven A. Beebe and Susan J. Beebe, from Steven A. Beebe and Susan J. Beebe, *Public Speaking: An Audience-Centered Approach,* Fourth Edition, copyright © 2000 by Allyn & Bacon. Reprinted by permission.

"Emergency Medical Technicians" by Joseph J. Mistovich, Brent Q. Hafen, and Keith J. Karren, from *Prehospital Emergency Care,* Sixth Edition by Mistovich/Hafen/Karren, copyright © 2000. Reprinted by permission of Prentice-Hall, Inc., Upper Saddle River, NJ.

"Internet Job Search" by A. C. "Buddy" Krizan, Patricia Merrier, Carol Larson Jones, and Jules Harcourt, from *Business Communication,* Fourth Edition, by A. Krizan, P. Merrier, C. L. Jones, and J. Harcourt, copyright © 1999. Reprinted with permission of South-Western College Publishing, a division of Thomson Learning, fax 1-800-730-2215.

Media and Popular Culture

"Taking Potluck" by Tom Bodett, from *Small Comforts* by Tom Bodett, copyright © 1987 by Tom Bodett. Reprinted by permission of Perseus Books Publishers, a member of Perseus Books, L. L. C.

"Color TV" by Richard Breyer. This article appeared in the March 2000 issue and is reprinted with permission from *The World and I,* a publication of *The Washington Times Corporation,* copyright © 2000.

"Breaking the Habit" by Mike Duffy. From the *Detroit Free Press,* April 23, 2000. Reprinted by permission of the *Detroit Free Press.*

"Shoeless Joe" by W. P. Kinsella. From *Shoeless Joe,* copyright © 1982 by William P. Kinsella. Reprinted by permission of Houghton Mifflin Company. All rights reserved.

"Elvis Culture" by Erika Doss, from *Elvis Culture: Fans, Faith, and Image,* by Erika Doss, published by the University Press of Kansas, copyright © 1999, www.kansaspress.ku.edu. Used by permission of the publisher.

"Dressing Down" by John Brooks. Reprinted by permission of Harold Ober Associates Incorporated, copyright © 1981 by John Brooks. First published in *The Atlantic Monthly.*

Fitness and Health

"Strive to Be Fit, Not Fanatical" by Timothy Gower, which originally appeared in the *Los Angeles Times,* June 7, 1999. Reprinted by permission of Timothy Gower.

"Procrastination and Stress" by Lester A. Lefton, from Lefton, Lester A., *Psychology,* Seventh Edition, copyright © 2000 by Allyn & Bacon. Reprinted/adapted by permission.

"Managing Time" by Rebecca J. Donatelle and Lorraine G. Davis. From *Health: The Basics,* Third Edition, by Rebecca J. Donatelle and Lorraine G. Davis, copyright © 1999 by Allyn & Bacon. Reprinted by permission.

"Computer Addiction Is Coming Online" by William J. Cromie, which appeared in the *Harvard Gazette,* January 21, 1999. Reprinted by permission of William Cromie, *Harvard University Gazette.*

"Playing for Keeps" by Andy Steiner, which appeared in *Utne Reader,* January–February 2000. Reprinted by permission of Andy Steiner, senior editor at *Utne Reader.*

"Can You Afford to Get Sick?" by Helen Martineau. Reprinted with permission from the October 1999, *American Health,* copyright © 1999 by The Reader's Digest Assn., Inc.

Nature and the Outdoors

"Journey of the Pink Dolphins" by Sy Montgomery, from *Journey of the Pink Dolphins: An Amazon Quest* by Sy Montgomery, copyright © 2000 by Sy Montgomery. Excerpted by permission of Simon & Schuster.

"In the Shadow of Man" by Jane Goodall, from *In the Shadow of Man* by Jane Goodall, copyright © 1971 by Hugo and Jane van Lawick-Goodall. Reprinted by permission of Houghton Mifflin Co. All rights reserved.

"Life in the Treetops" by Margaret D. Lowman, from Margaret D. Lowman, *Life in the Treetops: Adventures of a Woman in Field Biology,* published by Yale University Press, copyright © 1999. Reprinted by permission of Yale University Press.

"Nature's R_x" by Joel L. Swerdlow, excerpted from Joel L. Swerdlow, "Nature's R_x," *The National Geographic,* April 2000. Reprinted by permission of the National Geographic Society.

"Monarchs' Migration: A Fragile Journey" by William K. Stevens. Excerpted from "Monarchs' Migration" by William K. Stevens, from *The Science Times Book of Insects* (The Lyons Press, 1998). Reprinted by special arrangement with the publisher.

"Heavy Traffic on the Everest Highway" by Geoffrey Tabin. Reprinted from *Blind Corners,* copyright © 1998 by Geoffrey Tabin with permission from *The Globe Pequot Press,* Guilford, CT, 1-800-962-0973. www.globepequot.com.

"Death Valley" by Doug and Bobbe Tatreau, excerpted from *Parks of the Pacific Coast: The Complete Guide to the National and Historic Parks of California, Oregon and Washington* by Doug and Bobbe Tatreau, copyright © 1985 by Fast & McMillan Publishers, Inc.

Technology and the Future

"What'll They Think of Next?" by Melissa Melton and Barbra Murray, copyright, January 3, 2000, *U.S. News & World Report.* Visit us at our Web site at www.usnews.com for additional information.

"The 10-Minute Tech Inspection" by Peter Bohr, first appeared in *Westways* magazine, Auto Club of Southern California, 2000. Reprinted by permission.

"Tourist Trap" by James Hebert, which appeared in the *San Diego Union-Tribune,* January 1, 2000. Reprinted with permission from the *San Diego Union-Tribune.*

"Indistinguishable from Magic" by Robert L. Forward, excerpted from Robert Forward, *Indistinguishable from Magic,* Baen Books, copyright © 1995. Reprinted by permission of the publisher.

"The Mars Direct Plan" by Robert Zubrin. From "The Mars Direct Plan" by Robert Zubrin, in *Scientific American,* copyright © March 2000 by Scientific American, Inc. All rights reserved.

"The World After Cloning" by Wray Herbert, Jeffrey L. Sheler, and Traci Watson, copyright © March 10, 1997, *U.S. News & World Report.* Visit us at our Web site at www.usnews.com for additional information.

Index

"The Ambitious Generation," Barbara Schneider and David Stevenson, 35
"American Fish," R.A. Sasaki, 10
Asayesh, Gelareh; "Saffron Sky," 40

Banks, Sandy; "Boomer Parents," 23
Beebe, Steven A. and Susan J. Beebe; "The Rich Heritage of Public Speaking," 80
Beebe, Susan J. and Steven A. Beebe; "The Rich Heritage of Public Speaking," 80
Berk, Laura E.; "The Reading Debate," 63
Bodett, Tom; "Taking Potluck," 98
Bohr, Peter; "The 10-Minute Tech Inspection," 211
"Boomer Parents," Sandy Banks, 23
"Breaking the Habit," Mike Duffy, 109
"Breaking Through the Barriers," James M. Henslin, 75
Breyer, Richard; "Color TV," 103
Brooks, John; "Dressing Down," 127

"Can You Afford to Get Sick?," Helen Martineau, 159
Castro, Janice; "Spanglish Spoken Here," 29
"Color TV," Richard Breyer, 103

"Computer Addiction is Coming Online," William J. Cromie, 148
Cromie, William J.; "Computer Addiction is Coming Online," 148

Davis, Lorraine G. and Rebecca J. Donatelle; "Managing Time," 144
"Death Valley," Doug and Bobbe Tatreau, 199
Donatelle, Rebecca J. and Lorraine G. Davis; "Managing Time," 144
Doss, Erika; "Elvis Culture," 122
"Dressing Down," John Brooks, 127
Duffy, Mike; "Breaking the Habit," 109

"Elvis Culture," Erika Doss, 122
"Emergency Medical Technicians," Joseph J. Mistovich, Brent Q. Hafen, and Keith J. Karren, 85

Forward, Robert L.; "Indistinguishable from Magic," 222

Gabler, Robert E., Robert J. Sager, Daniel L. Wise, and James F. Petersen; "Humans and the Environment," 3
Goodall, Jane; "In the Shadow of Man," 171

245

246 ◆ *Index*

Gower, Timothy; "Strive to Be Fit, Not Fanatical," 134

Hafen, Brent Q., Joseph J. Mistovich, and Keith J. Karren; "Emergency Medical Technicians," 85
Harcourt, Jules, A. C. "Buddy" Krizan, Patricia Merrier, and Carol Larson Jones; "Internet Job Search," 91
"Heavy Traffic on the Everest Highway," Geoffrey Tabin, 193
Hebert, James; "Tourist Trap," 217
Henslin, James M.; "Breaking Through the Barriers," 75
Herbert, Wray, Jeffrey L. Sheler, and Traci Watson; "The World After Cloning," 233
Holmes, Linda Janet and Margaret Charles Smith; "Listen to Me Good," 18
"How to Write with Style," Kurt Vonnegut, Jr., 57
"Humans and the Environment," Robert E. Gabler, Robert J. Sager, Daniel L. Wise, and James F. Petersen, 3

"In the Shadow of Man," Jane Goodall, 171
"Indistinguishable from Magic," Robert L. Forward, 222
"Internet Job Search," A. C. "Buddy" Krizan, Patricia Merrier, Carol Larson Jones, and Jules Harcourt, 91

Jones, Carol Larson, A. C. "Buddy" Krizan, Patricia Merrier, and Jules Harcourt; "Internet Job Search," 91
"Journey of the Pink Dolphins," Sy Montgomery, 166

Karren, Keith J., Joseph J. Mistovich, and Brent Q. Hafen; "Emergency Medical Technicians," 85
Kennedy, Randall; "Suspect Policy," 46
Kinsella, W. P.; "Shoeless Joe," 116
Krizan, A. C. "Buddy," Patricia Merrier, Carol Larson Jones, and Jules Harcourt; "Internet Job Search," 91

Lefton, Lester A.; "Procrastination and Stress," 139
"Life in the Treetops," Margaret D. Lowman, 175
"Listen to Me Good," Margaret Charles Smith and Linda Janet Holmes, 18
Lowman, Margaret D.; "Life in the Treetops," 175

"Managing Time," Rebecca J. Donatelle and Lorraine G. Davis, 144
"The Mars Direct Plan," Robert Zubrin, 227
Martineau, Helen; "Can You Afford to Get Sick?," 159
Melton, Melissa and Barbra Murray; "What'll They Think of Next?," 206
Merrier, Patricia, A. C. "Buddy" Krizan, Carol Larson Jones, and Jules Harcourt; "Internet Job Search," 91
Mistovich, Joseph J., Brent Q. Hafen, and Keith J. Karren; "Emergency Medical Technicians," 85
"Monarchs' Migration: A Fragile Journey," William K. Stevens, 187
Montgomery, Sy; "Journey of the Pink Dolphins," 166

Murray, Barbra and Melissa Melton; "What'll They Think of Next?," 206

"Nature's Rx," Joel L. Swerdlow, 182

Petersen, James F., Robert E. Gabler, Robert J. Sager, and Daniel L. Wise; "Humans and the Environment," 3
"Playing for Keeps," Andy Steiner, 154
"Possible Lives," Mike Rose, 68
"Procrastination and Stress," Lester A. Lefton, 139

Quinones, Sam; "Stop!," 52

"The Reading Debate," Laura E. Berk, 63
"The Rich Heritage of Public Speaking," Steven A. Beebe and Susan J. Beebe, 80
Rose, Mike; "Possible Lives," 68

"Saffron Sky," Gelareh Asayesh, 40
Sager, Robert J., Robert E. Gabler, Daniel L. Wise, and James F. Petersen; "Humans and the Environment," 3
Sasaki, R. A.; "American Fish," 10
Schneider, Barbara and David Stevenson; "The Ambitious Generation," 35
Sheler, Jeffrey L., Wray Herbert, and Traci Watson; "The World After Cloning," 233
"Shoeless Joe," W. P. Kinsella, 116
Smith, Margaret Charles and Linda Janet Holmes; "Listen to Me Good," 18
"Spanglish Spoken Here," Janice Castro, 29
Steiner, Andy; "Playing for Keeps," 154

Stevens, William K.; "Monarchs' Migration: A Fragile Journey," 187
Stevenson, David and Barbara Schneider; "The Ambitious Generation," 35
"Stop!," Sam Quinones, 52
"Strive to Be Fit, Not Fanatical," Timothy Gower, 134
"Suspect Policy," Randall Kennedy, 46
Swerdlow, Joel L.; "Nature's Rx," 182

Tabin, Geoffrey; "Heavy Traffic on the Everest Highway," 193
"Taking Potluck," Tom Bodett, 98
Tatreau, Bobbe and Doug Tatreau; "Death Valley," 199
Tatreau, Doug and Bobbe Tatreau; "Death Valley," 199
"The 10-Minute Tech Inspection," Peter Bohr, 211
"Tourist Trap," James Hebert, 217

Vonnegut, Kurt, Jr.; "How to Write with Style," 57

Watson, Traci, Wray Herbert, and Jeffrey L. Sheler; "The World After Cloning," 233
"What'll They Think of Next?," Melissa Melton and Barbra Murray, 206
Wise, Daniel L., Robert E. Gabler, Robert J. Sager, and James F. Petersen; "Humans and the Environment," 3
"The World After Cloning," Wray Herbert, Jeffrey L. Sheler, and Traci Watson, 233

Zubrin, Robert; "The Mars Direct Plan," 227